Applying

Six Sigma

Using Minitab

Austin Texas
Dec/Nov 2015

Minitab ▶

QUALITY. ANALYSIS. RESULTS.

First published by Dog Ear Publishing
4011 Vincennes Road
Indianapolis, IN 46268
www.dogearpublishing.net

ISBN: 978-1-4575-3687-8

This book is printed on acid free paper.
Printed in the United States of America

Acknowledgement

Writing a book using material developed for Six Sigma methodology is not an individual undertaking. Many distinguished individuals have supplied ideas and updates to create the material used in this book. The authors wish to thank the following individuals for their ideas and efforts in creating this material: Eric Edwin, Jeff Jackson and Richard Lynch. Without their inputs this book may not have been created.

Special thanks goes to Adrienne Miller and the fine folks at Dog Ear Publishing for their help in completing this project. The people at Dog Ear Publishing helped in all aspects of this creative endeavor.

We also wish to thank Minitab Inc. for the support they provide. Minitab is a company that has shown a strong customer focus. No issue has ever been too small or large for their support. The website's knowledge database and their technical support is unmatched. While there are many statistical software programs available to use in a classroom setting, Minitab is, in the view of the authors, is the best. Thanks to all of the Minitab employees who have answered our questions, and helped the students to become connected.

Finally, we wish to thank our 20,000 plus students from over 4,000 organizations who allow us to continue doing what we love to do, teach. Without their kind comments and helpful suggestions this would simply be a job, and not a passion.

To find out more about SixSigma.us and the services offered, go to:

www.6Sigma.us

Table of Contents

Acknowledgement .... i i i

Introduction 1

   Six Sigma and Minitab: A Powerful Combination 1

   How This Book Is Constructed 2

   Datasets 2

   Minitab Review 2

      Dialog Boxes 2

      Input Data 3

      Opening Excel Files 8

      Worksheets 1 0

      Columns 1 4

      Random Data 1 9

      Patterned Data 2 0

   Data Manipulation 2 4

      Code Data 2 5

      Rank Data 2 6

      Sort Data 2 8

   Calculator 2 9

   Graph Options 3 0

      Brush points 3 0

      Update Graph Automatically 3 1

      Tile Graphs 3 2

   Minitab Shortcut Keys 3 3

   Minitab Macros 3 4

Define Phase 3 6

   Working With Data 3 6

   The Project Charter 3 7

Graphical Tools 4 0

    Dot Plot 4 0

    Histogram 4 3

    Box Plot 4 6

    Time Series Plot 5 1

    I-MR Chart 5 3

    Scatter Plot 5 7

    Pareto Plot 5 9

Measure Phase 6 6

The Importance of Assessment 6 6

Tools of the Measure Phase 6 7

Summary Statistics 6 7

Definitions of Statistical Terms 6 8

    Central Tendency 6 8

    Spread 6 9

    Shape 7 1

Using Minitab to Display Statistics 7 2

Checking Process Stability - SPC 7 4

Measurement System Analysis (MSA) 7 7

Accuracy and Precision 8 0

The Impact of Additive Propery 8 1

Repeatability and Reproducibility 8 1

Metrics 8 2

Acceptable Levels For P/T and %R&R Values 8 3

Creating the MSA Worksheet 8 3

Gage Run Chart 8 5

Performing the Gage Study 8 8

MSA for Attribute Data 9 5

Kappa Analysis 1 0 3

MSA - Audits 1 1 0

    Random Samples 1 1 0

    Stratified Samples 1 1 2

    Systematic Samples 1 1 5

Determining the Process Capability 1 1 8

    Metrics 1 1 8

Minitab's Capability Study 1 2 1

Process Capability Six Pack 1 2 7

Analyze Phase 1 3 0

Tools and Outcomes 1 3 0

Graphical Tools 1 3 0

Probability Plot 1 3 1

Multi-Vari Plot 1 3 6

Confidence Intervals 1 3 8

Confidence Intervals – Graphical Display 1 4 0

Interval Plots with Groups 1 4 3

Hypothesis Testing 1 4 4

Comparative Studies 1 5 0

One Sample t-Test 1 5 0

Two Sample t-Test 1 5 6

Test of Equal Variance 1 6 2

ANOVA Analysis 1 6 4

Chi–Square Analysis 1 6 8

Pareto Chart of Delivery Issues 1 6 9

Minitab's Chi-Square Analysis 1 7 4

Summary Table Option 1 7 7

Correlation 1 8 5

Simple Linear Regression Analysis 1 8 9

Residuals versus Fits 1 9 9

Residuals versus Run Order 2 0 0

Multiple Regression 2 0 2

Creating the Regression Equation 2 0 4

Factorial Experiments 2 1 2

General Factorial Designs 2 1 2

General Full Factorial Design Analysis 2 1 5

Paired t-Test 2 1 9

Balanced ANOVA 2 2 2

GLM 2 2 4

Fully Nested ANOVA 2 3 1

Multi-Vari Graph 2 3 3

Improve Phase 2 3 5

Tools And Outcomes..235

Background for Design of Experiments (DOE)..235

The Interactive Nature of Experimentation...236

Two Level Factorial Designs..237

    Design of Experiments (DOE)...238

    Analysis of the Full Factorial Experiment..240

    Reduced Model..248

    Design of Experiments (DOE) with Center Points...253

    Analyze Full Factorial with Center Points and Blocks.......................................256

Fractional Factorial Designs...267

    Creating a Fractional Factorial Design..267

    Analyze Fractional Factorial Designs...270

Response Surface Designs...277

    PtType..280

    Analyze RSM...281

    Graphical Display...289

    Multiple Response Optimization..291

    Modifying Designs..297

    Replicate Design...300

    Foldover..302

    Add Axial Points...305

Defining Custom Designs..308

    Opening an Excel spreadsheet in Minitab...308

    Custom Response Surface Designs...313

    Display Designs..317

Control Phase...320

Tools And Outcomes..320

Statistical Process Control (SPC)...321

    X Bar R Chart...326

    X Bar S Chart...330

Control Charts for Attribute Data..331

    P Chart..331

    NP Chart...333

    C Chart..334

    U Chart...335

Attribute Control Charts for Special Situations...336

P Chart Diagnosis 3 3 6

Laney P' Chart 338

U Chart Diagnosis 339

Laney U' Chart 340

Process Capability – Non Normal Data 342

Using Other Distribution Curves 345

Index 349

Introduction

Welcome to Applying Six Sigma Using Minitab. This book is specially designed to be an easy-to-understand and easy-to-use resource for Six Sigma practitioners of all experience levels. It is filled with explanations and 'hands on' demonstrations of the common and useful features in Minitab.

The authors understand that even experienced Six Sigma practitioners can use a Minitab refresher from time to time, especially since the program offers such a wide array of features and functionality. Just as importantly, experience has shown us that those new to Six Sigma need a solid reference resource as well.

And that's how this book came to be. It is written for the purpose of serving Six Sigma practitioners regardless of whether they are working on their first project or their one thousandth project. Of course, those new to Six Sigma will likely need access to a variety of resource materials so there's no claim that this is the 'only book needed', or some other such statement.

For those outside of Six Sigma this book offers plenty of information to meet basic needs. The practice of data analysis crosses many different industries and boundaries, so the concepts and ideas presented here are easily transferable to other applications.

Six Sigma and Minitab: A Powerful Combination

The Six Sigma process improvement methodology, more than any other methodology, demonstrates the critical importance of proper collection and analysis of data. From its roots in the manufacturing environment, the power of Six Sigma has found its way into virtually all areas of business, regardless of product, service, industry, or profession.

Some of the strongest proponents of Six Sigma methodology can be found in non-manufacturing disciplines. Why? Because those companies who use Six Sigma, reap the tremendous money savings and quickly recognize the value of this methodology. In fact, many of these non-manufacturing entities enjoy even greater savings than that typically generated in a manufacturing environment.

Minitab® Statistical Software is an exceptional tool for data analysis, especially in the context of Six Sigma methodology. It has been around since the 1970's, and over the last several decades has repeatedly proven itself to be one of the most useful and powerful statistical packages around. Portions if the input and output contained in this book are printed with permission of Minitab Inc. All material remains the exclusive property and copyright of Minitab Inc. All rights reserved.

How This Book Is Constructed

The text in this book follows the DMAIC (Define Measure Analyze Improve Control) phases of Six Sigma methodology. While the book's flow is DMAIC in nature, its applications are not limited to this particular process. Data analysis is the same no matter what process is used. Furthermore, this book is not designed to analyze manufacturing projects differently than transactional projects. If something can be measured, it can be analyzed.

Throughout the book, various data sets are presented to demonstrate specific statistical analysis tasks and tools. Minitab Projects carry the extension .MPJ; worksheets within projects are referenced by their title only, and individual Minitab worksheets saved outside of a project carry the extension .MTW.

Datasets

Datasets used in this book can be downloaded at: **www.6sigma.us/applyingsixsigmausingminitab**

Minitab Review

Dialog Boxes

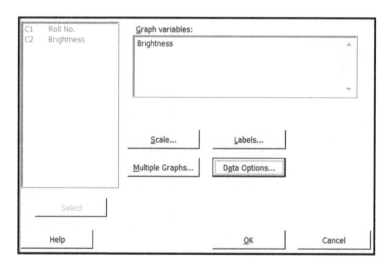

In Minitab, dialog boxes present areas for column inputs and buttons for additional options. Generally, a large variables area as shown here (labeled 'Graph variables:') indicates the possibility of multiple columns. Remember that Minitab sees spaces as delimiters so a name such as Roll No. is viewed as two columns. To input Roll No. as a single column requires single quotes around the name, 'Roll No.'.

Note: Every Dialog box contains a Help button; when selected, it opens the help files for that specific Dialog box.

With a dialog box open, there are four ways to input columns:
1. Double click the column name
2. Type the column number (C1, C2 etc.)
3. Type the column heading (Brightness, 'Roll No.')
4. Click the desired column(s) name(s) and then click the **Select** button

Minitab will only display columns that contain the appropriate data type for the requested input. If the dialog box requires numeric data, the text and date/time column names will not be displayed.

Hint: Changes to the options within a dialog box remain in place until the Minitab session is closed. Press the **F3** key to reset the dialog box and all associated options to the default condition.

Input Data

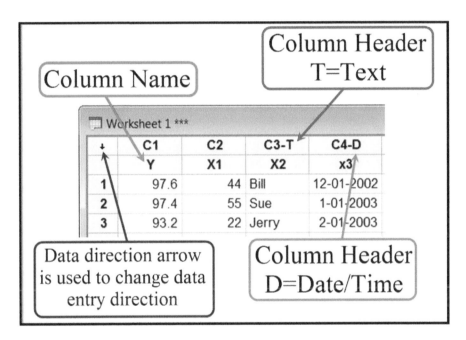

Minitab allows several methods to input data. The first is simply to type in the values. The column header (cell number C1, C2 etc.) indicates the type of data that exists in the column. Minitab allows only one type of data per column.

A column header that contains only the column number (C1, C2) indicates the data is numeric; no text or date-time stamp is allowed. A 'T' (C3-T) indicates a text column; it can contain numerals, but they are left justified and treated as text. Statistical analysis cannot be performed on a text column.

A '-D' indicates a Date/Time column. Date/Time column formatting will be discussed later.

Typing data into Minitab

Typing information directly into a cell is easy, but there are times when it becomes tedious. For instance, to populate a column with one data value, doing it cell by cell is very slow so it's easier to populate the entire column at once.

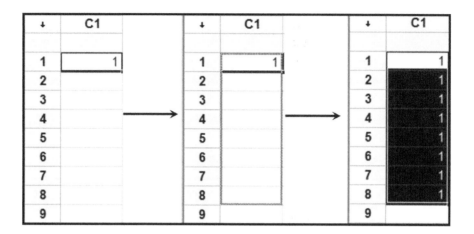

To accomplish this task, perform the following steps:
- Type the value into one cell
- Select the cell
- Place the cursor over the lower right corner of the cell
- Click and hold the left mouse button, then drag down to the final cell of the repeated values.
- Release the left mouse button

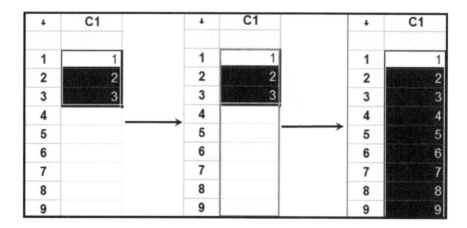

To continue a sequence of numbers, perform the following steps:
- Highlight the cells that define the sequence
- Place the cursor over the lower right corner of the last cell
- Click and hold the left mouse button, then drag down to the final cell to be populated.
- Release the left mouse button

Minitab has now filled in the values in the sequence.

To repeat a pattern of text or data, highlight the pattern and select *Edit > Copy* (shortcut key Crtl+c).).
Next, highlight the destination cells and select *Edit > Paste* (shortcut key Crtl + v).

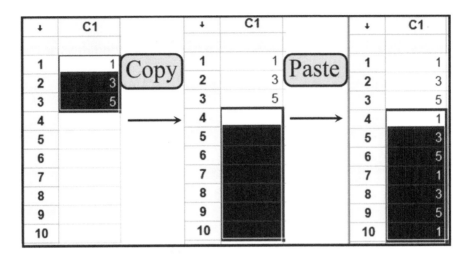

Minitab requires each column to have a unique name. When a column is copied within a worksheet, Minitab automatically adds '_#' to the new column's heading.

C1	C2	C3-T	C4-D	C5-T	C6-D
Y	X1	X2	X3	X2_1	X3_1
97.6	44	Bill	12-01-2002	Bill	12-01-2002
97.4	55	Sue	1-01-2003	Sue	1-01-2003
93.2	22	Jerry	2-01-2003	Jerry	2-01-2003
*	*	Missing	3-01-2003	Missing	3-01-2003
92.0	22	Sue	4-01-2004	Sue	4-01-2004
93.0	33	Jerry	5-01-2004	Jerry	5-01-2004

Here the column C3 was copied to C5, so Minitab added '_1' to the name X2.

A column or worksheet filled with data values is meaningless unless information regarding the data is known, so Minitab allows a description for each column, the worksheet, or both. This allows information to be accurately transferred from one user to the next.

To add a description, use the Editor function. For a specific column, place the cursor in a cell from that column; for the entire worksheet, place the cursor in any cell on the worksheet.

Minitab Project: **Intro to Minitab**

Minitab Worksheet: *Response Time*

Menu command: *Editor > Column > Description* **(for column descriptions)**

Menu command: *Editor > Worksheet > Description* **(for worksheet descriptions)**

Input a description for the column.

Click **OK**.

Input a description for the worksheet.

Click **OK**.

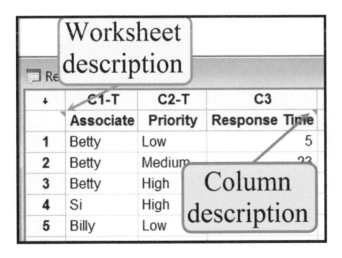

The final worksheet contains small red triangles, indicating descriptions are available.

Opening Excel Files

Be cautious when opening an Excel spreadsheet in Minitab; because Excel allows multiple data types in a single column. This results in some very strange looking Minitab worksheets.

Minitab command: *File > Open Worksheet*

Using the 'Look in:' entry, select the directory containing the desired Excel file.

Use the pull down menu for 'Files of type:' and select Excel (*.xls) files only.

In the 'File name:' input, select the file;

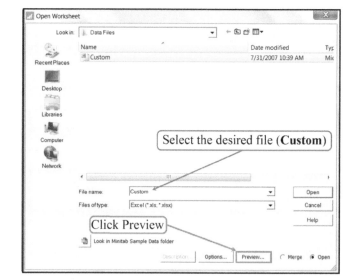

Select the directory and file.

Click the **Preview** button.

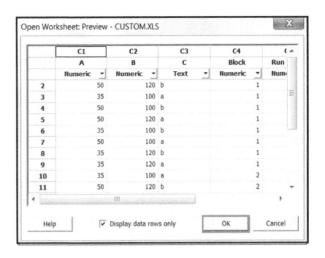

If the information looks acceptable, click **OK**.

If there are issues with the worksheet, click **OK** and then select the **Options** button in the **Open Worksheet** dialog window.

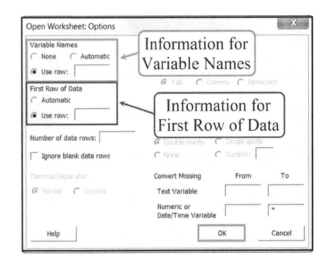

Minitab assumes the column headings are in row one. If this is not the case, formatting issues arise.

For the variables (column) names select the appropriate option. (Note: Minitab assumes row one contains the names.)

If no column names exist, select **None**.

If they exist in another row, select '**Use row:**' and type in the proper row number.

Supply the rest of the information as needed.

Click **OK** then click **Open** in the Open Worksheet dialog box.

The final Excel spreadsheet opened in Minitab.

C1	C2	C3-T	C4	C5	C6
A	B	C	Block	Run Order	Result
50	120	b	1	1	76
35	100	a	1	2	67
50	100	b	1	3	56
50	120	a	1	4	78
35	100	b	1	5	74
50	100	a	1	6	66
35	120	b	1	7	66
35	120	a	1	8	65

Worksheets

The following worksheet is designed to demonstrate Minitab's worksheet functions.

Minitab Project: **Intro to Minitab**

Minitab Worksheet: *Time Card Errors*

Split

Splitting a worksheet creates multiple worksheets based on a specific column. The number of new worksheets depends upon the number of unique entries in the selected column.

Minitab command: *Data > Split Worksheet*

Select the column to use for the split (**Location**).

Click **OK**.

Multiple worksheets are created, each containing the rows for a specific location.

Note: If a column with 50 unique values is selected, Minitab will create 50 new worksheets. The original worksheet is unchanged.

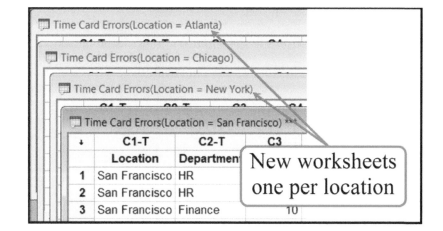

Subset

Subsets of worksheets are created based on one of three situations:
- Selection of specific rows
- Rows associated with brushed graph points
- A specific condition defined by the user

Note: Brushed points will be discussed later in this chapter.

Minitab command: *Data > Subset Worksheet*

Choose to change or accept the default name for the new worksheet.

Choose to include or exclude the rows that match the specified situation.

Select how the rows are selected, using one of three options:
- Select specific rows by typing in the row numbers
- Select the rows that result from brushing data values displayed on certain graphs
- Select the rows that match a specific condition

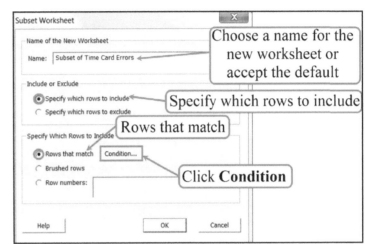

For 'Include or Exclude' select 'Specify which rows to include'.

For 'Specify Which Rows to Include' select 'Rows that match'.

Click the Condition button.

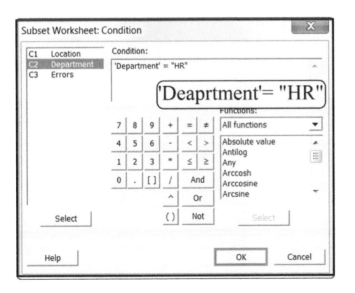

Set the condition as **'Department' = "HR"** (The single and double quotes are required.)

Click **OK** (twice).

Subset of Time Card Errors

C1-T	C2-T	C3
Location	**Department**	**Errors**
Chicago	HR	11
Chicago	HR	4
New York	HR	5
New York	HR	6
Atlanta	HR	3
Atlanta	HR	6
San Francisco	HR	10

The new worksheet contains all rows that have HR as the Department.

Merge

Merging two worksheets places the columns from one worksheet next to the columns from the other worksheet.

Minitab Project: **Intro to Minitab**

Minitab Worksheet: *Time Card Errors(Location = San Francisco)*

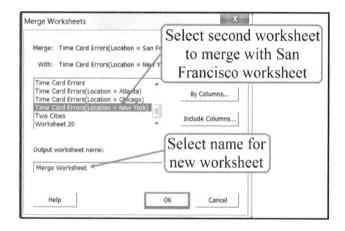

(Created from the Split worksheet command.)

Minitab command: *Data > Merge Worksheets*

The active worksheet is Time Card Errors(Location = San Francisco).

Select the worksheet to merge with the active worksheet (Time Card Errors(Location = New York). Choose a name for the new worksheet. Click **OK**.

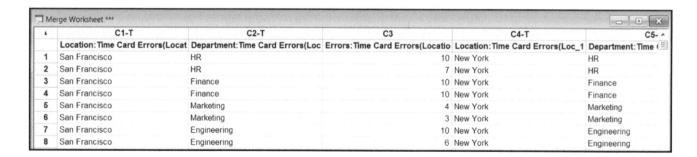

The first worksheet (San Francisco) appears in the left three columns of the worksheet. The second worksheet (New York) appears in columns C4 – C6. To present the information in a columnwise format, additional manipulation is required.

Minitab command: *Data > Stack > Block of Columns*

On the first line select the first 3 columns associated with the San Francisco worksheet.

On the second line select the three columns associated with the New York worksheet.

Select the name for a new worksheet and use the variables names in the subscript column.

Click **OK**.

C1	C2-T	C3-T	C4
Subscripts			
1 San Francisco	HR		10
1 San Francisco	HR		7
1 San Francisco	Finance		10
1 San Francisco	Finance		10
1 San Francisco	Marketing		4
1 San Francisco	Marketing		3
1 San Francisco	Engineering		10
1 San Francisco	Engineering		6
1 San Francisco	Safety		8
1 San Francisco	Safety		3
2 New York	HR		5
2 New York	HR		6

Completed **Two Cities** table.

To reformat the table, delete the first column (Subscripts) and type column headings for C1-T, C2_T, and C3 (**Location**, **Department** and **Errors**).

C1-T	C2-T	C3
Location	Department	Errors
San Francisco	HR	10
San Francisco	HR	7
San Francisco	Finance	10
San Francisco	Finance	10
San Francisco	Marketing	4
San Francisco	Marketing	3
San Francisco	Engineering	10
San Francisco	Engineering	6
San Francisco	Safety	8
San Francisco	Safety	3
New York	HR	5
New York	HR	6

Completed worksheet.

Columns

Stacking Columns

Many functions in Minitab require the data to be presented in a columnwise manner. Columnwise is a format in which output is contained in one column and all other columns contain designated factors that provide the unique qualifiers.

For instance, look at the cycle time for a particular activity. One approach is to assign each associate to a separate column and populate with his/her data. The columnwise method, on the other hand, would put cycle time data for all operators in one column, with a separate column containing the associate's designation for each value in the main column.

Minitab Project: *Intro to Minitab*

Minitab Worksheet: *Columns*

The worksheet contains cycle times for 3 associates; each associate is listed in a separate column. To create the columnwise format the columns must be placed one on top of the other.

Minitab command: *Data > Stack > Columns*

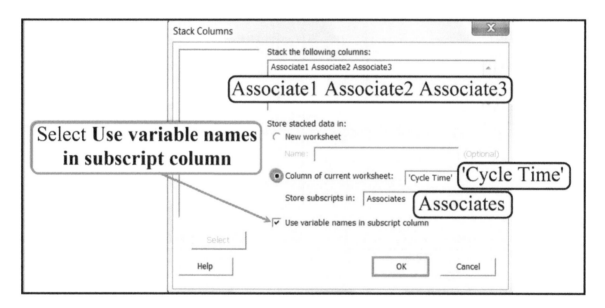

Select the columns for the stack (**C1 (Associate1)**, **C2 (Associate2)** and **C3 (Associate3)**).

Determine where to place the stacked column. The column for subscripts is optional, but recommended.

Click **OK**.

C1	C2	C3	C4	C5-T
Associate1	Associate2	Associate3	Cycle Time	Associates
51	41	55	51	Associate1
54	34	45	54	Associate1
50	44	51	50	Associate1
42	42	33	42	Associate1
49	62	38	49	Associate1
44	52	46	44	Associate1
33	50	46	33	Associate1
32	36	44	32	Associate1
46	56	45	46	Associate1

Column C4 (Cycle Time) is the column of stacked data with the subscripts appearing in column C5 (Associates).

Only the first 10 rows are shown.

Unstack

Minitab also offers a method to unstack data. With this method, the designated column is separated into a number of new columns depending upon the number of unique entities in the specified column.

Minitab command: *Data > Unstack Columns*

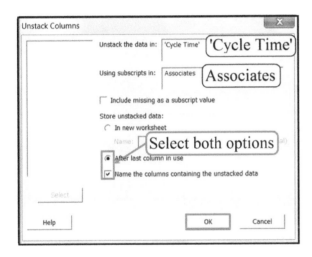

Select the column containing the data (**'Cycle Time'**).

Select the column containing the unstacking criteria (**Associates**).

Determine where to place the unstacked information.

Click **OK**.

C6	C7	C8
Cycle Time_Associate1	Cycle Time_Associate2	Cycle Time_Associate3
51	41	55
54	34	45
50	44	51
42	42	33
49	62	38
44	52	46
33	50	46
32	36	44
46	56	45

Here are the first few rows of the final table.

The cycle time information is separated (C6 to C8) based on the associate.

Hint: Use caution in selecting the '**Use subscripts in**' column. The number of new columns created is equal to the number of unique entities in this column.

Copy Columns

When a column is copied, Minitab automatically adds an "_#" (underscore and number) to the column name because every column must have a unique name. Once the copy is complete however, it is a good idea to edit the column heading and give it a name that best fits the project's needs.

Select the desired column to be copied by placing the cursor over the column number and performing a left mouse click. In this example the column is C1.

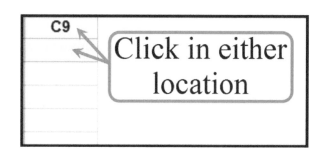

↓	C1	C2	C3
	Associate1	Associate2	Associate3
1	51	41	55
2	54	34	45
3	50	44	51
4	42	42	33
5	49	62	38
6	44	52	46
7	33	50	46
8	32	36	44
9	46	56	45

Once the column is selected, use the shortcut keys Ctrl + c or use the menu command: *Edit > Copy Cells*.

Select the location for the copy by clicking in either the column number cell or the column heading cell.

Paste the cell using the shortcut key (Ctrl + v) or the menu command: *Edit > Paste Cells*.

C9	Click in either location

Edit the column heading as needed.

C9
Associate1_1
51
54
50
42
49

Format columns

To change the format of a numeric column, select:

Editor > Format Column > Numeric

Or: right click one of the column's cells and select:

Format Column > Numeric.

For a **Text** column select: *Editor > Format Column > Text*. (Right click in the cell will provide the same options.)

To format a **Date/Time** column, right click the cell and select *Format Column > Date/Time*.

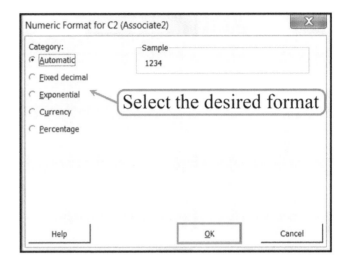

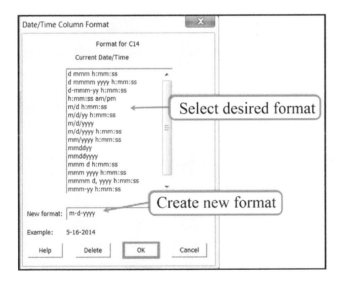

The Date/Time formats available in Minitab are seen below.

Select from the formats on the Minitab list, or create a new custom format.

Click **OK**.

Formulas

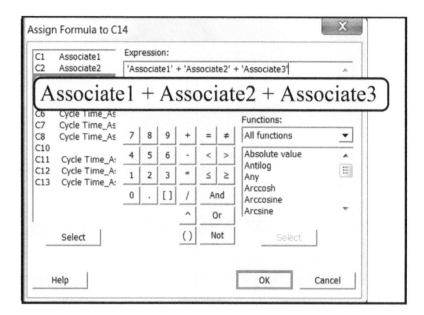

Formulas may be assigned to columns or used as a onetime calculation.

To assign a formula to a column, right click in the column and select

Formulas > Assign Formula to Column

Create the formula in the 'Expression:' window.

Click **OK**.

C14
147
133
145
117
149
142
129
112
147

The green check sign in the corner of the column number indicates a formula is associated with that column.

A second option is to use the **menu command** *Calc > Calculator*. This option will be discussed later in the chapter.

Random Data

Columns of random data may be assigned based on different distributions.

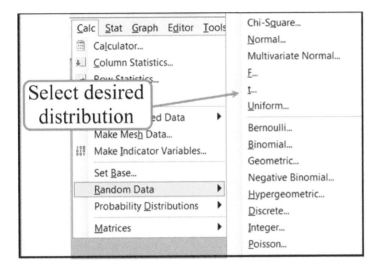

To populate a column with random data select *Calc > Random Data*.

Select the desired distribution.

This example uses the Normal distribution.

Select the number of rows to be populated (50).

Select the columns to contain the random data; multiple columns may be selected.

For the normal distribution, select the mean and standard deviation that defines the population.

Click **OK**.

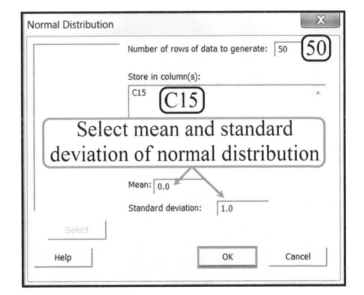

The columns are now populated with the requested data.

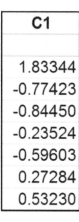

C1
1.83344
-0.77423
-0.84450
-0.23524
-0.59603
0.27284
0.53230

Patterned Data

If specific patterns of data are required, Minitab provides options to input numeric, text, or date/time values.

Minitab command: *Calc > Make Patterned Data*

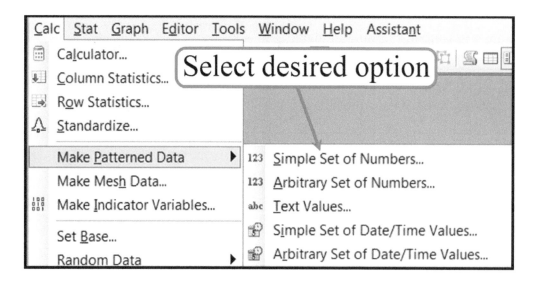

Select the type of patterned data.

This example uses the 'Simple Set of Numbers'.

Select the column for the patterned data. Only one column can be populated at a time.

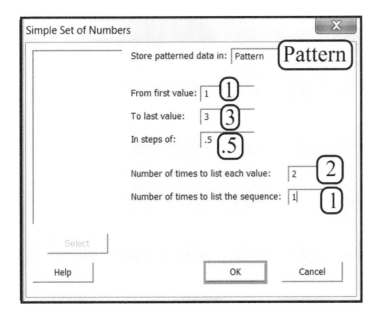

Input the first and last values of the series (1 and 3) and select the step increments.

This example uses steps of .5, so the values are 1, 1.5, 2, 2.5 and 3.

Each value is displayed twice before moving to the next value, and the entire sequence is displayed once.

Change these settings to match the desired result.

Click **OK**.

C3
Pattern
1.0
1.0
1.5
1.5
2.0
2.0
2.5
2.5
3.0
3.0

Now each value is displayed twice in steps of .5.

The Text value option uses the following dialog box. Type the name of the column to store the patterned list.

Menu: *Calc > Make Patterned Data > Text Values*

For **Text values**, double quotes are required for names with a space. Without the double quotes, Minitab sees it as two separate names.

Select the number of times to list each text value and the number of time to repeat the sequence.

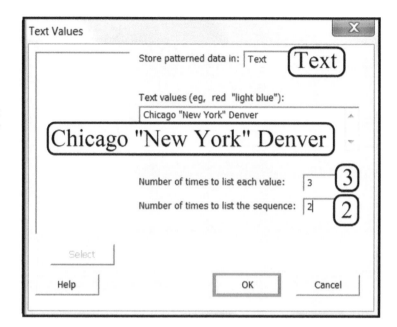

C4-T
Text
Chicago
Chicago
Chicago
New York
New York
New York
Denver
Denver
Denver

Only the first set of city names are shown.

Date/Time options are seen here: Inputs for the Date/Time pattern are similar to those found in the pattern number window.

Menu: *Calc > Make Patterned Data > Simple Set of Date/Time Values*

Input starting and ending dates.

Input the steps for the change in dates.

Select the number of times to list each value.

Select the number of times to list the sequence.

Click **OK**.

The 'Step unit:' option is unique. It contains the following:

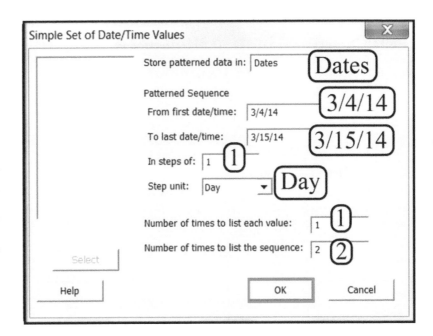

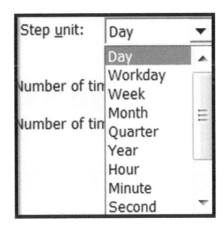

Data Manipulation

Minitab allows data manipulations in many different forms. This section covers the following:
- Change Data Type
- Code Data
- Rank Data
- Sort Data

Minitab Project: **Intro to Minitab**

Minitab Worksheet: *Data Manipulation*

C1-T	C2	C3-T
Location	Percent	Max
Green Bay	4.5	40
Green Bay	6.0	34
Boston	2.3	42
Boston	8.0	47
Austin	4.2	55
Austin	3.1	32
Seattle	4.5	48
Seattle	6.0	72
Green Bay	2.1	45

Change Data Type

If numeric data appears in a column left justified and the column heading has a '–T', Minitab considers the values to be text and no statistical analysis is possible. This issue often appears if a file is opened from another program into Minitab.

To correct this issue, change the data type.

Minitab command: *Data > Change Data Type > Text to Numeric*

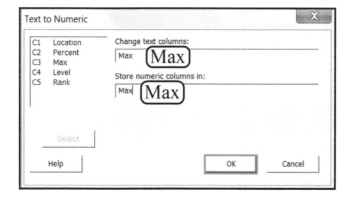

Select the column of text to be changed (Max).

Select the column (either a new column or the original column) to store the changed values.

Click **OK**.

The results show the old text column is now numeric.

Hint: Text columns changed to numeric will lose the cells with letters. The cell appear with the * indicating a missing value.

C1-T	C2	C3
Location	Percent	Max
Green Bay	4.5	40
Green Bay	6.0	34
Boston	2.3	42
Boston	8.0	47
Austin	4.2	55
Austin	3.1	32
Seattle	4.5	48
Seattle	6.0	72
Green Bay	2.1	45

The Max column is now numeric.

Code Data

Coding data allows for values (numeric, text, or date/time) to be replaced by other values.

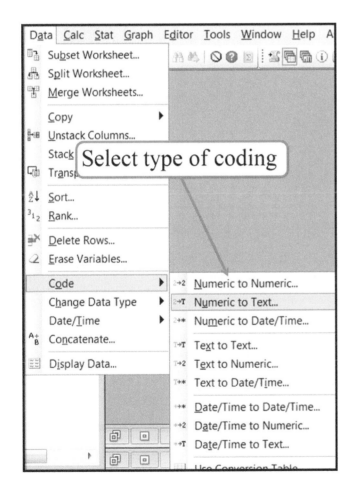

Minitab command: *Data > Code*

Select the type of coding desired. All combinations are possible.

The example presented will be a numeric to text coding.

Select the initial column with the numeric values (Max).

Select the column to store the coded information (**Level**).

For the original values, use either a single value or a set of values. The colon (**:**) between values indicates all numbers inclusive. The listings cannot have any overlapping values between groups.

Click OK.

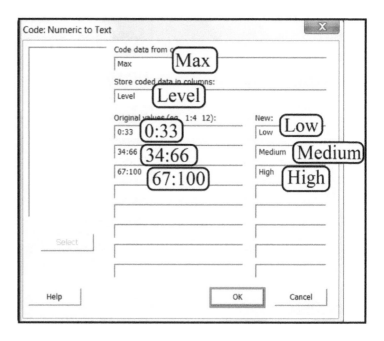

C3	C4-T
Max	**Level**
40	Medium
34	Medium
42	Medium
47	Medium
55	Medium
32	Low
48	Medium
72	High

The new column contains the coded information.

Rank Data

To determine the rank of n values, sort the data low to high. Assign a rank of 1 to the lowest value and a rank of n to the largest value. In the case of a tie between values, Minitab averages the ranks of the common values. So for instance, if ranks 5, 6, 7, and 8 are tied, they will all receive the rank of (5+6+7+8)/4 = 6.5.

Minitab command: *Data > Rank*

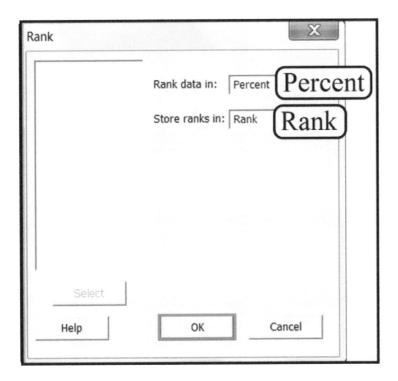

Select the column containing the data (**Percent**).

Select the column to store the rank values (**Rank**).

Click **OK**.

C1-T	C2	C3	C4-T	C5
Location	Percent	Max	Level	Rank
Green Bay	4.5	40	Medium	17.0
Green Bay	6.0	34	Medium	24.5
Boston	2.3	42	Medium	4.0
Boston	8.0	47	Medium	30.5
Austin	4.2	55	Medium	13.0
Austin	3.1	32	Low	8.5
Seattle	4.5	48	Medium	17.0

Column C5 contains the rank values.

Sort Data

Sorting data is a common actions performed on data.

Minitab command: *Data > Sort*

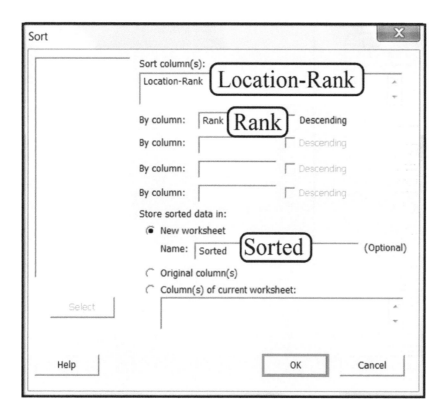

Select the columns for the sort. The hyphen between the two column names indicates all columns between those two are included in the sort.

The 'By column:' is the column used to determine the sort. Notice that 4 levels of sorts are possible.

Determine where to place the sorted columns. They can be placed in a new worksheet or back in the original columns.

Hint: To place the sorted columns back into the original columns, keep an index column available to re-sort to the original positions.

C1-T	C2	C3	C4-T	C5
Location	Percent	Max	Level	Rank
Seattle	1.6	54	Medium	1.0
Green Bay	2.1	45	Medium	2.0
Boston	2.3	42	Medium	4.0
Austin	2.3	55	Medium	4.0
Boston	2.3	61	Medium	4.0
Seattle	2.5	78	High	6.0
Austin	2.8	43	Medium	7.0
Austin	3.1	32	Low	8.5
Green Bay	3.1	25	Low	8.5

Worksheet sorted by the column **Rank**.

Calculator

Activate Worksheet *Calculator*.

To use Minitab's calculator, select *Calc > Calculator*

Select the output column, and create the equation in the '**Expression**' location. Mathematical and Statistical functions are available in the Functions option.

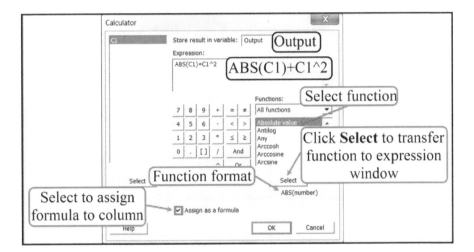

Click the function name, The format appears below the **Select** button.

Click the **Select** button to place the function in the Expression window. Input the necessary parameters.

To assign the formula to the column select the **Assign as a formula** box.

Click **OK**.

C1	C2
	Output
1.83344	5.19494
-0.77423	1.37366
-0.84450	1.55768
-0.23524	0.29058
-0.59603	0.95128
0.27284	0.34728

C2 is the new column with the expression's results.

Graph Options

Minitab offers many options to spice up a graph; so many in fact, that it's not possible to cover them all in this chapter. This section will present a few of these options. Additional options appear later in the Measure chapter.

Brush points

Brushing an individual point on a graph highlights the point and places a dot next to the row number corresponding to that point in the worksheet. The row numbers are also listed in the upper left corner of the graph. The following example will demonstrate brushing with the '**I-MR**' chart.

Minitab Project: **Graph Options**

Minitab Worksheet: **Graph**

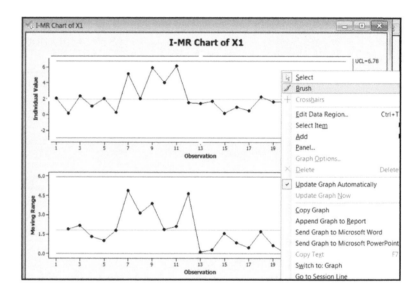

Select the I-MR chart.

Place the cursor in the graph window and right click.

Select **Brush**.

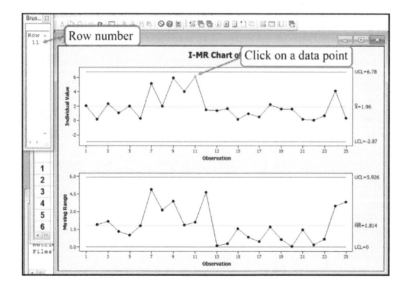

The cursor changes to a hand with the index finger extended.

Point the hand at a data point and click the left mouse button.

The point changes color and the row number appear in the '**Brush**' window in the upper left corner of the screen.

The row corresponding to this point will have a dot next to the row number.

8	2.04481	62	New York
9	5.93346	59	Denver
10	4.07405	65	Chicago
· 11	6.16035	70	New York
12	1.52732	56	Denver
13	1.43558	65	Chicago
14	1.69547	54	New York
15	0.17306	48	Denver

The brushed point is located in row 11.

A diamond appears to the left of the brushed row's number.

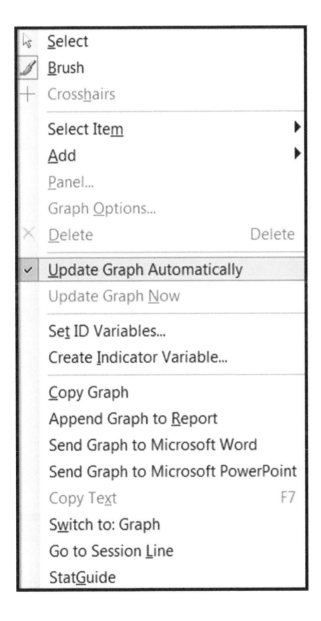

Update Graph Automatically

Minitab now offers the option of automatically updating graphs created in Minitab. This is a very useful function when manipulating data in the worksheet.

To activate automatic update, place the cursor in the graph and right mouse click.

Select **Update Graph Automatically**.

Any changes subsequently made to the worksheet will automatically be reflected in the graph.

Tile Graphs

The tile function is very useful because it allows multiple graphs to be displayed in a single Minitab window. The graphs (as well as the worksheet, if selected) are formatted to fit in the window, but including too many graphs at the same time causes them to appear very small.

Select the Graph folder icon on the Main Menu.

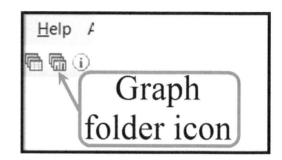

The **Project Manager** window appears.

Select the desired graphs, holding down the Ctrl key to make multiple selections.

Point at one of the selected graphs and perform a right mouse click.

Select **Tile** from the list.

The graphs now appear next to one another in the Graph window.

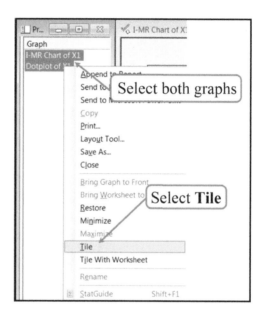

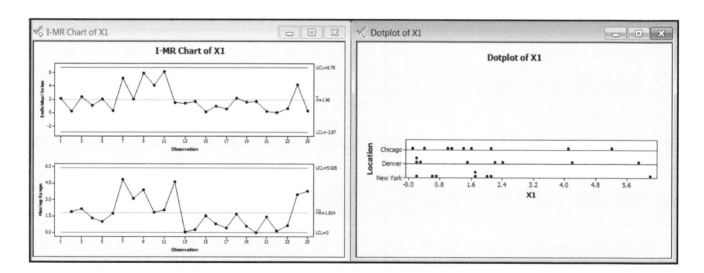

Hint: DO NOT use the menu selection *Window > Tile*. This will cause every worksheet and graph (plus the session window) to tile.

Minitab Shortcut Keys

Below is a list of some useful shortcut keys. For a complete list, select *Help > Help > Intro to Minitab*, or click the Help Icon.

Command	Keys	Description
FileNew	Ctrl+N	Create a new Minitab project or worksheet
FileOpenProject	Ctrl+O	Open an existing Minitab project
FilePrintWindow	Ctrl+P	Print the contents of the active window
FileSaveProject	Ctrl+S	Save Minitab Projects
EditCommandLineEditor	Ctrl+L	Edit and submit session commands
EditCopy	Ctrl+C	Copy the selection and put it on the Clipboard
EditCut	Ctrl+X	Cut the selection and put it on the Clipboard
EditLastDialogBox	Ctrl+E	Reopen the most recently used dialog to rerun the command of modify settings
EditPaste	Ctrl+V	Paste the contents of the Clipboard
EditRedo	Ctrl+Y	Reverse the previous undone action
EditSelectAll	Ctrl+A	Select all of the contents in the active window
EditUndo	Ctrl+Z	Undo previous action
Reset Dialog Box	F3	Resets active dialog box to default settings

Minitab Macros

Minitab macros can help with repetitive tasks by creating a series of session commands. These are one line commands strung together to create a Macro. Macro's are either Global in nature (these allow the user to analyze data in an active worksheet), or Local (macros that can accept arguments and have their own subcommands). For more information on creating macro's, contact Minitab. A library of macros are available from Minitab at www.minitab.com. To view the command lines that are being used while running Minitab, select the History icon.

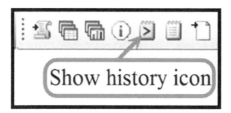

To display an example of the macro command lines, after performing a series of actions in Minitab, click on the Show History icon.

> **History**
> Worksheet "3LevelANOVA.MTW"
> VarTest 'Sue' - 'Jerry';
> Unstacked;
> Confidence 95.0;
> GInterval;
>   NoDefault;
> TMethod;
> TBonferroni;
> TTest.

Above is an example of the commands Minitab used to create a Test of Equal Variance for the factors Sue, Fred, and Jerry.

Define Phase

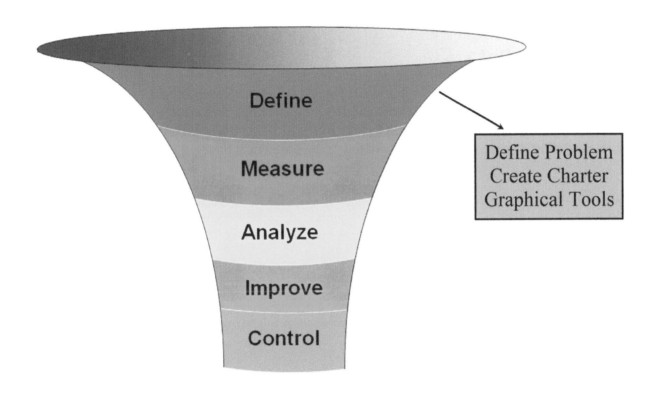

Define
Measure
Analyze
Improve
Control

Define Problem
Create Charter
Graphical Tools

Define Phase

Many Six Sigma practitioners argue this is the critical phase of any Six Sigma project. Why? Because selecting the right project and accurately scoping that project form the basic foundation for the ultimate success of the project as a whole. This is also the phase where those new to Six Sigma first encounter a major difference of this process compared to other processes. In the past, organizations relied on 'gut feelings' and anecdotal observations as the primary sources of information to create a project definition.

Perhaps this method occasionally bore fruit, but in the majority of cases it likely caused the entire project to go astray. The reason, because 'gut feelings' and anecdotal observations are simply not reliable sources of information on which to base a critical improvement project. In other words, thinking something is a problem is one thing, being able to show it with data is something else.

Working With Data

The Six Sigma process is different (and effective) because it relies on measurable data. This usually requires some initial and basic analysis of available data to determine where a problem exists and its overall extent. It is a detailed and precise process which can be frustrating for those unaccustomed to this level of scrutiny. The process is critical, however, to accurately defining the problem at hand.

In the Define phase, team efforts focus on exploring data relating to issues within an organization. This allows the team to determine where and how resources should be allocated to produce the desired improvements. Specific metrics are also established during this phase, allowing for an accurate determination of the business case for proceeding as well as measuring the ultimate success of the project.

While the initial project selection process typically begins at a high organizational level, it is then scoped down to a level appropriate for either a Black Belt or Green Belt to pursue. An effective method often used to aid in scoping a project is to create a series of graphs based on available data. Graphs are an excellent visual representation of the information under investigation. They allow team participants to 'see' the information in new ways.

In addition, graphs can demonstrate clearly whether there have been recent changes in the metric, and/or if the variation in the metric are due to a second factor. Graphs are also used to visualize and demonstrate whether changes in the process instituted by the team has improved or degraded the metric. This chapter includes samples of several different graphs using Minitab.

The Project Charter

Following project definition, the next step is to create a Project Charter. A project charter is a written 'road map', used to define the issues identified and clearly state how the team will proceed through the project.

There are many different types and styles of project charters, but they all have similar requirements and specific components.

State the practical problem under consideration. It is important for every improvement team to understand exactly what it is they are working on, and defining the 'practical problem' is one way of achieving this objective. This is where the basic issue at hand is explained and described.

2. **Project Description: what is the "Practical Problem"**	Problem and goal statement (project's purpose)

Examples might include:
- Customers are dissatisfied with our on-time delivery.
- Department 47 creates too much scrap.
- Invoices have too many errors.
- Customers complain about the wait times when they call in.
- Claims take too long to process.

Next, each general issue needs a 'problem and goal statement'; again using the examples above, potential statements include:
- Customer on-time delivery is currently averaging 74%. The goal of this project is to raise the on-time delivery to 95%.
- Department 47's scrap costs are 33% of sales. The goal of this project is to reduce this to 10% of sales.
- The current 12.8% of the invoices have errors. The goal of this project is to reduce this to 1%.
- The current customer wait time is 5.5 minutes. The goal of this proj-ect is to reduce the wait time to 45 seconds.
- The current claims process takes 21 days. The goal of this proj-ect is to reduce the claims process to 5 days.

Assign metrics to the problem. At this point, each general issue must also have a metric assigned to it that ties into the overall practical problem. Using the examples above, potential metrics might include:
- Measure Percent on-time delivery, or actual time to deliver.
- Measure scrap as a percent of product or as a gross weight.
- Measure the number of errors per invoice, or the number of errors per line on an invoice.
- Measure customer wait times.
- Measure time to process a claim.

3. Objective:		Project Y's	Baseline	GOAL	Entitlement	units
	What improvement is targeted and what will be the impact on Rolled Throughput Yield (RTY), Cost of Poor Quality (COPQ) and Capability index C-P, back orders, costs?					
	The "Statistical Problem" - the measurable variable(s	Metric 1				%
		Metric 2				$/A
		Metric 3				units/A

The Charter includes three categories of metrics: baseline (the current situation), goal (the level that indicates a successful project) and entitlement (the best that can be expected or perfection). Along with the critical metrics, another type of metric is important to consider. These are referred to as 'secondary' metrics. Secondary metrics are those that the team needs to keep-an-eye on. For instance, if a team is tasked with reducing a cycle time by 30%, their secondary metric would be defects. It's easy to reduce cycle times if defect levels are allowed to soar. So in this case whatever is the defect's baseline, this would also be the goal. By reducing cycle times the team cannot allow the defects to increase.

Using the first project as an example, where the primary metric is on-time delivery. This primary metric could be improved by sending out partial shipments or keeping a large inventory of finished goods on hand and available for shipping. Stepping back from the primary metric, however, neither of these solutions is acceptable because they would create other, much greater problems elsewhere in the organization. Therefore, a secondary metric might include: 1) inventory levels, or 2) percent shipments complete.

For another example, look at the third project where the primary metric is measuring the number of errors per invoice. This primary metric could be improved by ensuring multiple individuals inspect each invoice, but again, this solution is not acceptable. It would greatly increase the cycle time for each invoice, causing a negative impact elsewhere in the organization. The secondary metrics in this case could be: 1) cycle time and 2) man-hours per invoice.

Refine the project scope. At this point in the process, many projects are far too broad to be accomplished within the target of four to six months. The scope is simply too large and must be reduced, generally by performing some preliminary analysis on primary metric. Simple graphs are quite useful in helping to refine the scope of a project.

6. Project Scope:	Which part of the process will be investigated and excluded.

Scope reduction begins with looking at data taken from the process in question, or from customer surveys if applicable. If this kind of data is not readily available then the team should start collecting it.

Examples of useful types of data to collect include;
- Cycle times
- Defects
- Count of issues
- Sales volume
- Number of new clients per month

Before data analysis can begin, it is important to determine the critical metrics. Critical metrics come from internal customers (individuals or groups within a company who receive or are affected by a process output) or external customers (those who receive the output of a process but are not part of the company). Once critical metrics are determined and data is gathered, the team can determine if the results indicate a problem does indeed exist.

It is important to remember that during this Define phase, only an initial assessment is performed. More detailed analyses occur later on in the Measure and Analyze phase; it is these later analyses that will associate specific critical inputs (X's) with the critical outputs (Y's), allowing proactive process control to occur.

The Define phase, then, should set in motion the path to improvement.

Graphical Tools

Graphical tools are critical to the Define phase because they are quite often the best way to analyze date related to the processes at hand. Of course there are many different methods for analyzing preliminary data, and Six Sigma teams should not hesitate to use other methods as well. However, graphs are particularly useful because they add a helpful visual component to the process.

No single graph is right for every occasion and situation, so the team should have a good understanding of a) different kinds of graphs, and b) when and where it is appropriate to use each type of graph. This portion for the Define section will discuss the following types of graphs:
- Dot Plot
- Histogram
- Box Plot
- Scatter Plot
- Run Chart
- I-MR Chart
- Pareto Plot

Dot Plot

Tool Use

Use a Dot Plot to display individual data points. It provides an excellent visual representation for the data set's center and range. It also provides a satisfactory indication for the shape of the distribution.

Data Type

A Dot Plot requires numeric data.

Minitab Project: **QualityTools.MPJ**

Worksheet: *Check in Time*

This data represent the number of seconds it takes to check in customers at the front desk of a hotel. Fifty data points were collected on each of three associates.

Menu command: *Graph> Dotplot > Simple*

Input **Cycle Time** as the Graph variables:

Click **OK**.

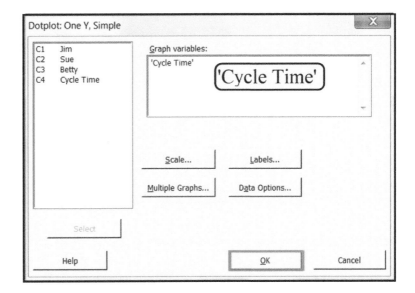

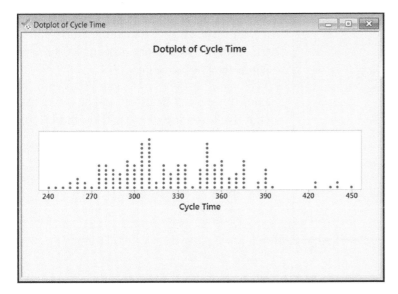

The individual values are shown, with equal values stacked upon one another.

The range of values is evident; the minimum is 240 and the maximum is 450, therefore the range is 450 – 240 = 210.

The center can be approximated as around 330.

Following an initial look at the process data, it might be desirable to determine if various individuals are behaving differently. To accomplish this, it is necessary to show which values are associated with which associate.

In the worksheet, this information is produced by the Associate column. There are three associates listed, so to determine if Cycle Times differ for each associate, produce a graph showing the values for each associate. The Dot Plot with groups is useful for making this comparison.

The Associate in this case would be considered an X; whether this is a critical X is determined later.

To create the Dot Plot with groups, use the following command.

Menu command: *Graph > Dotplot > With Groups*

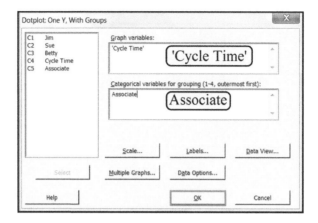

Input **Cycle Time** as the Graph variables: and **Associate** as the Categorical variables.

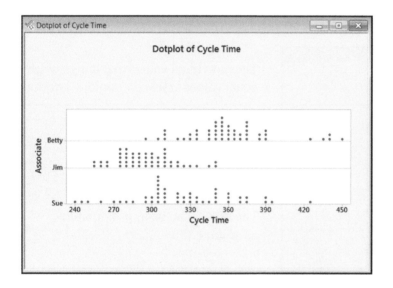

Click OK.

This graph shows the same information as the Simple Dot Plot, only now the data is separated by associate.

Looking at this graph it might be suspected that Jim has a lower cycle time than Betty.

To make the final determination, a t-Test or ANOVA analysis is required. These tests are explained in the Analyze section.

The Dot Plot can be used with more than one output, as well as with and without groups.

Select *Graph > Dotplot* to bring up this window:

While there are other options available, don't create a graph that will be too complex or confusing for the audience. Keep it simple.

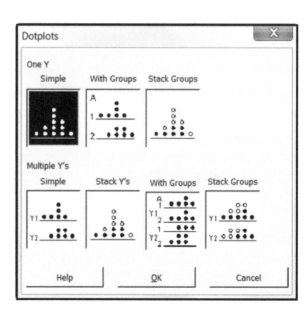

Histogram

Tool Use: Use a Histogram to show the general shape, center and spread of data. It does not provide individual data values.

Data Type: The Histogram requires numeric data.

Minitab Project: **QualityTools.MPJ**

Worksheet: *Check in Time*

Menu command: *Graph> Histogram > Simple*

Input **'Cycle Time'** as the Graph variables:

Click **OK**.

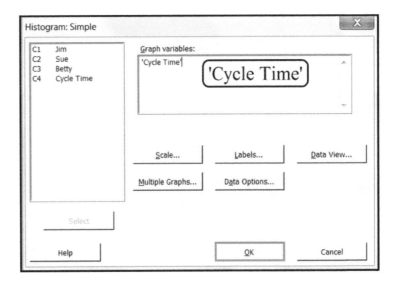

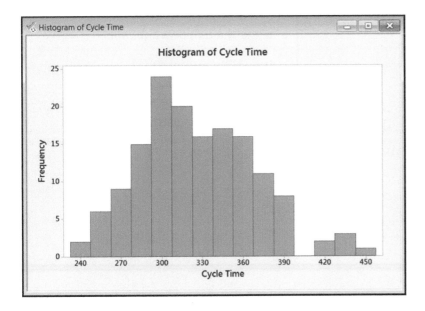

Data are binned into non-overlapping groups. The number of values in each bin is indicated by the height of the bar (frequency).

A Histogram is useful to visualize a sample's parent distribution. Minitab uses the Normal distribution as its default, and will also create curves relative to the distributions listed below.

Use these steps to create a Histogram with one of the distributions overlaid:

Menu command: *Graph> Histogram > With Fit*

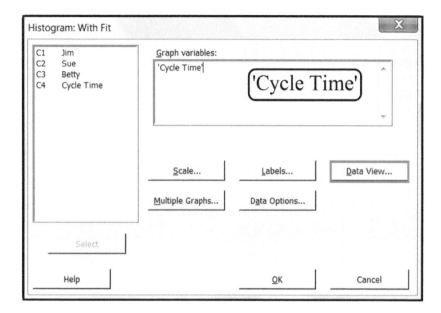

Select **'Cycle Time'** as the Graph variables;

Click **Data View**.

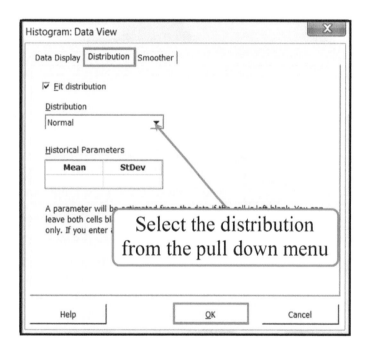

Click the **Distribution** tab and choose the distribution by using the pull down menu.

Input **Parameters** for the specific distribution if they are known; if no parameters are input, Minitab uses the sample data to estimate the values.

Click **OK** (twice).

Distributions available in Minitab

Normal
Lognormal
3-parameter lognormal
Gamma
3-parameter gamma
Exponential
2-parameter exponential
Smallest extreme value
Weibull
3-parameter Weibull
Largest extreme value
Logistic
Loglogistic
3-parameter loglogistic

This final graph shows the same histogram, but now with the normal curve superimposed.

The normal curve has a mean of 326.7 and a standard deviation of 42.52. The values are provided in the upper right corner of the graph.

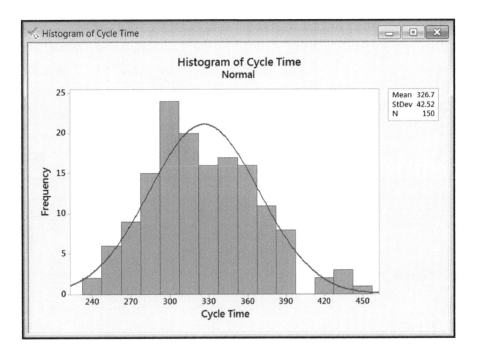

Box Plot

Tool Use: Use a Box Plot to display a summary of the data set. It provides the Median and the range of data values.

Data Type: The Box Plot requires numeric data.

Minitab Project: **QualityTools.MPJ**

Worksheet: *Check in Time*

Menu command: *Graph > Boxplot > Simple*

Input **Cycle Time** as the Graph variables:

Click **OK**.

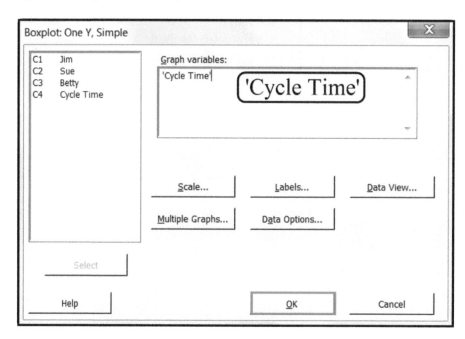

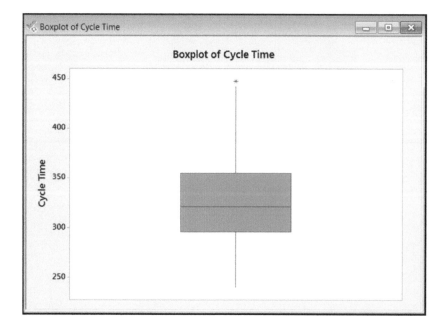

The Box Plot (also known as a Box and Whiskers plot) is so named because the design forms a box representing the middle 50% of the data.

The upper portion of the box represents the value below which 75% of the data resides.

The line inside the box represents the Median (the middle or 50% value).

The bottom portion of the box is the value below which 25% of the data resides.

The whiskers extend to the upper and lower values, unless the value extends beyond the predetermined limit referred to as the 'outlier indicator'.

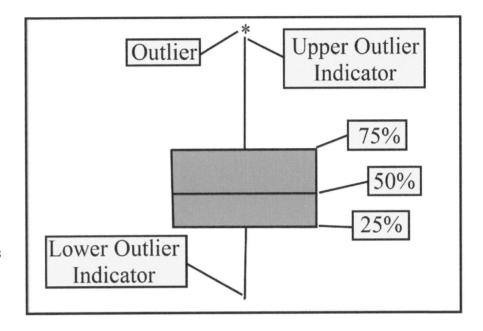

Any value beyond a length of 1.5 times the box height (referred to as the IQR or Inner Quartile Range) will be considered an outlier.

Remember this is a designation only. An outlier does not refer to a bad or incorrect value, only one that is different than the rest of the values in the data set.

Outliers should be investigated to be sure an error wasn't made in the recording or collection of the value.

The Box Plot will also display different groups of data for a side-by-side comparison.

Menu command: *Graph > Boxplot > With Groups*

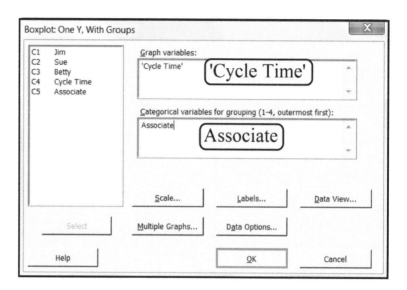

Input **Cycle Time** as the Graph variables

Select **Associate** for the Categorical variables

Click **OK**

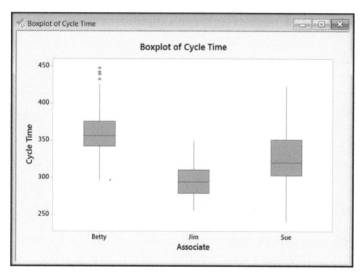

The Box Plots are displayed side by side for easy comparison.

Jim's information shows less spread (shorter lines) and a tighter middle 50% of data (smaller box). His cycle times appear lower than Betty's, and may also be lower than Sue's.

The analytical tools to make this determination are covered in the Analyze chapter.

Additional options for Box Plots include displaying individual values.

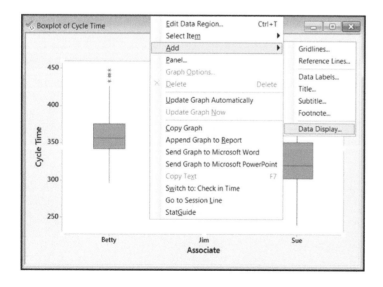

Right click inside the graph

Select **Add** then **Data Display**.

Select **Individual symbols**.

Click **OK**.

Other options are available as listed in the window.

Select the desired options and click **OK.**

When there are multiple values close to one another, it becomes difficult to see each data point. To alleviate this issue, Minitab will separate the circles (referred to as jittering the points).

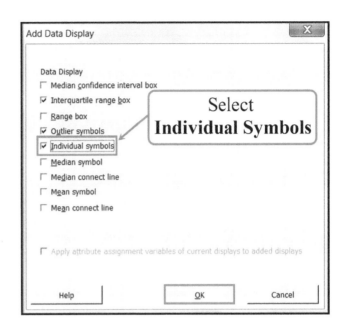

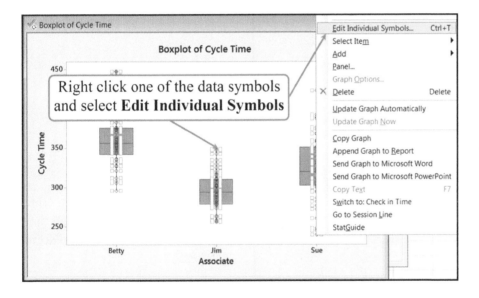

Right mouse click one of the circles and select **Edit Individual Symbols**.

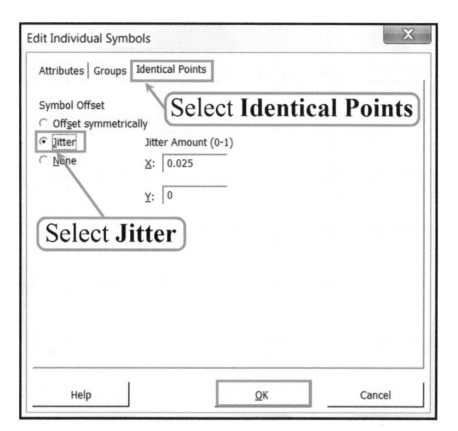

Click the **Jitter** button

Click **OK**.

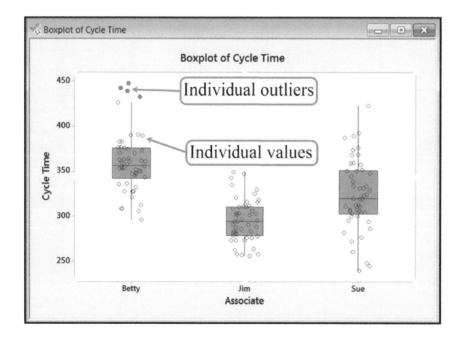

The individual values are thus jittered (moved) to the left and right so they become distinct entities.

Time Series Plot

Tool Use: The Time Series Plot displays data in time sequence. It will display shifts, trends or cyclic events that might help the team determine sources of variation.

Note: Minitab assumes data is arranged in a time sequence from earliest to recent.

Data Type: The Time Series Plot requires numeric data.

Worksheet: *Check in Time*

Menu command: *Graph > Time Series Plot > Simple*

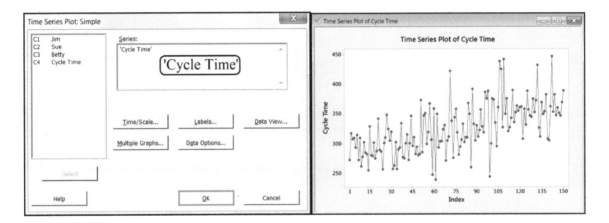

Select **Cycle Time** as the Series.

Click **OK**.

This graph indicates data on the right side might be higher than on the left.

Using the by variable option will show grouped values for the individual associates.

Right mouse click on one of the graph symbols and select **Edit Symbols**.

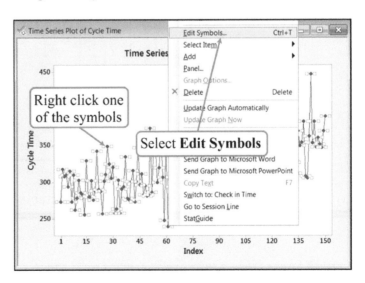

Select the Groups tab.

Choose **Associate**

Click **OK**.

The graph now shows each operator as a different color.

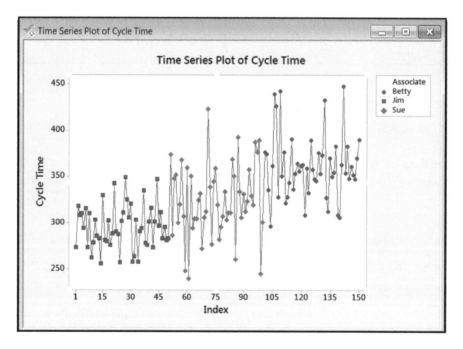

It is now evident why the values are increasing; it is attributable to the differences among the associates.

I-MR Chart

Tool Use: The I-MR Chart mimics the Time Series Plot, but contains three additional lines.

Data Type: The I-MR Chart requires numeric data.

Sample I-MR Chart:

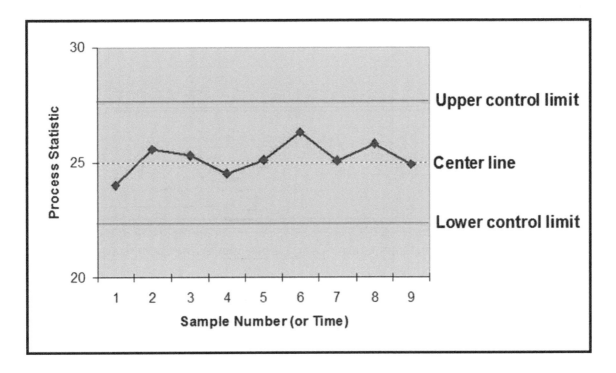

The Center line is the average of the selected values. It is expected that the values follow a random pattern around the Center Line.

The upper and lower lines are called the Upper and Lower Control Limits. Using statistically calculated values, these lines represent the values between which almost 100% (99.73% to be exact) of the values are expected to reside.

Values outside of these limits indicate a potentially abnormal condition existed during those process runs.

Worksheet: *Check in Time*

Menu command: *Stat > Control Charts > Variables Charts for Individuals > I-MR*

Select **Cycle Time** as the Variable.

Click **OK**.

The I-MR Chart looks the same as a Time Series Plot, except for the Control Limits.

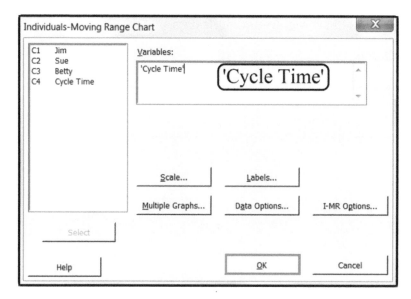

Note: More detailed information about Control Charts is provided in the Control chapter of this book.

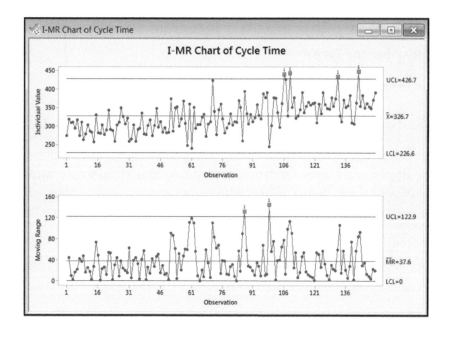

For the time being, it is important to simply understand that any point above the upper red line (Upper Control Limit) or below the lower red line (Lower Control Limit) indicates an Out-of-Control condition.

In this example, several values are above the UCL; this should be investigated further.

It was suggested earlier that differences exist among the associates. To observe this with a control chart, select:

Menu command: *Stat > Control Charts > Variables Charts for Individuals > I-MR* **Choose the I-MR Options button.**

Another advantage of the I-MR chart is the ability to compare the process mean and control limits between two groups. In the Check in Time worksheet, the fourth column represents three different employees. To compare the three employees on a single graph, return to the Individuals Moving Range Chart input screen and select the I-MR Options button.

Select **Cycle Time** as the Variables.

Click the **I-MR Options** button.

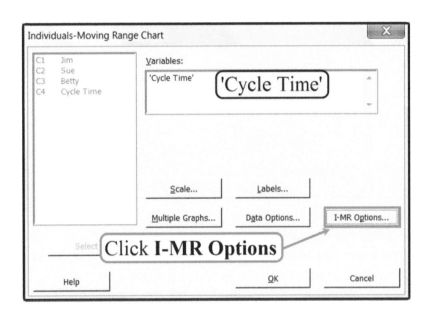

Select the **Stages** tab.

Choose **Associate** for the Define Stages.

Click **OK** twice.

The chart now demonstrates information for each associate.

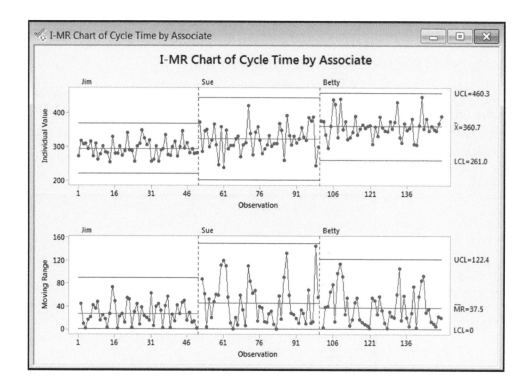

There is a difference between the means; the center lines for the groups are not the same. Whether this difference is significant requires analytical tools that will be discussed in the Analyze chapter of this book.

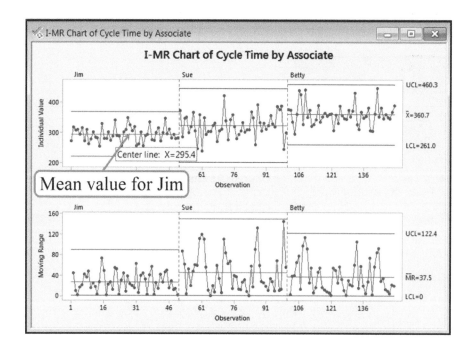

Hint: Notice that the mean for Betty is shown on the right (360.7).

To find the mean value for Jim or Sue, place the cursor over the mean line in the chart.

The value of the line appears.

Scatter Plot

Tool Use: Use a Scatter Plot to determine whether a relationship exists between two variables.

Data Type: A Scatter Plot requires numeric data for both inputs.

Minitab Project: **QualityTools.MPJ**

Worksheet: *SnowRain*

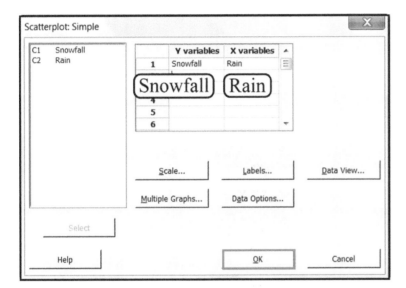

Menu command: *Graph > Scatterplot > Simple*

Select **Snowfall** as the Y variable and **Rain** as the X variable.

Click **OK**.

The relationship between Rain and Snowfall is clear; higher Rain levels correspond to higher levels of Snowfall.

Note: Further analysis of this relationship is provided in the Regression portion of the Analysis chapter in this book.

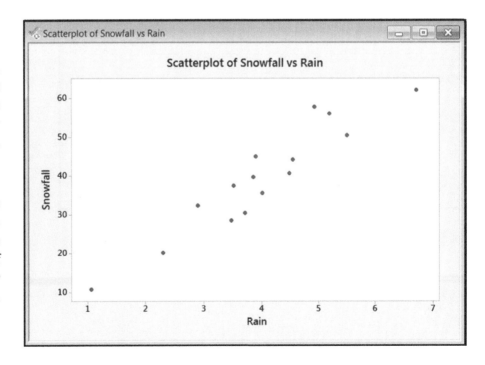

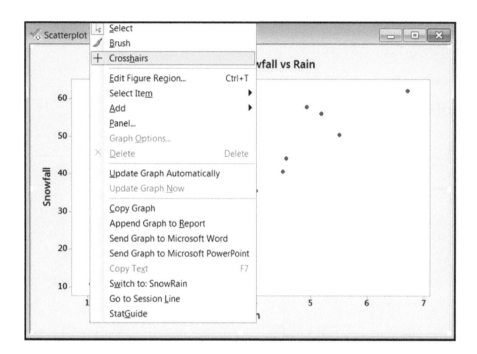

Hint: To obtain values for individual points, right click inside the graph and select **Crosshairs**.

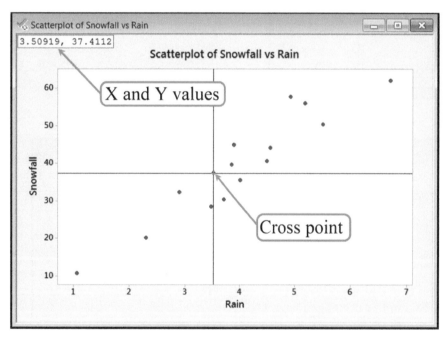

Move the crosshairs over the desired location, and the X and Y values appear in the upper left corner of the graph.

Pareto Chart

Tool Use: The Pareto Plot is a bar chart sorted left to right (highest to lowest); it is commonly used to indicate the frequency of issues. It is particularly easy to understand, and is an excellent way to shed light on the major issues or problems facing a company. Use a Pareto Chart to help prioritize issues related to the project.

Data Type: A Pareto Plot requires counts of issues in different categories.

Minitab Project: **QualityTools.MPJ**

Worksheet: *Quality*

Data for a Pareto Plot is collected in one of two ways:
1. Record each issue as a separate entry in the worksheet

or

2. Perform a summary analysis and present the information as a summary table.

Both methods are demonstrated in this section.

Menu command: *Stat > Quality Tools > Pareto Chart*

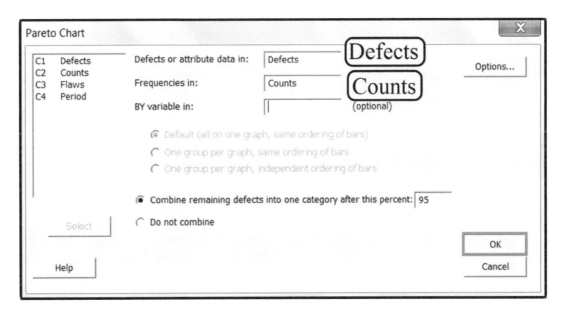

Input **Defects** for Labels in:

Select **Counts** for Frequency in:

Click **OK**.

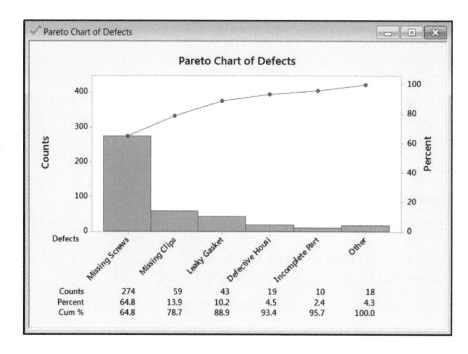

The top categories comprising 95% of the issues are shown. The remaining groups are placed in a category labeled 'Other'.

To display all of the defect categories, return to the Pareto Chart input screen (Ctrl+e) and select the 'Do Not Combine' option.

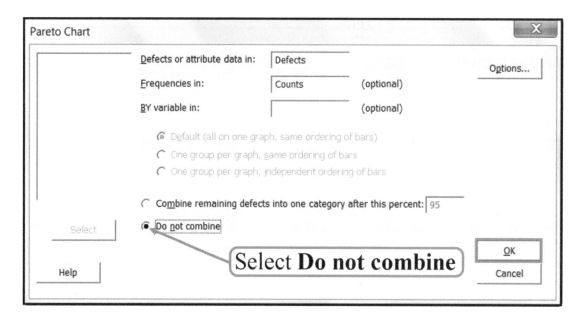

Select **Defects** for Labels in:

Select **Counts** for Frequencies in:

Select the 'Do not combine' option.

Click **OK**.

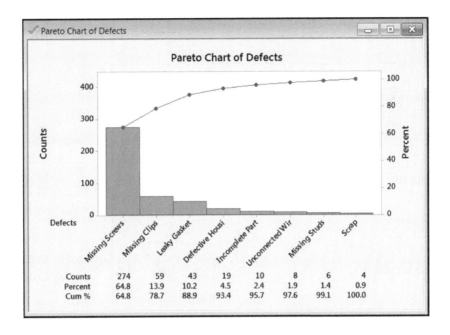

Now all defect categories are shown. Use this view with caution, because the chart can easily become overcrowded if there are too many categories.

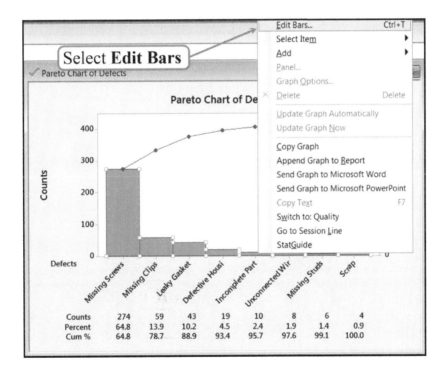

Hint: To change the color, pattern or outline of a bar, first click on any bar; this will select all bars. Next, click the bar to be changed; this will select that individual bar. Finally, double click on the bar to display the option window.

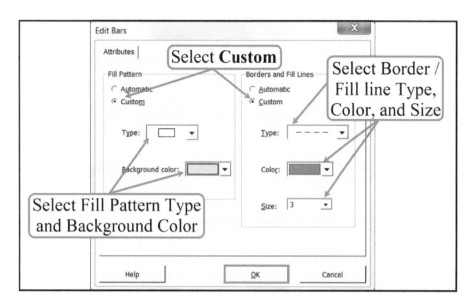

Select both **Custom** options.

Use the pull down menu to select the type and color of the Fill Pattern.

Use the pull down menu to select the Type, Color and Size of the Borders and Fill Lines.

Click **OK**.

Here is the updated graph, with new color and lines for first bar.

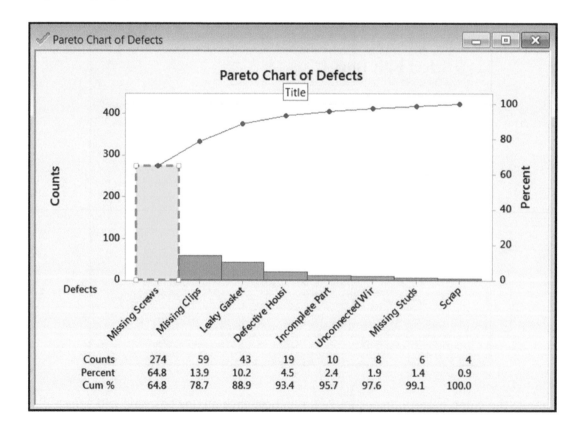

Minitab also allows the user to create a chart divided by a second category. To create a chart that's divided by a column representing the shift where the defect occurred, first, look at the defects as a single group.

Menu command: *Stat > Quality Tools > Pareto Chart*

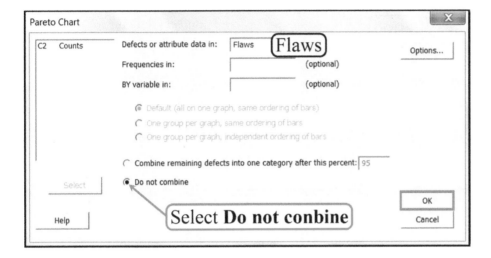

Select **Flaws**.

Choose the '**Do not combine**' option.

Click **OK**.

Edit these bars as shown previously.

For instance, highlight the first two bars (Peel and Scratch) to emphasize which defects are targeted for reduction.

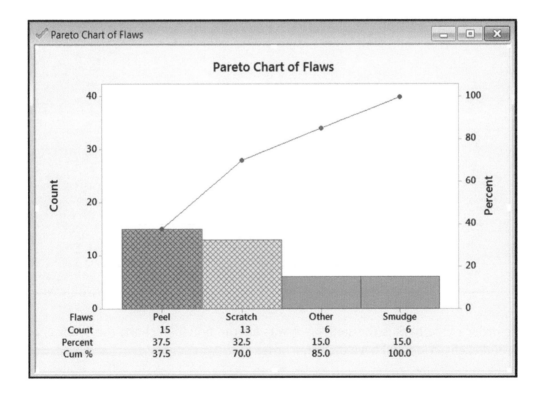

The chart can also be edited to show defects by period. To do so, first return to the Pareto Chart menu (ctrl+e).

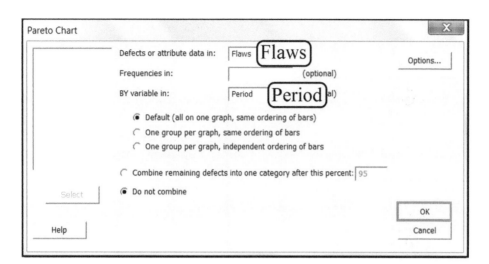

Select **Flaws** for Chart defects data in:

Choose **Period** for By variable in:

Click **OK**.

Now the chart shows defects by period.

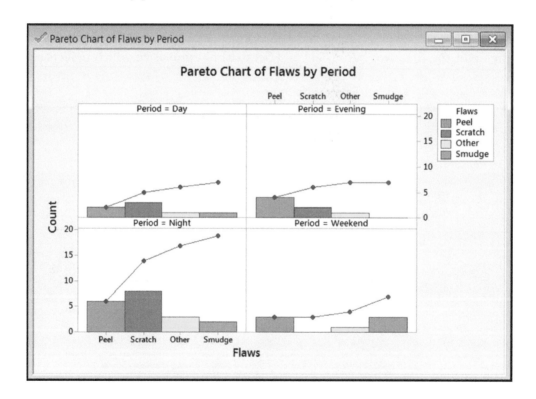

Notice that the order of the bars is the same as it was for the previous chart; the order is dictated by the overall pareto, and each period will have the same order.

This allows for a comparison between different categories to determine if one has a higher incidence of a specific flaw. Pareto Charts with this type of division are referred to as Second Level Paretos.

Measure Phase

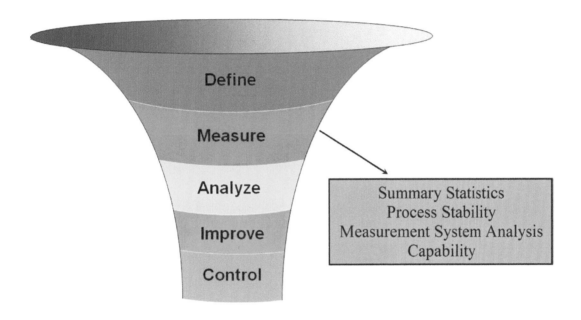

Measure Phase

- The Measure phase of a Six Sigma process produces a number of important outcomes. The top two are:
- Determine the critical outputs (Y's) the project intends to improve
- Determine the inputs (X's) that affect the critical outputs

Knowledge-based tools are critical to this part of the process, as they are used to analyze various inputs and determine their appropriate categorization. Some of the commonly used knowledge-based tools include the Process Map; the Cause and Effect Matrix; and the Failure Modes and Effects Analysis (FMEA). These tools use the team's current knowledge of the process, so while statistical analysis is possible it is generally not emphasized at this point.

Also in the Measure phase, the team performs an assessment of measurement systems for the critical Y's. This is necessary to verify the project is indeed working on an issue that is important to the company, and it requires a critical look at the data to determine if the measurements are reliable.

The Importance of Assessment

It may be tempting to skip over this assessment and just assume the measurement systems are appropriate and accurate; however, skipping these assessments increases the changes of discovering later on that the true project issue was simply a measurement problem. The time spent in checking the measurement systems early more than makes up for the frustration that occurs later when it's discovered the data initially analyzed is useless.

If the measurement systems are not acceptable, the team must fix it and collect new data. All previously collected data is suspect at best, and cannot be trusted. It is not unreasonable to completely disregard previous data and wait for new data, just to be on the safe side.

Once assessment is complete and measurement systems are found to be acceptable and accurate, the team can move on to assessment of the Y's. This assessment includes analyzing Y's for stability and capability.

Throughout this book, our assumption is the user will analyze sample information of a particular process of interest to their organization.

Tools of the Measure Phase

Common tools used in the Measure phase fall into two categories: Statistical Tools and Outcomes. Some examples of each include the following:

Statistical Tools	Outcomes
Summary Statistics SPC (Statistical Process Control) for process stability MSA (Measurement Systems Analysis) Capability Studies	Baseline Capability Project Goals Measurement Systems assessment

Summary Statistics

Statistical analysis and summary statistics serve an important purpose - to provide estimates of the population (process) parameters under investigation. Depending on the specifics of an issue, this may be as simple as estimating the defects found in customer orders, or as complicated as understanding the relationship among several factors in the manufacturing of a computer chips.

In this chapter, use of the term 'statistic' refers to sample values (average, range, standard deviation, etc.), and the term 'parameters' refers to the population values these statistics are estimating. To put it in simple terms, sample statistics are used to estimate population parameters.

Throughout this book population parameters are written as bold font Greek letters. Sample statistics are written as bold letters. The following chart is set up as a reference:

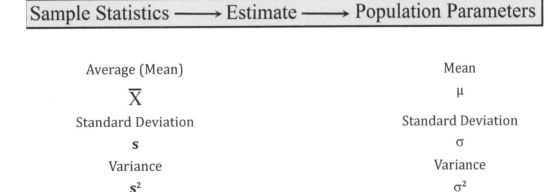

Sample Statistics ⟶ Estimate ⟶ Population Parameters

Average (Mean)	Mean
$\overline{X}$	μ
Standard Deviation	Standard Deviation
s	σ
Variance	Variance
s^2	σ^2

This chapter also contains simple mathematical formulas for some common statistics, but it is not necessary to know how to perform the calculations. What is important, though, is to understand what each statistic represents and how to use it properly.

Definitions of Statistical Terms

Central Tendency

Values that define the center of datasets include the Mean, Trimmed Mean, Median, and Mode.

Mean (Average)

The sample mean, or average, is a commonly used statistic. To calculate the mean, simply sum all of the values in a dataset and divide by the number of values in the dataset. For example, if the dataset contains five values (5, 8, 2, 6 and 4), the sum is 25. Twenty five divided by 5 produces an average of 5.

The formula for determining the mean is written as follows:

$$\textbf{Mean } (\overline{\textbf{X}}) = \frac{1}{n} \sum_{i=1}^{n} X_i$$

Trimmed Mean

The trimmed mean is based on a calculation similar to that used to find the mean. The only difference is that before performing the arithmetic operation, a percentage of the values on either end of the dataset are eliminated. For example, to calculate a 90% trimmed mean, first remove 5 % of the upper values and 5% of the lower values. The mean is then calculated on the remaining 90% of values in the dataset.

The trimmed mean is a useful statistic to use when there are suspect values on either end of the dataset. The formula for trimmed mean is the same as that used to determine mean, after removal of the desired percentage of points.

Median

The median is simply the center value of a dataset. To determine the median, arrange the values in an ascending order and determine the center; that is, the value with an equal number of data points above and below it. Go back to the example dataset used in the definition of mean. The sorted numbers are 2, 4, 5, 6, and 8. The value 5 is the median because there are two values above it (6 and 8) and two values below it (2 and 4).

If the dataset contains an even number of values, then the median is the average of the center two values. For example, say the dataset contains the values 4, 4, 7, 2, 6, and 11. When these values are sorted in ascending order, the dataset appears as 2, 4, 4, 6, 7, and 11; the middle two values are 4 and 6, and the average of these two values is 5, so the median is 5. Even though the value 5 is not in the dataset, it is still the median of these values.

There are two variations on the formula used to determine median – one for an odd number of values in the dataset and one for an even number of values in the dataset.

When the number of values is odd:

Median (sorted data) = (n+1)/2 where n is the number of data points.

When the number of values is even:

The median is the average of the n/2 and n/2 + 1 data values.

Comparing Mean and Median

While mean and median both indicate central tendencies, their respective benefits differ slightly. It is important to understand these differences in order to use the appropriate metric for the issue under investigation.

The Mean is a commonly used statistic, but it is problematic when there are outliers in the dataset; that is, when some data points are far removed from the majority of data. Because the mean uses all data points in a set, outliers have an excessive influence on the final value. The Median, on the other hand, is not used as often as the mean. However, it offers the significant benefit of eliminating the problem of outlier influence.

Here is an example of how this works. Suppose the dataset contains the values 5, 9, 2, 8, and 6; the mean is 6 and the median is also 6. Now, replace the value 9 with the value 99 – a significant outlier. The new mean is 24, but the median remains at 6.

So which is better, mean or median? The answer is 'it depends'. The mean is used in other calculations and is the statistic of many comparison studies, so it should not be neglected; however keep in mind the possible effects of outliers in the data set.

The best approach is to calculate both mean and median, then compare them. Symmetric datasets will produce two values close to one another, while dataset with outliers will produce values farther apart from each other. If there is a significant discrepancy between the mean and median, the team should investigate further using graphs and a thorough examination of the data.

Mode

Mode is defined as that value which occurs most often. For a symmetric dataset the mode is a good indicator of the center, but small datasets often contain multiple modes. Unimodal, bimodal and trimodal describe the number of modes in a dataset.

For example, a unimodal dataset contains a single major peak, while a bimodal dataset contains two major peaks. In terms of descriptive value, these terms are useful in determining if a dataset contains data from a single population (unimodal) or is potentially contaminated with data from multiple populations (bimodal or trimodal).

Spread

Values indicating the spread of data include the Range, Variance, Standard Deviation, and Coefficient of Variation (CV).

Range

Range represents the spread of a dataset. It is simply the highest value minus the lowest. The formula is:

Range = High value – Low value.

This is an easy value to calculate, but it has a couple of limitations. First, it ignores all but two data values, and second, it doesn't indicate how the rest of the data is distributed. For example, if a dataset contains 100 values, the range provides information on two of the data points. It does not, however, indicate how the remaining 98 values are grouped.

Variance (s²)

Variance uses all data point to indicate the data's spread. It is defined as the average squared deviation from the mean. Datasets with larger variances have a larger spread compared to those with smaller variances. The formula for the variance is:

$$s^2 = \frac{\sum_{i=1}^{n}(X_i - \overline{X})}{n-1}$$

Because the difference between the data values and the mean is squared, there are implications with outliers. As with the mean, outliers will have a large influence on the variance. It doesn't matter if the outlier value is low or high; because the difference is squared, it will always add to the variance.

An important property of variance is referred to as the additive property. This means the total variance for a process is the sum of variances for the individual components (assuming the components are independent). This is expressed in statistical terms as follows:

$$\sigma^2_{Total} = \sigma^2_1 + \sigma^2_2 + \ldots + \sigma^2_n$$

A more thorough examination of the additive property of variances will occur in the Measurement System Analysis (MSA) section.

Standard Deviation

Standard deviation is the square root of the variance. It is a metric used to express information in the same units as mean value. Why is this useful? Because the squared units used in variance make it difficult to visualize the spread of values, and standard deviation helps overcome this difficulty. The formula for standard deviation is:

$$s = \sqrt{s^2}$$

Coefficient of Variation (CV)

The final value used to indicate spread is coefficient of variation, or CV. It shows the spread relative to the sample mean. The formula is:

$$CV = \frac{s}{\bar{X}}$$

A common problem in datasets with high means is that they tend to have high variances. The CV makes it easier to compare unrelated datasets because the calculation produces a dimensionless value, better showing the relative spread of the datasets.

Shape

Values indicating the shape of data include skewness and kurtosis.

Skewness

Skewness indicates the relative size and direction of a dataset's asymmetry, sometimes described as a tail in the dataset. A positive skew indicates a tail to the right, or in the positive direction, while a negative skew indicates a tail to the left, or in the negative direction. A dataset with normal (or symmetric) distribution will have a skew value of 0.

The formula for skewness is fairly complicated, so it will not appear here. Instead, it can be found in the Minitab help menu.

Kurtosis

Kurtosis indicates the flatness of a dataset. A negative kurtosis indicates a flat distribution while a positive kurtosis indicates peaked distributions. A normal distribution will have a kurtosis of 0.

Using Minitab to Display Statistics

Minitab allows users to control the display of various statistics:
- Summary information on critical Y's produces a wide variety of values representing the center, spread and shape of data
- Summary statistics, along with graphical analysis, display vital information before proceeding with the process improvement project

Data Type: Summary statistics require numeric data.

Minitab Project: **QualityTools.MPJ**

Worksheet: *Check in Time*

Menu command: *Stat > Basic Statistics > Display Descriptive Statistics*

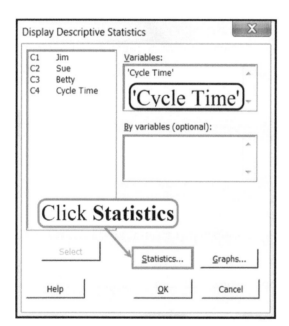

Input **Cycle Time** as the variable.

Click **Statistics**.

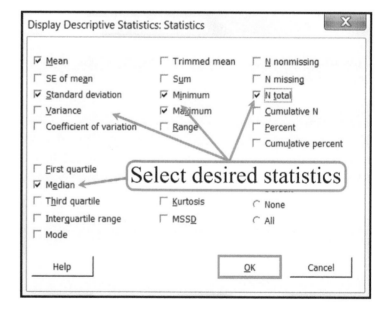

Select the items shown and click **OK** (twice).

For more information regarding the statistics, click the **Help** button.

Session Window output

Descriptive Statistics: Cycle Time

Variable	Total Count	Mean	StDev	Minimum	Median	Maximum
Cycle Time	150	326.66	42.52	239.84	321.21	447.85

Minitab creates a Graphical Summary option that contains both graphical and analytical information. The user cannot change the analytical options, but those provided in the program are sufficient for most applications.

Menu command: *Stat > Basic Statistics > Graphical Summary*

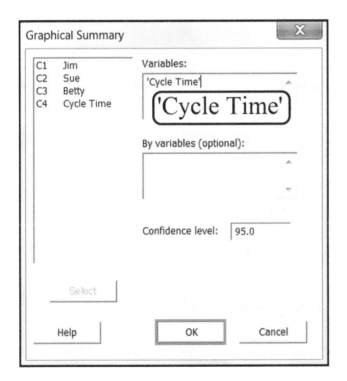

Input **Cycle Time** as the variable.

Click **OK**.

The user can change the confidence level by simply typing a desired value in place of the default value (95.0).

Hint: Use this display cautiously when giving presentations. The Graphical Summary, while very informative, presents a great deal of information in a manner that may be confusing if the audience is not well-informed about statistical values. Depending on the situation, this graph may not be the appropriate choice for communicating with a broad audience.

This graph shows a histogram with the normal curve; this type of graph will appear in the Analyze chapter.

The analytical portion of the graph includes the Anderson-Darling Test, the Mean, StDev (Standard Deviation), Variance, Skewness, and Kurtosis, along with the sample size N.

The next section of the graph helps to define the Box Plot graph. It includes information about the Minimum, 1st Quartile, Median, 3rd Quartile, and Maximum.

Finally, it shows information for the 95% confidence intervals. Intervals are calculated for the Mean, Median and Standard Deviation. Confidence intervals appear in more detail in the Analyze chapter.

Checking Process Stability - SPC

Before beginning any improvement activity, a team must determine process stability. This is important because an unstable process may occur as a result of multiple processes contaminating each another. What's more, to establish a baseline on an unstable process will create misleading information.

An excellent way to determine the stability of a process is to use an SPC chart. This is a specialized run chart with statistically based control limits added. More information about control charts is presented in the Control chapter.

Tool Use: Use an SPC chart to determine if a process is running under a Common Cause variation (stable condition), or if a Special Cause variation (unstable condition) exists. If special cause variation exists, the sources of variation should be found and eliminated.

A stable process has a constant mean and a constant standard deviation or spread. Running under a common cause variation condition allows the process owner to make predictions on future process output.

Here is an example of a stable process:

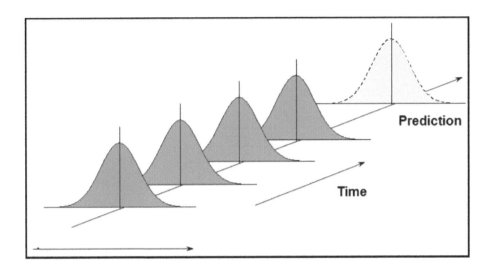

This demonstrates that the output remains the same over time so there's a high degree of predictability as to what will happen in the future.

Data Type: SPC charts can use either continuous or discrete data.

Note: For the purposes of this chapter, the discussion of Control Charts will be quite limited. A closer examination will occur in the Control chapter..

A popular control chart used during an initial investigation is the I-MR chart; it uses either continuous or count data collected as individual values. At least 25 data points should be used to assess process stability.

Minitab Project: **QualityTools.MPJ**

Worksheet: *Check in Time*

Menu command: *Stat > Control Charts > Variables Charts for Individuals > I-MR*

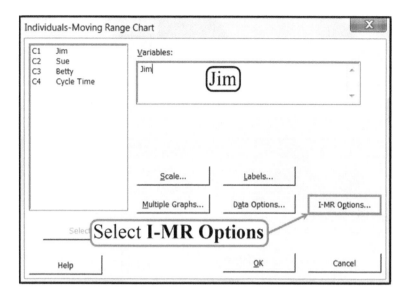

Select **Jim** as the variables.

Click the **I-MR Options** button. In the Options screen, click the **Tests** tab.

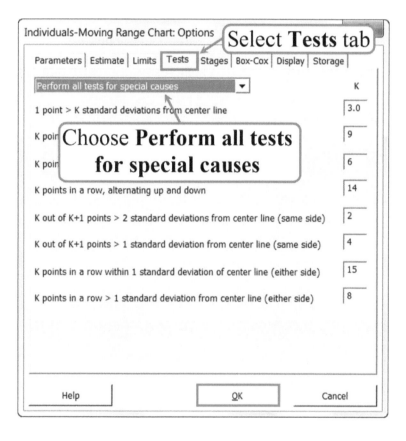

Use the pull down arrow and choose **Perform all tests for special causes**.

Click **OK** twice.

Note: This screen allows the user to change the parameters for each rule, which should only be done with great caution.

Examine the resulting graph carefully.

If no points are outside the control limits (red lines) and no obvious shifts have occurred, the process is stable.

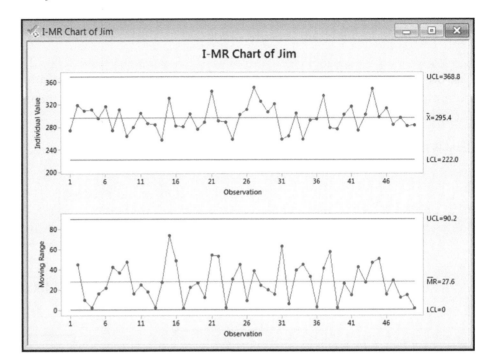

Additional discussion about Control Charts and unstable processes occurs in the Control chapter.

Measurement System Analysis (MSA)

Tool Use: Perform a Measurement System Analysis (MSA) on all critical outputs (Y's). Any inadequate measurement system must be corrected; if not corrected, the team cannot accurately measure improvements. A similar MSA should be performed on all critical X's to determine their reliability as well.

Data Type: An MSA can be performed on either continuous or discrete (attribute) data. This chapter includes examples that will:
1. Follow the lines of a traditional MSA for manufactured parts
2. Demonstrate an MSA for a transactional process
3. Show how to perform an analysis of files in a database

Overview: Before proceeding with any project, teams must use an MSA to determine if the available data (or collected data) is trustworthy. If the measurement system is poor or even flawed, the data it produces is suspect at best.

Remember, an MSA is not simply a test of the equipment; rather, it includes tools, procedures, operators and environment. The MSA creates values associated with Repeatability and Reproducibility to address all of these issues.

Types of MSA studies include:
1. GR&R Study - Gauge Repeatability and Reproducibility
2. Attribute MSA
3. Audit

The observations in a dataset should represent the true process variation; however, the values represent not only the process variation, but also the variation caused by the measurement system used to produce the values.

This is represented by the following:

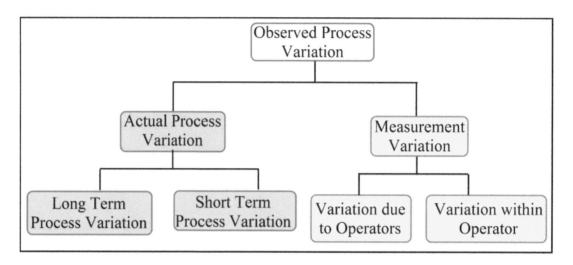

Note: Long and short term process variation will be discussed in more detail in the process capability section.

Variation in a measurement system is divided into two domains – variation due to operators (Reproducibility) and variation within operator (Repeatability).

Issues in the first domain (variation due to operators) are usually the result of slight differences in technique from one operator to another. To resolve issues of this kind conduct a thorough review of procedures and institution of best practices.

Issues in the second domain (variation within operator) may be a result of the operator not performing procedures consistently, or a result of the tool itself.

Hint: Avoid issues related to a particular tool by having the tool serviced and calibrated by the manufacturer before performing the MSA.

The purpose of an MSA study is to determine variation caused by the measurement system, and to assess its impact on the observed process variation.

If measurement variation is small relative to process variation, then the measurement system is adequate to proceed with the improvement project.

However, if measurement variation is large relative to process variation, the measurement system needs improvement. If improvements are not made, it will be impossible to accurately measure improvements due to Six Sigma team efforts.

It is also important to assess measurement system variation relative to process specifications. Minitab produces metrics for both situations.

Metrics: To assess a measurement system, it is necessary to develop metrics linked to the system in terms of the process and customer specifications as well as to the system itself. MSA output metrics include the following:

1. Standard deviation of the measurement system. $\sigma_{Sigma\ measurement\ system}$
2. Standard deviation repeatability. $\sigma_{reproducibility}$
3. Standard deviation reproducibility. $\sigma_{reproducibility}$
4. P/T – the precision to tolerance ratio. (Also listed as %P/T)
5. % R&R – the percent Repeatability and Reproducibility.
6. % Agreement – the percent agreement for studies of attribute data.

The first three of these metrics (Standard deviation of the measurement system; Standard deviation repeatability; Standard deviation reproducibility) assess the system itself. The fourth (P/T ratio) relates the measurement system to customer specifications. This is important because if the system is unable to distinguish a good from a bad part, it is of little use.

The fifth metric (%R&R) relates the measurement system to process variation. If this value is large, the system is unable to measure improvements in the process variation. The final metric (%Agreement) is used with attribute (good, bad) analyses. It measures the percent of time operators agree with either themselves or other operators. The following material will discuss each of these six metrics in more detail.

Accuracy and Precision

Accuracy and precision are two often misused terms when discussing measurement systems. In other disciplines they may be used interchangeably, but in Six Sigma they each have a separate, distinct definition.

Accuracy

Accuracy is defined as the difference between actual value and the average of multiple readings. It is also known as the systems bias. Bias can only be determined using a known standard, one that has traceable standards with known values. Analysis of bias in a measurement system is generally conducted by the equipment maintenance group.

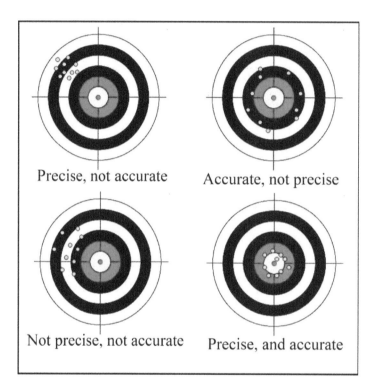

Precision

Precision is defined by the spread of multiple readings; the smaller the spread of reading, the more precise they are, while the larger the spread the less precise they are.

This illustration demonstrates these concepts:

The upper left image is precise (tight cluster of points) but is not accurate (the average shot is off target).

The upper right is accurate because the average of all shots is close to the target, but the spread is large so it is not precise.

The Impact of Additive Property

In the Summary Statistics section, variances were mentioned as being additive. This additive property is used to divide measurement system variation into its component parts, as shown here:

$$\sigma^2_{Measurement\ System} = \sigma^2_{Repeatability} + \sigma^2_{Reproducibility}$$

In measurement system analysis, teams must calculate both for variances and for standard deviation. This is where the terms repeatability and reproducibility come into play.

Using the additive property of variances, the following condition exists:

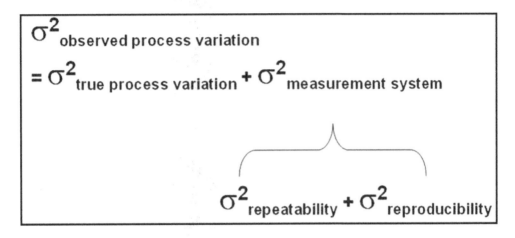

The observed process variance equals the sum of the true process variance and the measurement system variance; the measurement system variance is the sum of the variance from repeatability and reproducibility. Values for all factors are provided by Minitab.

Repeatability and Reproducibility

Repeatability - Repeatability is the variation between successive measurements of the same sample, same characteristic, by the same person using the same instrument. It is also known as the *test- retest error*, and is used as an estimate of *short-term variation*.

Reproducibility - Reproducibility is the variation that results from different conditions used to make measurements. This results from different operators, different setups, different samples, and different environmental conditions. It is also known as *long-term variation*.

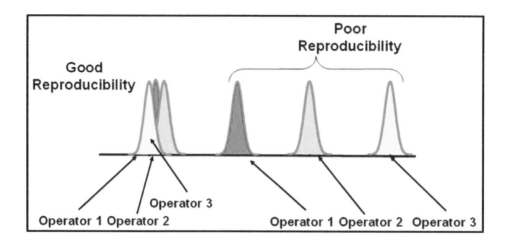

Metrics

%R&R: This metric relates measurement system variation to process variation. The formula is:

$$\%R\&R = \frac{\sigma_{\text{measurement system}}}{\sigma_{\text{observed process variation}}} * 100\%$$

%R&R indicates the measurement system's proportion of the total observed variation. This is a useful metric for the Project Leader because it reveals whether or not a measurement system is capable of measuring improvements in process variation.

In Minitab this is the % Study Variation or %SV.

%P/T: This metric compares measurement system variation to process tolerance. If the value of this ratio is too high, it indicates the system is unable to distinguish between good product and bad product. The formula is:

$$\%P/T = \frac{6 * \sigma_{\text{measurement system}}}{\text{USL - LSL}} * 100\%$$

Hint: The value 6 in the numerator was originally listed as 5.15 (99% of the area under the normal curve) in earlier approaches to Six Sigma process improvement; however, many companies are now moving to 6 (99.73% of the area).

Acceptable Levels For P/T and %R&R Values

Guidelines for acceptable levels of P/T and %R&R values are as follows:

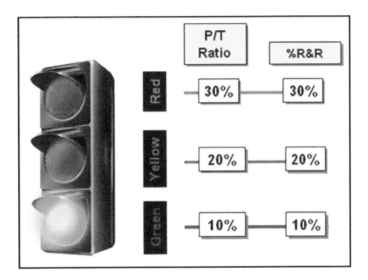

Typically, levels below 10% indicate an excellent system. Levels between 10% and 20% indicate the system is good for the current process, but as process variation decreases %R&R will increase, so it should be re-checked periodically. In fact, a dramatic decrease in process variation could cause a previously good measurement to become bad.

When level fall between 20% and 30%, the system is still considered acceptable but improvement plans should be investigated. If levels are above 30% the system is not acceptable and should not be used with the current procedures.

Creating the MSA Worksheet

A typical MSA for manufactured parts consists of obtaining material from the production line, having several operators measure the items multiple times, and then analyzing the results to determine where the major sources of variation exist.

The first step in this MSA process is to create a worksheet.

Menu command:

Stat > Quality Tools > Gage Study > Create Gage R&R Study Worksheet

It is important to use common sense when determining resource requirements to run an MSA.

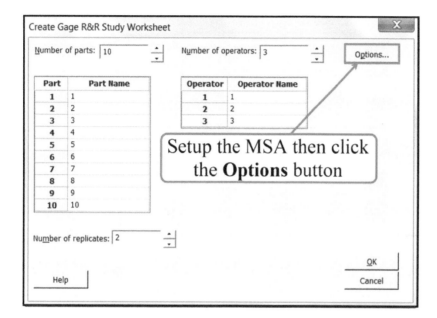

Select the number of parts, the number of operators and the number of replicates.

This example uses the default format, ten parts, three operators, and two trials.

Note that Minitab allows each part to have an identifier, and for each operator to be listed by name.

After filling in the proper information, click the **Options...** button.

The Options screen offers additional choices, including different levels of randomization. These choices range from the order of parts to be inspected to the order of operators performing the measurements.

Proper randomization is essential for proper assessment of a measurement system because it prevents operators from remembering what they measured on previous trials.

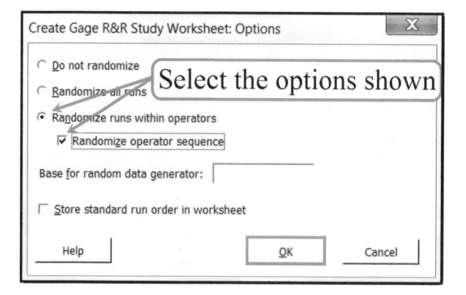

The default option (**Randomize runs within operators)** is the typical method of running a MSA study; additionally, using the option to **Randomize operator sequence** is an excellent way to eliminate issues associated with the same operator performing the initial measurement for each replication.

Select options as shown above and click **OK** (twice).

C1	C2-T	C3-T
RunOrder	Parts	Operators
1	7	3
2	9	3
3	8	3
4	2	3
5	3	3
6	6	3
7	4	3
8	5	3
9	10	3
10	1	3

Run the MSA as listed in the Run Order column to maintain the desired randomization.

The worksheet shown was used to perform the following MSA. To access analysis, use the following steps:

Minitab project MSA.MPJ Worksheet *WaterMSA*

Begin the analysis with the Gage Run chart. This chart will show if there are any obvious issues between or within operators.

Gage Run Chart

Menu command: *Stat > Quality Tools > Gage Study > Gage Run Chart*

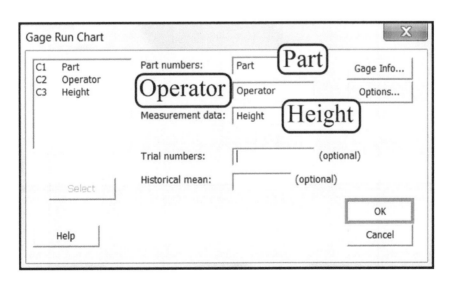

Input **Parts**, **Operators** and **Height**.

Click **OK**.

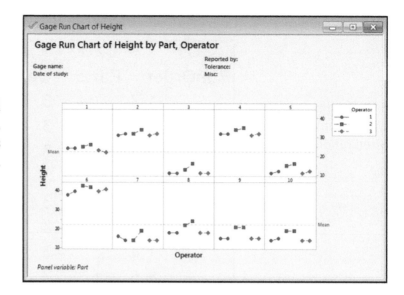

Each reading is displayed by operator, part, and trial. Look for obvious differences between operators or trials.

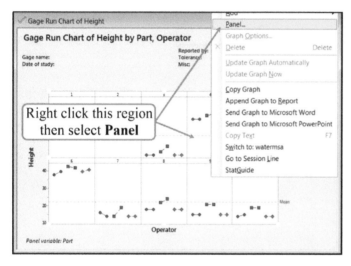

To observe all parts on a single row, **right click** within the graph and select **Panel**.

Select **1** for rows and **10** for columns.

Click **OK**.

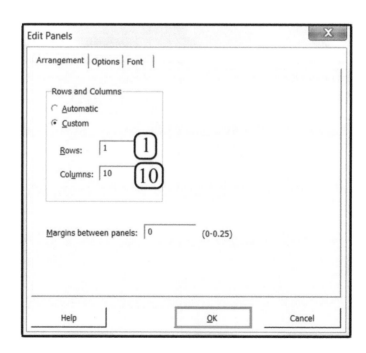

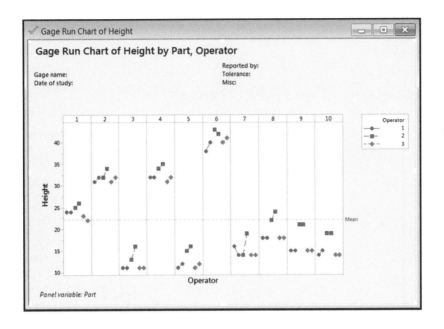

The readings for each operator by part can be compared on one line.

Repeatability of the measurement system is indicated by the difference between readings within each part for each operator. A larger average difference indicates the measurement system suffers from a repeatability (short term) issue.

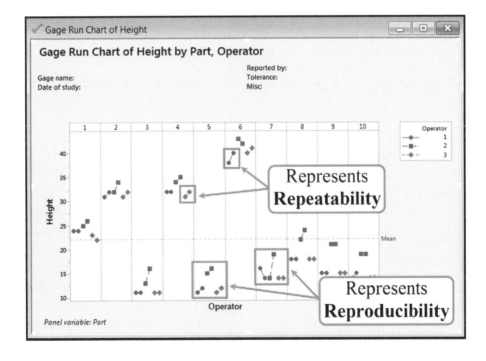

Reproducibility is indicated by the difference between operators within each part. Operator differences are obvious, such as the case for parts 8 to 10 where operator 2 produces readings consistently higher than the other two operators.

Performing the Gage Study

Menu command:

Stat > Quality Tools > Gage Study > Gage R&R (Crossed)

Insert the Part numbers
(**Parts**), Operators
(**Operators**) and
Measurement Data (**Height**).

Click **Options**.

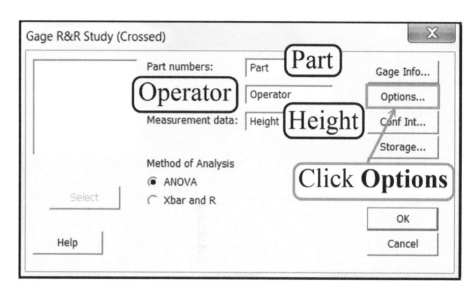

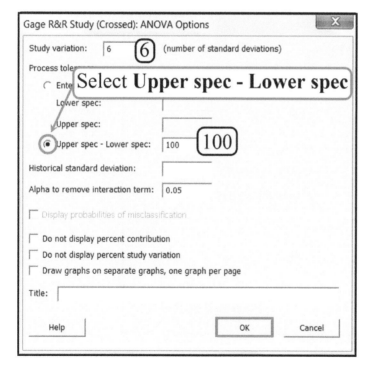

In the Options window, type
6 for Study variation.

Note: Some companies are still using 5.15.
Follow the company's policy for this value.

The Process tolerance for this example
process (Upper spec – Lower spec) is **100**.

Click **OK** twice.

The analysis contains both graphical and
analytical information. Two values of
particular interest are the **%R&R** and
% P/T ratios. The first metric, **%R&R**
relates variability of a measurement
system to process variation, while **%P/T**
relates variability of a measurement
system to the specification window.

There are two important questions to answer when reviewing a measurement system:
1. Is the system acceptable as a means of determining whether the product is within specification?
2. Is the system acceptable to measure improvements made to the variability of the process?

%P/T answers the first question and % R&R answers the second question. The quality of a measurement system is considered acceptable if **%R&R** and **%P/T** are below 30%, and excellent if those values are below 10%.

The important outcome of a MSA is to understand where variation exists and determine if it is worthwhile to improve or replace the current system.

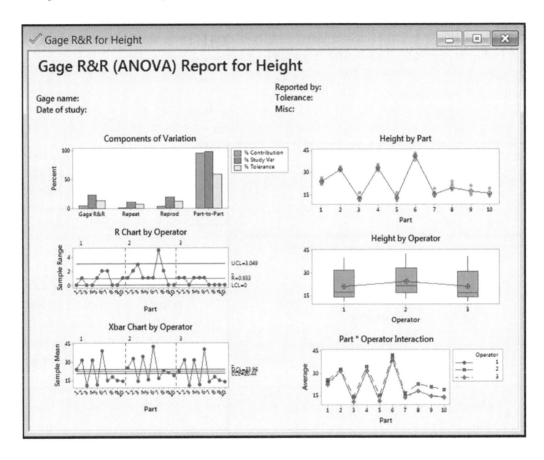

Each of these graphs will be investigated individually.

The Component of Variation chart depicts **%R&R** and **%P/T** ratios graphically. In a good measurement system, the three groups of bars on the left side should be small relative to the Part-to-Part bars on the right.

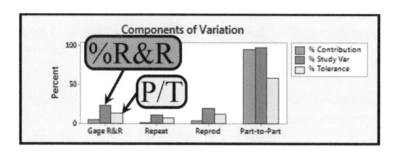

Remember, typical goals for **%P/T** and **%R&R** are as follows:
- **<10%** = Ideal
- **10%** to **30%** = Acceptable
- **>30%** = Unacceptable

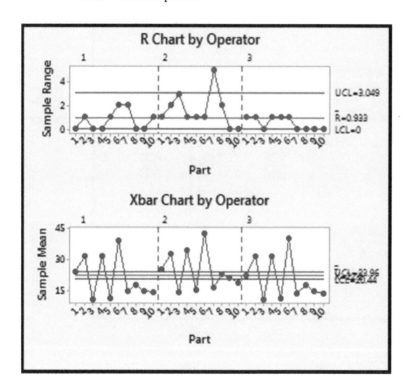

Any variability in the X chart should be outside the Control Limits; this indicates that the measurement system is able to distinguish the difference between samples.

If no Sample to Sample variability exists, the study samples probably did not represent true process variation. It may also indicate a measurement system is unable to distinguish differences between parts because it sees them all as the same.

This graph shows the average (connected circles) and spread of values for each sample.

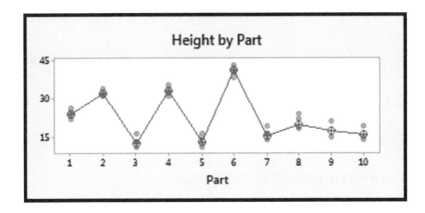

The ideal situation would have minimal spread within each sample and a spread between samples representing the current process variability.

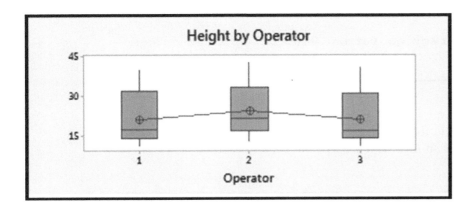

The Box Plots show the Mean (Circles), Median (line within box), and the spread of data for each operator.

The line connecting the means should be straight (horizontal). The overall spread (size of box and length of whiskers should be approximately equal.

Parallel lines with no crossing indicate no interaction. Interactions between operators and parts are indicated by crossing lines.

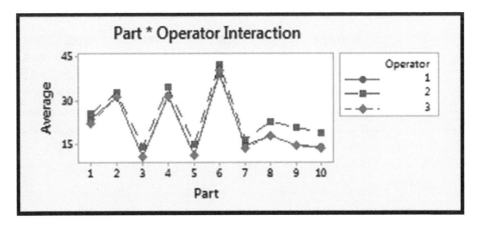

Any Operator/Part interactions must be examined and resolved. In the above example, all three operators have a matching pattern for the first seven parts but then something changes for operator two. The readings from this operator are much higher on the last three parts. A discrepancy exists, so individual parts should be kept and reviewed to determine the cause.

The ANOVA table is a statistical assessment of factors (parts and operators plus their interaction). Low p-values indicate that statistically there is a difference between levels within the factor; however, this does not indicate whether the measurement system is or is not acceptable.

Results for: watermsa

Gage R&R Study - ANOVA Method

Two-Way ANOVA Table With Interaction

Source	DF	SS	MS	F	P
Part	9	5170.27	574.474	331.074	0.000
Operator	2	159.10	79.550	45.845	0.000
Part * Operator	18	31.23	1.735	1.679	0.102
Repeatability	30	31.00	1.033		
Total	59	5391.60			

α to remove interaction term = 0.05

Since the p-value for the Parts*Operator interaction is greater than the alpha (a) to remove value of .05, Minitab produces an ANOVA table without the interaction.

Two-Way ANOVA Table Without Interaction

Source	DF	SS	MS	F	P
Part	9	5170.27	574.474	443.087	0.000
Operator	2	159.10	79.550	61.356	0.000
Repeatability	48	62.23	1.297		
Total	59	5391.60			

The VarComp table uses variances to calculate the portion each component of the measurement system contributes to the overall variation. This table takes advantage of additive property of variances.

```
Gage R&R
                                    %Contribution
Source                  VarComp     (of VarComp)
Total Gage R&R            5.209             5.17
  Repeatability           1.297             1.29
  Reproducibility         3.913             3.88
    Operator              3.913             3.88
Part-To-Part             95.530            94.83
Total Variation         100.739           100.00

Process tolerance = 100
```

Since the variance is a squared value, the guidelines are not the same as for Repeatability and Reproducibility using standard deviations.

Values less than 7% for the Total Gage R&R (%Contribution) are considered acceptable. If the analysis exceeds this value, then determine which portion (Repeatability or Reproducibility) has the largest portion.

Remember, the Total Gage R&R Variance Component (VarComp) (5.209) is equal to the sum of the Repeatability (1.297) and Reproducibility (3.913) Variance Component.

The Reproducibility VarComp is equal to the Operator plus the Operator * Part interaction. Since the interaction was removed from the model, the Reproducibility (3.913) component is the same as the Operator. Recall that some operator issues revolve around techniques.

The Variance Component method does not relate the value to the process specification. (There's no %P/T calculated with Variance Components.)

The following chart shows standard Gage R&R values:

Source	StdDev (SD)	Study Var (6 × SD)	%Study Var (%SV)	%Tolerance (SV/Toler)
Total Gage R&R	2.2824	13.6942	22.74	13.69
Repeatability	1.1387	6.8319	11.34	6.83
Reproducibility	1.9780	11.8683	19.71	11.87
Operator	1.9780	11.8683	19.71	11.87
Part-To-Part	9.7739	58.6435	97.38	58.64
Total Variation	10.0369	60.2212	100.00	60.22

Number of Distinct Categories = 6

The **%Study Var (%SV)** column shows the **%R&R** value of **22.74%**, and the **%Tolerance (SV/Toler)** shows the **%P/T** value of 13.69%.

Use the %R&R value for process improvement efforts, and the %P/T for acceptance of product to specification.

The Distinct Categories should be at least 5 for proper discrimination in process improvement efforts.

Again, values less than 30% for **%R&R** and **%P/T** are considered acceptable. Another way to determine how well a measuring system distinguishes parts that are truly different is to look at the number of distinct categories. There should be at least five distinct categories for the chart to be useful for process improvement purposes.

MSA for Attribute Data

There are a variety of ways to perform a MSA for attribute data. The simplest is one which checks the system via a "Good" and "Bad" set of criteria for each item. The items can range from actual products produced in a manufacturing environment to assessment of inputs for order forms or invoices. A more detailed MSA for attribute data is to assess the system in terms of the type of defect found.

An attribute MSA may be applied to any part of any business.

Hint:

Remember, attribute data contains less information than continuous data, therefore, an attribute MSA requires a larger sample size of at least 50 items or more. The example below contains only ten items for demonstration purposes.

The first attribute MSA example contains a simple situation. In this study, ten items were selected for a Good/Bad assessment. Each of three operators looked at the items two times, and recorded them as either Good or Bad.

Minitab project   **MSA.MPJ**

Worksheet   *Attribute*

C1	C2	C3	C4-T
Sample	Operator	Replicate	Rating
1	1	1	Good
2	1	1	Bad
3	1	1	Good
4	1	1	Good
5	1	1	Bad
6	1	1	Good
7	1	1	Good
8	1	1	Good
9	1	1	Good
10	1	1	Bad

A Gage Run Chart would show which operators did not agree with themselves, or others. To display the Gage Run Chart the text column must be coded.

Coding Data: Select the worksheet **Attribute**

Menu command: *Data > Code > Text to Numeric*

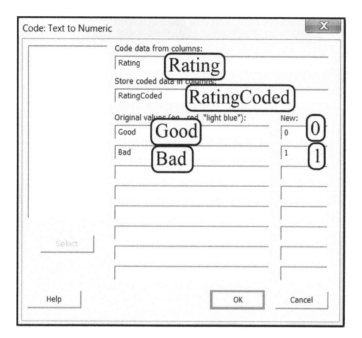

Select the text column Rating and type the name of the new column RatingCoded.

For Original values type Good and Bad. The text must match the column values exactly, including capitalizations.

For New, type **0** for Good and **1** for Bad.

Click **OK**.

C1	C2	C3	C4-T	C5
Sample	Operator	Replicate	Rating	RatingCoded
1	1	1	Good	0
2	1	1	Bad	1
3	1	1	Good	0
4	1	1	Good	0
5	1	1	Bad	1
6	1	1	Good	0
7	1	1	Good	0
8	1	1	Good	0
9	1	1	Good	0
10	1	1	Bad	1

Here is the updated worksheet with the new column RatingCoded.

Create the Gage Run Chart as shown previously.

Menu command: *Stat > Quality Tools > Gage Study > Gage Run Chart*

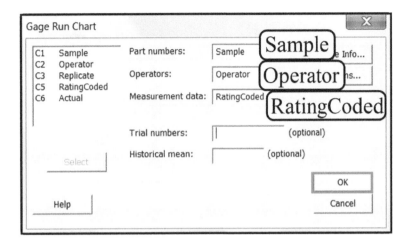

Select the Part numbers, Operators and Measurement data (Sample, Operator and RatingCoded respectively).

Click **OK**.

Any line that is not horizontal indicates a disagreement between the two trials.

In this example, operator 1 did not agree with themselves for part 3 and part 9. Operator 3 did not agree on part 7. Operator 2 agreed on all parts.

For this simple situation, the graph provides information on operator issues. Several different methods are available to improve a visual quality inspection. These include:

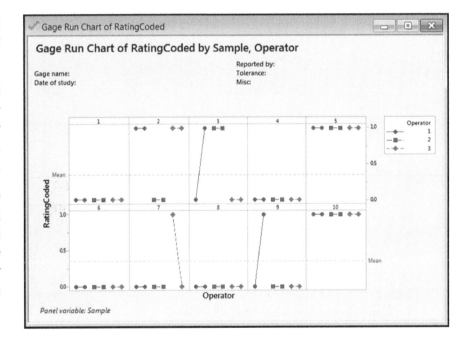

1. Improve lighting
2. Magnification of item
3. Display photos of good and bad conditions
4. Refresher classes on the criteria

Attribute Agreement Analysis:

Stat > Quality Tools > Attribute Agreement Analysis

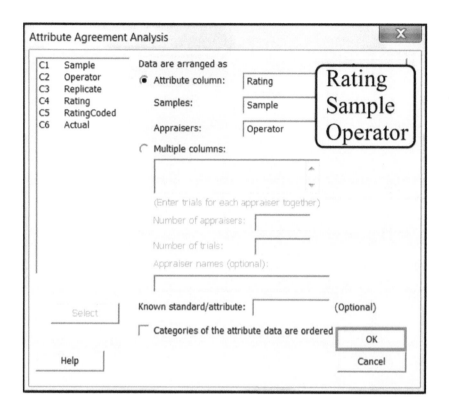

Input the Attribute Column (Rating), Samples: (Sample), Appraisers: (Operator).

Click **OK**.

Graphical output displays the Percent agreement within the operators. The dot represents the actual value while the lines indicate a 95% confidence interval.

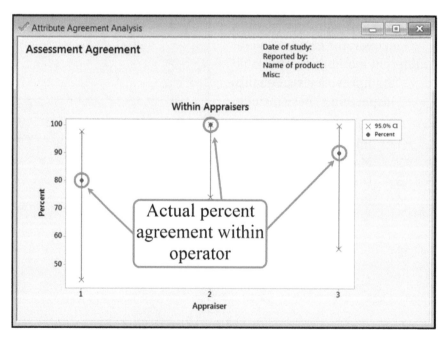

The Session window contains additional information.

The first portion of the Session window shows the same information displayed in the graph.

Attribute Agreement Analysis for Rating

Within Appraisers

Assessment Agreement

Appraiser	# Inspected	# Matched	Percent	95% CI
1	10	8	80.00	(44.39, 97.48)
2	10	10	100.00	(74.11, 100.00)
3	10	9	90.00	(55.50, 99.75)

\# Matched: Appraiser agrees with him/herself across trials.

The number of matches and the percent match. The 95% CI is the 95% confidence interval for the population percent agreement.

The second section shows the agreement between operators.

Between Appraisers

Assessment Agreement

# Inspected	# Matched	Percent	95% CI
10	6	60.00	(26.24, 87.84)

\# Matched: All appraisers' assessments agree with each other.

If an operator did not agree with themselves, they couldn't agree with the other operators.

Again, a 95% confidence interval is displayed. Information on the Kappa statistic will be covered in the next example.

The next example shows attribute data in which the operator must not only identify a defect, but must also classify the defect. This worksheet also demonstrates the use of an expert or standard; in other words, the correct answer.

Up to this point, the tests have compared operators within and between themselves, but with no mention of whether they were correct. The Expert or Standard column contains the correct answer, so now the test will compare operators within and between themselves as well as with the expert (or correct) answer.

Minitab Project: **MSA.MPJ**

Worksheet: *Attribute_Standard*

C1	C2-T	C3-T	C4-T
Samples	Operators	Results	Standard
1	OP 1	Scratch	No Defect
2	OP 1	No Defect	No Defect
3	OP 1	Smudge	Mottle
4	OP 1	Pickle	Pickle
5	OP 1	No Defect	Smudge
6	OP 1	Mottle	Pickle
7	OP 1	Scratch	No Defect
8	OP 1	Scratch	No Defect
9	OP 1	Smudge	Smudge
10	OP 1	Mottle	Pickle

The data structure in Minitab is important to consider when performing an Attribute MSA.

The initial worksheet can be created in the same manner as found in the previous MSA study. However, for the attribute study add a column representing the correct answer.

In this worksheet, this represents the correct defect classification. This column is required to determine not only whether the measurement system is repeatable between and within operators, but also whether it is accurate.

Even if the nature of the project output is an attribute, such as a go/no go assessment or a determination of a defect, assessment of the measurement system is still required. Minitab provides tools necessary to determine if the attribute measurement system needs improvements.

To create the Gage Run chart, a coded system is required.

In this example, the categories of defects are Scratch; Smudge; Pickle; Mottle; and No Defect.

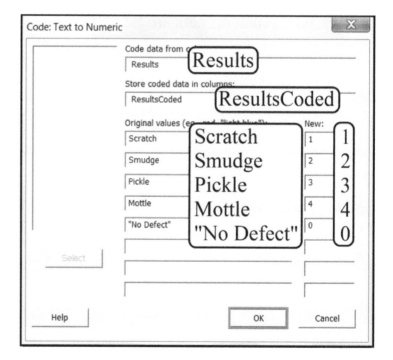

C1	C2-T	C3-T	C4-T	C5
Samples	Operators	Results	Standard	ResultsCoded
1	OP 1	Scratch	No Defect	1
2	OP 1	No Defect	No Defect	0
3	OP 1	Smudge	Mottle	2
4	OP 1	Pickle	Pickle	3
5	OP 1	No Defect	Smudge	0
6	OP 1	Mottle	Pickle	4
7	OP 1	Scratch	No Defect	1
8	OP 1	Scratch	No Defect	1
9	OP 1	Smudge	Smudge	2
10	OP 1	Mottle	Pickle	4

Assign a value to each category and code the Results

Create the Gage Run chart as shown previously.

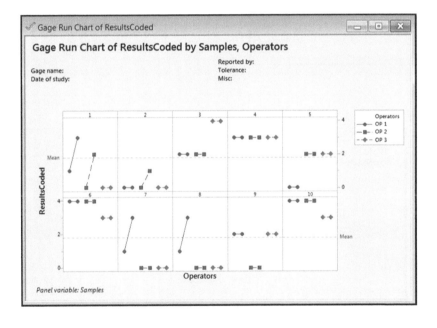

The graph shows the agreement within and between operators.

It also indicates what the disagreement was within and between operators.

Run the Attribute Agreement Analysis

Menu command:

Stat > Quality Tools > Attribute Agreement Analysis

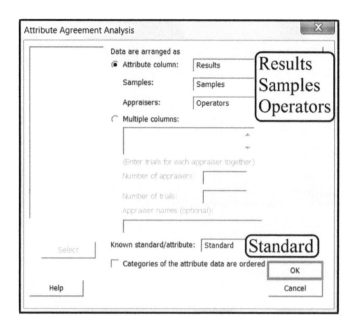

Input **Result**, **Sample** and **Operator** as shown. Under Known standard/attribute select the **Standard** column.

Click **OK**.

In the graph on the left, the dot shows the actual percent agreement within each operator.

The lines represent the 95% confidence interval for the population mean for each operator. (Confidence Intervals are discussed in the Analyze chapter.)

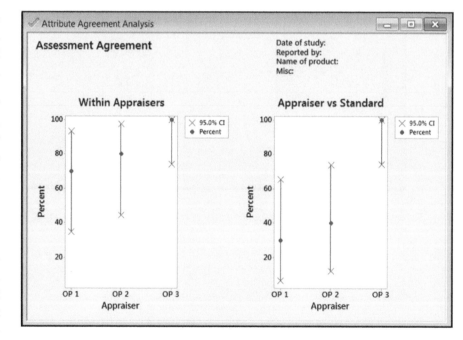

The graph on the right shows the percent agreement each operator had with the correct answer. Again, the dot represents the sample average while the lines represent the 95% confidence interval for the population mean.

Kappa Analysis

Minitab performs an analysis using the Fleiss' Kappa statistic. It provides a measure for the consistency of agreement within and between operators as well as between operator and expert. Kappa is calculated using the following equation:

$$\text{Kappa} = \frac{P_{observed} - P_{chance}}{1 - P_{chance}}$$

where:

$P_{observed}$ = Proportion of units classified in which the raters agreed

P_{chance} = Proportion of units for which one would expect agreement by chance

Results of the calculation can be categorized as follows:

Kappa = 1.0	Kappa = 0.0	Kappa < 0.0
Perfect agreement.	Agreement the same as would be expected by chance alone.	Agreement less than would be expected by chance alone.

Each Kappa value has an associated p-value, based on the Kappa Hypothesis:

H_o: Agreement is due to chance

H_a: Agreement is not due to chance

It is generally agreed that a Kappa >.7 indicates an acceptable measurement system.

Attribute Agreement Analysis for Results

Within Appraisers

Assessment Agreement

```
Appraiser  # Inspected  # Matched  Percent      95% CI
OP 1               10          7    70.00  (34.75,  93.33)
OP 2               10          8    80.00  (44.39,  97.48)
OP 3               10         10   100.00  (74.11, 100.00)


# Matched: Appraiser agrees with him/herself across trials.
```

Session window output

Session window results show summary information for each operator. Anything short of 100% agreement indicates an operator has an issue with repeatability.

This chart shows each operator's ability to determine a specific quality characteristic.

P-values greater than .05 indicate categories that may have kappa = 0; operators are having problems discerning issues in these categories. Use this output to verify if an operator has trouble consistently identifying a specific issue.

Fleiss' Kappa Statistics

Appraiser	Response	Kappa	SE Kappa	Z	P(vs > 0)
OP 1	Mottle	1.00000	0.316228	3.16228	0.0008
	No Defect	1.00000	0.316228	3.16228	0.0008
	Pickle	0.20000	0.316228	0.63246	0.2635
	Scratch	-0.17647	0.316228	-0.55805	0.7116
	Smudge	1.00000	0.316228	3.16228	0.0008
	Overall	0.62264	0.159617	3.90084	0.0000
OP 2	Mottle	1.00000	0.316228	3.16228	0.0008
	No Defect	0.58333	0.316228	1.84466	0.0325
	Pickle	1.00000	0.316228	3.16228	0.0008
	Scratch	-0.05263	0.316228	-0.16644	0.5661
	Smudge	0.73333	0.316228	2.31900	0.0102
	Overall	0.72414	0.181485	3.99006	0.0000
OP 3	Mottle	1.00000	0.316228	3.16228	0.0008
	No Defect	1.00000	0.316228	3.16228	0.0008
	Pickle	1.00000	0.316228	3.16228	0.0008
	Scratch	*	*	*	*
	Smudge	1.00000	0.316228	3.16228	0.0008
	Overall	1.00000	0.196915	5.07833	0.0000

* When no or all responses across trials equal the value, kappa cannot be computed.

This chart shows a comparison of operators' results to standard or known values.

Each Appraiser vs Standard

Assessment Agreement

Appraiser	# Inspected	# Matched	Percent	95% CI
OP 1	10	3	30.00	(6.67, 65.25)
OP 2	10	4	40.00	(12.16, 73.76)
OP 3	10	10	100.00	(74.11, 100.00)

Matched: Appraiser's assessment across trials agrees with the known standard.

This report shows how each appraiser compares to the expert.

```
Fleiss' Kappa Statistics

Appraiser  Response      Kappa   SE Kappa          Z  P(vs > 0)
OP 1       Mottle     -0.17647   0.223607   -0.78920     0.7850
           No Defect   0.04762   0.223607    0.21296     0.4157
           Pickle      0.13805   0.223607    0.61738     0.2685
           Scratch           *          *          *          *
           Smudge      0.37500   0.223607    1.67705     0.0468
           Overall     0.07138   0.124534    0.57319     0.2833
OP 2       Mottle     -0.17647   0.223607   -0.78920     0.7850
           No Defect   0.56932   0.223607    2.54607     0.0054
           Pickle      0.37500   0.223607    1.67705     0.0468
           Scratch           *          *          *          *
           Smudge      0.28750   0.223607    1.28574     0.0993
           Overall     0.31223   0.129727    2.40683     0.0080
OP 3       Mottle      1.00000   0.223607    4.47214     0.0000
           No Defect   1.00000   0.223607    4.47214     0.0000
           Pickle      1.00000   0.223607    4.47214     0.0000
           Scratch           *          *          *          *
           Smudge      1.00000   0.223607    4.47214     0.0000
           Overall     1.00000   0.139240    7.18185     0.0000


* When all sample standards and responses of a trial(s) equal
the value or none of them equals the value, kappa cannot be
computed.
```

The analysis shows the defect categories for each appraiser. In this case, appraiser 3 has the perfect score for all categories. The other 2 appraisers have issues with all categories.

The Between Appraiser assessment shows the overall number of items matched between appraisers. In this example, only one item is consistently matched for all assessments.

Between Appraisers

Assessment Agreement

```
# Inspected  # Matched  Percent      95% CI
        10           1   10.00  (0.25, 44.50)
```

`# Matched: All appraisers' assessments agree with each other.`

Fleiss' Kappa Statistics

Response	Kappa	SE Kappa	Z	P(vs > 0)
Mottle	0.424000	0.0816497	5.19292	0.0000
No Defect	0.310000	0.0816497	3.79671	0.0001
Pickle	0.391162	0.0816497	4.79074	0.0000
Scratch	-0.071429	0.0816497	-0.87482	0.8092
Smudge	0.430442	0.0816497	5.27182	0.0000
Overall	0.344501	0.0439899	7.83138	0.0000

This last table shows overall agreement with the standard.

All Appraisers vs Standard

Assessment Agreement

```
# Inspected  # Matched  Percent      95% CI
        10          1    10.00  (0.25, 44.50)
```

```
# Matched: All appraisers' assessments agree with
the known standard.
```

Fleiss' Kappa Statistics

```
Response      Kappa  SE Kappa         Z  P(vs > 0)
Mottle     0.215686  0.129099   1.67070     0.0474
No Defect  0.538980  0.129099   4.17492     0.0000
Pickle     0.504350  0.129099   3.90668     0.0000
Scratch           *         *         *          *
Smudge     0.554167  0.129099   4.29256     0.0000
Overall    0.461204  0.075811   6.08362     0.0000
```

```
* When all sample standards and responses of a
trial(s) equal the value or none of them equals
the value, kappa cannot be computed.
```

To be a match, all appraisers on all trials must match the known value. Each defect category is displayed with the associated Kappa value. In this example, the low overall Kappa indicates a measurement system that's unable to consistently describe the correct defect.

MSA - Audits

The final measurement system to analyze is one where the data is pulled from a database – a very common situation for many Six Sigma projects. If these databases contain errors then the data used for the project is wrong.

To determine the 'correctness' of data in a database, an audit is required. The audit will not look at every record, because a task of this magnitude would be beyond the team's resources. Instead, check a sample of records for accuracy and completeness.

It is important to obtain a sample that represents the entire database if the audit is to be correct. Several methods are available to obtain an appropriate sample, these include random, stratified, and systematic sampling.

Random Samples

To create a random sample using Minitab, create a column that contains a list of all records. This can be a simple string of numbers from 1 to the last record. The number of records to be selected is dependent upon the resources available, to perform the audit.

If there are 500 records available and the team wants to check 50 of them, create a column in Minitab with the values from 1 to 500.

C1 Record No.
1
2
3
4
5
6
7
8
9
10
11

Menu command:

Calc > Random Data > Sample From Columns

Select **50** as the Number of rows to sample. (This is the final sample size).

For 'From columns:' enter **'Record No.'**. The single quotes are required because the column heading contains a space.

For 'Store samples in:' enter **Sample**.

Click **OK**.

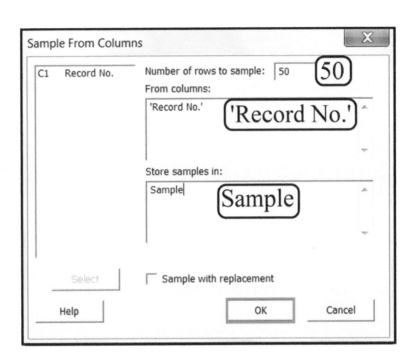

C1	C2
Record No.	**Sample**
1	237
2	441
3	203
4	349
5	378
6	171
7	360
8	179
9	437
10	82
11	210

Hint: *Do not select the 'Sample with replacement' box, or there is a chance the same record could be selected more than once.*

The worksheet contains a new column (Sample) with the desired 50 record numbers. These are the records to be selected and analyzed for accuracy and completeness.

The record numbers appear in a random order, but they may be sorted if it makes the audit process easier. (Only the first 11 record numbers are shown.)

Stratified Samples

A stratified sample is used when there are specific criteria associated with the database of records and the team wants to see the sample represent the proportion of records that fall into each group. Examples of such criteria might include gender; income; size of client; types of material purchased; health care procedures performed; size of loans; and the like.

To perform a stratified sample, begin with the desired sample size and then determine the percentage of each group in the final database. The sample size of each stratum corresponds to the percentage of the records they represent.

Example: The team is working with loans and they want to check the database for accuracy and completeness. There are three categories (strata) of loans: small (< $100,000), medium ($100,000 to $500,000), and jumbo (>$500,000). The approximate proportion of each category is 45%, 35% and 20% respectively.

The teams wants to use a sample size of 75 records, so according to the general proportions of different types of loans the sample should contain 33.75 records of small loans; 26.25 records of medium loans; and 15 records of jumbo loans.

(Collect 34 small loans, 26 medium and 15 jumbos.)

C1	C2
Record No.	Loan Value
1	$54,519
2	$302,166
3	$326,474
4	$190,575
5	$4,522,418
6	$1,045,457
7	$91,674
8	$80,424
9	$100,453
10	$82,000
11	$52,128

To obtain the desired records using Minitab, begin with the entire list of records and a column indicating the three loan sizes.

Create a column coding the loan amounts

Select Worksheet: *Loan*

Menu command: *Data > Code > Numeric to Text*

Use defined values for the Small, Medium and Jumbo categories.

Click **OK**.

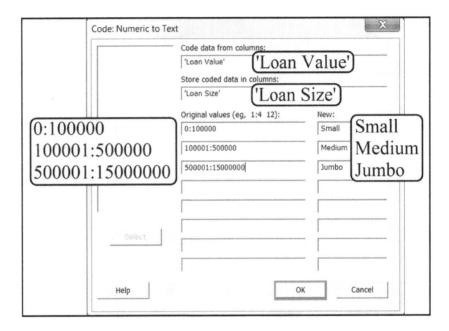

C1	C2	C3-T
Record No.	**Loan Value**	**Loan Size**
1	$54,519	Small
2	$302,166	Medium
3	$326,474	Medium
4	$190,575	Medium
5	$4,522,418	Jumbo
6	$1,045,457	Jumbo
7	$91,674	Small
8	$80,424	Small
9	$100,453	Medium
10	$82,000	Small
11	$52,128	Small

Use the column 'Loan Size' to split the worksheet. Splitting the worksheet creates new sheets without removing the original sheet.

Menu command: *Data > Split Worksheet*

Select the column containing the correct criteria for the split.

Three new worksheets are created - one for Small loans, one for Medium loans, and one for Jumbo loans.

Select the desired number of samples from each worksheet as shown with the random sampling example. For Small loans, select 34 samples; for Medium loans, select 26; and for Jumbo loans, select 15. This generates the required 75 records to audit.

Systematic Samples

Systematic samples are often used as a simple matter of convenience for the team. In this type of sampling, items are selected based on a pre-determined system (every 10th item, every 20th item, etc.). This method will usually produce a good quality sample, but sometimes there is an issue with an unknown sequence that mimics the sampling system.

For instance, if the system calls for collecting every 10th item; however, based on the manufacturing and arrival patterns of these items, every 10th item comes from the same source. If this is the case, then the entire sample will come from one source and no other; this is certainly not a desirable condition. Issues of an unknown sequence mimicking the sample system are relatively rare, but it is worth double checking before proceeding with this type of sample.

To select the records for this type of sample, determine the percent of the records to audit and create a column containing numbers representing that percent. For instance, if 10% of the records are desired, use the numbers 1 to 10; if 20% of the records are required, use the values 1 to 5; and so on. To select 5% of the records, a column with the numbers 1 to 20 is required. Use Minitab to create this column.

Minitab command:

Calc > Make Patterned Data > Simple Set of Numbers

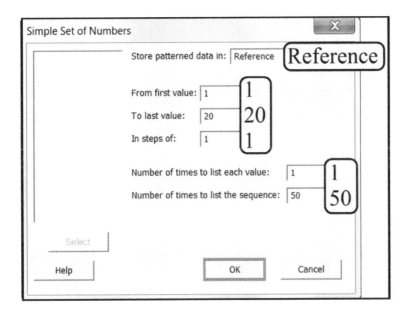

Select the column to store the patterned data (Reference).

For the sequence, begin with the value 1 (first value) and go to 20 (last value). Move in steps of 1 (in steps of).

Each value is listed once (number of times to list each value) before moving to the next value.

This creates the sequence 1 to 20; if there are 1000 records this sequence (1 to 20) must occur 50 times (Number of times to list the sequence) to include all 1000 records in the sampling system.

Click **OK**.

This is the final worksheet with reference numbers

Split the worksheet based on the reference number to create 20 new worksheets, and then select one of these new worksheets to obtain the samples.

Another method is to select one of the values and create a worksheet with just that one value. This is accomplished using the subset option.

C1	C2	C3-T	C4
Record No.	Loan Value	Loan Size	Reference
1	$54,519	Small	1
2	$302,166	Medium	2
3	$326,474	Medium	3
4	$190,575	Medium	4
5	$4,522,418	Jumbo	5
6	$1,045,457	Jumbo	6
7	$91,674	Small	7
8	$80,424	Small	8
9	$100,453	Medium	9
10	$82,000	Small	10
11	$52,128	Small	11
12	$4,848,451	Jumbo	12

Minitab command: *Data > Subset Worksheet*

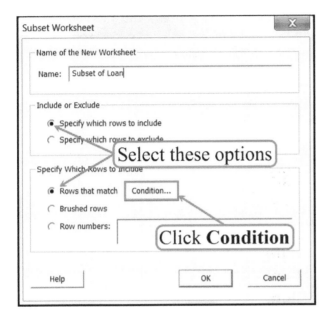

Type the name of a new worksheet, or accept the default setting of 'Subset of (name of worksheet)'.

Choose 'Specify which rows to include'.

Choose 'Rows that match'.

Click **Condition**....

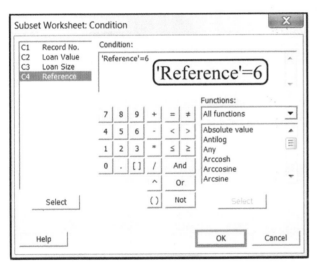

For Condition, select the column with the patterned numbers and set it equal to a value. Here the value is six.

The subset will create a worksheet with only the rows that have the number 6 in the 'Reference' column.

Click **OK** twice.

Subset of worksheet.

C1	C2	C3-T	C4
Record No.	Loan Value	Loan Size	Reference
6	$1,045,457	Jumbo	6
26	$13,696	Small	6
46	$93,310	Small	6
66	$4,320,172	Jumbo	6
86	$477,621	Medium	6
106	$1,810,388	Jumbo	6
126	$72,052	Small	6
146	$84,278	Small	6
166	$70,677	Small	6
186	$1,845,177	Jumbo	6
206	$4,976,233	Jumbo	6
226	$22,234	Small	6

The Record No. column contains the records for the audit.

Selected files can now be analyzed for accuracy and completeness; classification of errors can follow the same method as used previously.

Determining the Process Capability

A process capability analysis is the connection between the voice of the process and the voice of the customer. The capability study provides information on the percent of a process that is outside of customer specifications, so without customer specifications the capability study is simply not possible.

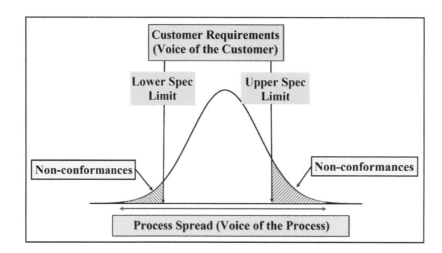

The initial evaluation of process capability provides a baseline from which a goal is determined, and the amount of progress from the baseline to the goal determines the success of the project.

Process capability analysis requires an estimate of the process spread based on the sample information. Customer requirements are then overlaid, and the percent of the process outside these specifications is determined. This type of display makes it much easier to evaluate process spread vs. customer specs.

Metrics

Process Capability metrics help to compare unrelated processes. The values calculated allow process owners to determine the need for improvements. The formula used is as follows:

$$Cp = \frac{USL - LSL}{6 * s}$$

(where s is the standard deviation based on the subgroup size)

Cp compares the process specification window to the spread of the process represented by 6 standard deviations (or 99.73% of a normally distributed process).

Cp calculations assume a process is centered within specifications, which means a Cp calculation offers no indication of whether the process is on target. It is possible, then, for a process to have a high Cp value and yet also have a high percent of the process outside of the specifications.

Cpk is the metric that looks at the process mean in relation to the specifications. It is the minimum of **Cpu** and **Cpl**, shown as follows:

$$\mathbf{Cpk = Min(Cpu, Cpl)}$$

Where:

$$\mathbf{Cpu} = \left(\frac{\mathbf{USL} - \overline{\mathbf{X}}}{\mathbf{3 * s}} \right)$$

and

$$\mathbf{Cpl} = \left(\frac{\overline{\mathbf{X}} - \mathbf{LSL}}{\mathbf{3 * s}} \right)$$

Minitab offers several options for estimating standard deviation when calculating Cp and Cpk, based on sample size. For a sample size of 1, Minitab will use, as an estimate of σ, the Average Moving Range divided by a correction factor based on the number of values used to calculate the moving range. The default is to use 2 values for the moving range.

With a moving range of size 2, the formula becomes:

$$\mathbf{s} = \frac{\overline{\mathbf{MR}}}{1.128}$$

For subgroup sizes larger than 1, several other options exist; Minitab allows for use of either the average Range, the average Standard Deviation, or a Pooled Standard Deviation.

Pp and **Ppk** are calculated in the same manner as **Cp** and **Cpk**, only the standard deviation is based on the overall standard deviation, not a subgroup standard deviation. This is the same value as the standard deviation calculated using the;

Calc > Column Statistics, or *Stat > Basic Statistics* options.

By definition, a Six Sigma process has a Pp ≥ 2.0 and a Ppk ≥ 1.5; however, **Cpm** is the proper metric for use when the target value is not centered within the specifications. Information on the calculation for **Cpm** is available in the Minitab help menu.

Z values

Minitab calculates three Z values: Z bench, Z LSL, and Z USL. Z LSL and Z USL are equal to 3*Cpl or Ppl and 3* Cpu or Ppu. Z bench is calculated based on the cumulative normal distribution function. The exact formulas are found in the Minitab help menu.

DPU

DPU (Defects per Unit) is calculated by taking the total number of defects in a sample and dividing by the number of units in that sample. It is assumed that a unit may have more than one defect.

DPMO

When the quality level of a process improves the DPU value decreases, often to a level where the DPU is a very small fraction that shows up as .000 on spreadsheets. To improve the discrimination of this metric, the DPMO (Defects per Million Opportunities) metric was developed. With DPMO, defects are measured in relation to defects that could potentially exist.

The formula for DPMO is as follows:

$$\textbf{DPMO} = \frac{\textbf{Defect count} * \textbf{1,000,000}}{(\textbf{\# Units}) * \left(\textbf{Opportunities} \middle/ \textbf{Unit}\right)}$$

The **Opportunity** is defined as the number of chances of not meeting a customer's requirement.

Percent Defective

Describing an item as either good or bad is one way to determine if an item is defective, but this is not the same thing as identifying a specific defect because an item classified as bad may have one or more defects.

When measuring defectives, gather a sample of items and determine the percent of items that fall into the defective category. Calculate the percent of the total and post it as the percent defective. To properly measure the percent defective of a process, the sample size should have on average five defective items. This means as a process improves, the sample size required to properly measure defective rate increases.

Minitab's Capability Study

Minitab's capability study produces within and overall capability values. Cp and Cpk are considered within capabilities and are used as an internal guide to how good a process could become; Pp and Ppk are considered overall capabilities and are what the customer sees. As a first step, teams try to move the process from current (Pp and Ppk) levels to Cp and Cpk levels. If this does not satisfy the project goals, additional work is needed.

Minitab project: **Capability.MPJ**

Worksheet: *Form_A*

Menu command: *Stat > Quality Tools > Capability Analysis > Normal*

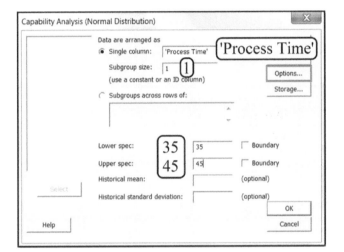

For Single column, select **Process Time.**

The subgroup size is **1**.

The Lower spec is **35** and the Upper spec is **45**.

Click the **Options** button.

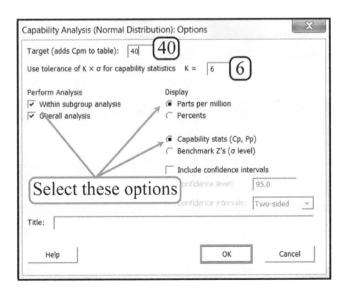

The target value is optional. With a target, (**40**) Minitab will calculate a Cpm value. The tolerance of k*sigma is set to **6**.

Note: Some companies still use the value 5.15

For the Perform Analysis, select both options.

Click **OK** (twice).

The results are displayed in both graphical and analytical form.

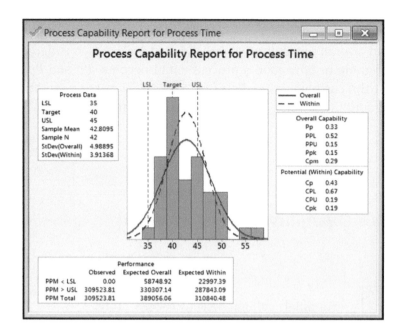

The graph displays a bar chart with 2 normal curves, one for the within estimate and one for the overall.

The process information is located on the upper left while the capability information is located on the right.

Calculations for the PPM, both within and overall, are located below the bar graph.

Some users prefer to have the defective information listed as a percent. To change the PPM to a percent, and to display the Z values, return to the options window on the previous page and select Percents and Benchmark Z's under the Display section.

Leave the other inputs as shown before.

Click **OK** twice.

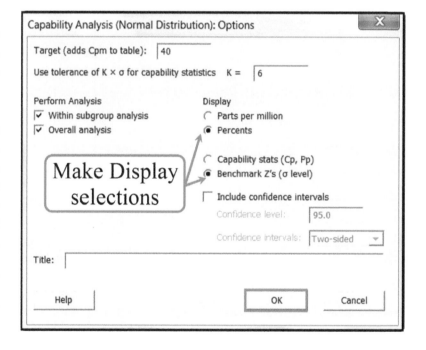

The Pp, Ppk and Cp, Cpk values are replace by the Z values. The PPM output is replaced with the % outside specification.

This graph is used during presentations, but it can be overwhelming to those not familiar with the terminology. To simplify the output, delete information that is not pertinent to the presentation. The basic information supplied by this chart is the amount of the process outside the customer's requirements.

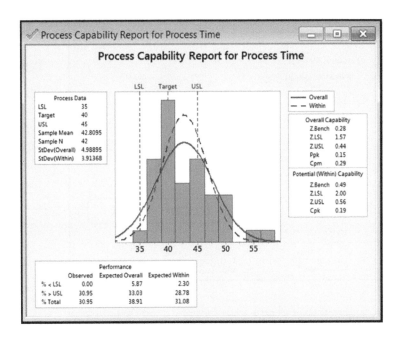

Hint:

To remove specific information, click the desired square and hit the delete button.

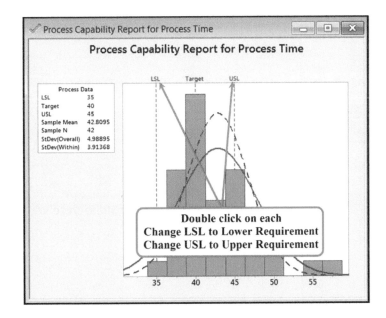

Next, change the LSL and USL to Lower Requirement and Upper Requirement.

Double Click on LSL:

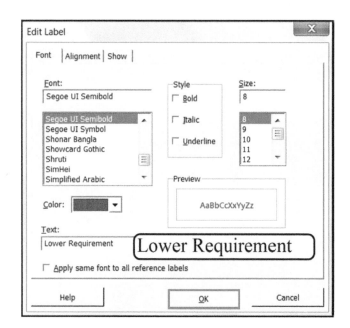

Select the **Font** tab.

Type in the desired text; **Lower Requirement**.

Click **OK**.

Repeat with USL, changing it to **Upper Requirement**.

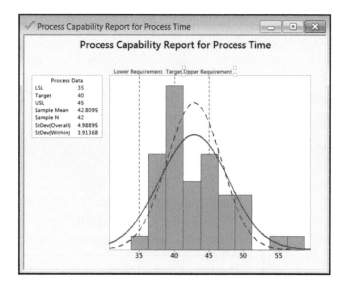

The graph could be simplified further by removing the normal curves.

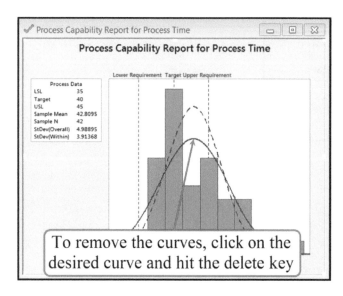

Click on the curve and hit the **delete** key.

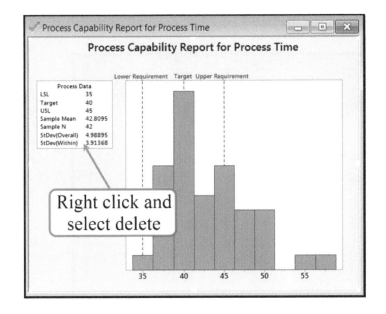

To remove the StDev (Within), right click to select the data section, then click on the value and select delete.

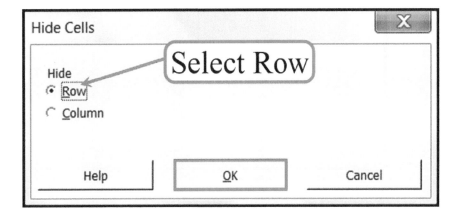

In the Hide Cells window, select Row and click **OK**.

To remove the Overall designation, **double click** StDev (Overall) and edit the text.

Click **OK**.

Final Graph

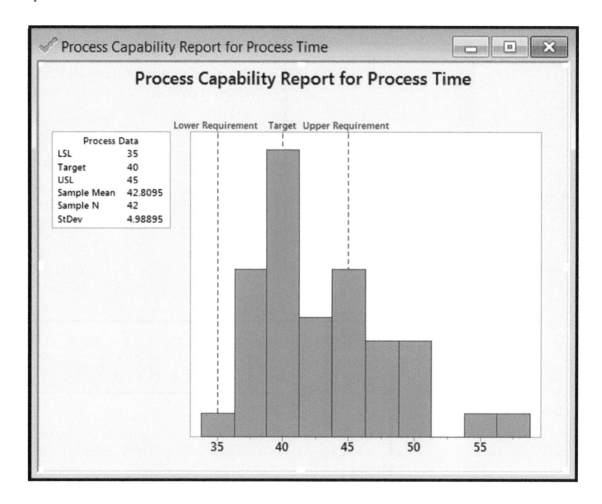

Process Capability Six Pack

Minitab also offers a capability analysis that includes several additional graphs. It is called the Capability Sixpack option.

Menu command: *Stat > Quality Tools > Capability Sixpack > Normal*

The inputs are the same as those used for the Capability chart.

Click **Options**.

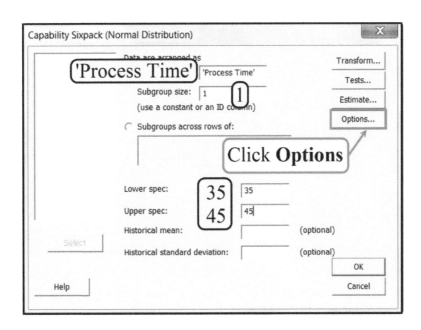

Input the target of 40.

Click **OK** (twice).

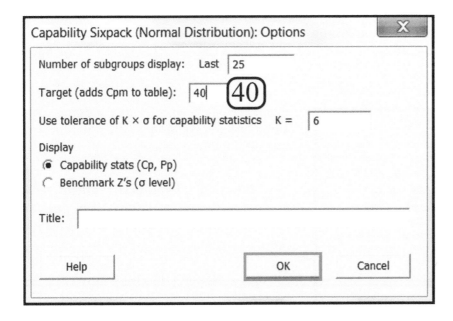

The Six Pack graphs test the stability and normality of the data.

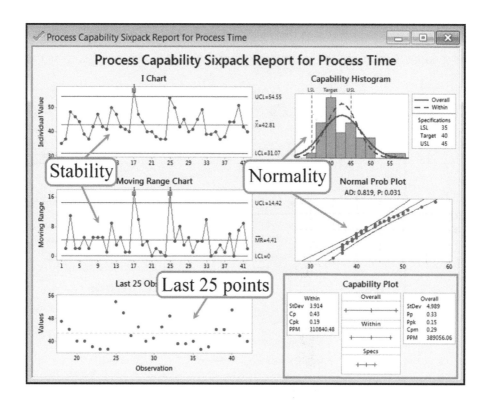

The I and Moving Range Charts are used for a sample size of 1. If the user selects a sample size greater than 1, the graph will be an Xbar-R chart or Xbar-S chart depending upon the estimate selected.

The chart on the lower left shows the last 25 data points; this chart is especially effective when there is a large amount of data in the worksheet. The two charts on the upper right represent the normality of the data. The Normal Prob Plot contains the Anderson Darling normality test statistic. A p-value less than .05 provides evidence that the data is not from a normal distribution. If this is the case, the resultant capability values are suspect.

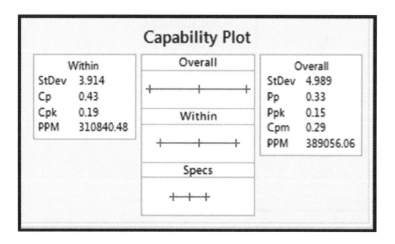

Finally, the lower right contains the summary information for the within and overall capability values:

The Within and Overall metrics are the same as for the Capability Study. And, like the Capability study, the Sixpack does have the option to display the Benchmark Z values.

The graph displays the width of the process (plus and minus 3 standard deviation) based on the within and overall calculations. The spread of these distributions are compared to the customer specifications. The graph above shows a process that produces output much in excess of the customer requirements.

Analyze Phase

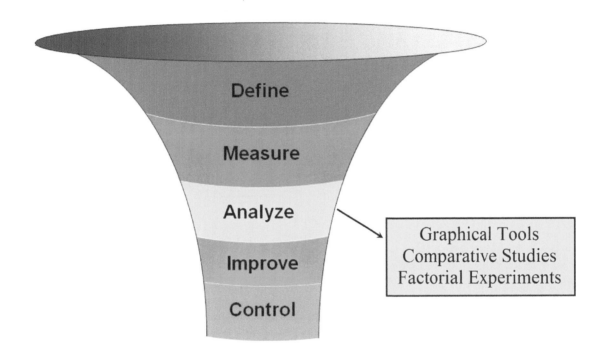

Analyze Phase

The Analyze phase of a Six Sigma process focuses on investigation and examination of potential critical inputs (X's) as identified in the Measure phase.

Statistical analysis and graphs become the primary focus of teams during this phase, as they attempt to identify links between inputs (X's) and critical outputs (Y's). What's more, **Minitab** becomes an increasingly critical instrument because it provides users with the computing power necessary to definitively show those links and relationships.

Tools and Outcomes

During the Analyze phase teams use a variety of tools, including:
- Graphical Tools
- Comparative Studies
- Factorial Experiments

These tools help teams generate the clear evidence necessary to achieve the major outcome of this phase; that is, they can clearly demonstrate which input factor(s) (X's) have the greatest affect on the critical outputs (Y's). Knowing which factors are important and where they have influence is the first step toward creating lasting process improvement.

Note: Through the remainder of this book, process outputs will be referred to simply as Y's, and inputs will be referred to simply as X's.

Keep in mind, however, that a solution to the overall problem is not expected in this phase; that occurs during the final part of the process, the Improve phase.

Graphical Tools

In the Measure phase, detailed analysis is performed on critical Y's to make an initial assessment of their stability, normality and capability. In the Analyze phase, attention turns to determining whether any X's under investigation do indeed have an effect on those Y's. A common method of making this determination is through the use of analytical tests.

Before launching into analytical tests, however, teams must first take a look at the data collected to see if there are any obvious relationships or issues of concern.

The following graphs are used to make this determination:
- Probability Plot
- Multi Vari Plot
- Interval Plot

Probability Plot

Tool Use: Use a Probability Plot to determine if a data set was obtained from a population with a specific distribution, usually the normal distribution.

Data Type: The Probability Plot requires numeric data.

Minitab Project: **QualityTools.MPJ**

Worksheet: *Check in Time*

Many analytical tools used for data analysis assume a normal distribution of data. Minitab includes a Normality Test function to check this assumption.

Menu command: *Stat > Basic Statistics > Normality Test*

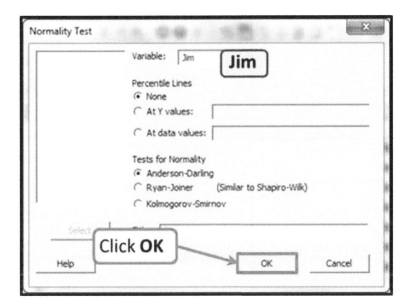

Select **Jim** as the Variable.

Click **OK**.

Summary information provided:

Mean, Standard Deviation (StDev), Sample size (N), Anderson-Darling test for normality (AD) and the associated p-value.

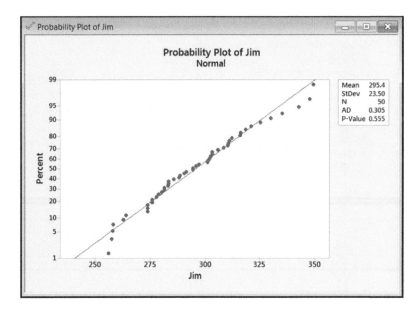

Hypothesis testing associated with the Anderson-Darling criteria is discussed later in this unit. For now, simply stated, if the p-value is greater than .05 the assumption is that data originated from a population with a normal distribution. In the example above, the result for Jim is a p-value = .555, which cannot reject the assumption of a population with a normal distribution.

Minitab can also perform a test for distributions other than the normal; the selection of the distribution is located under the Graph menu. Use the normal distribution to demonstrate this command, comparing it to the Normality test above.

Menu command: *Graph > Probability Plot > Single*

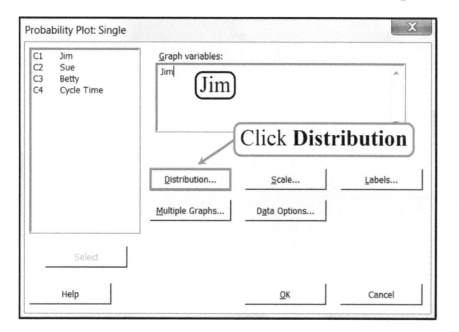

Input **Jim** as the Graph variables.

Click **Distribution**.

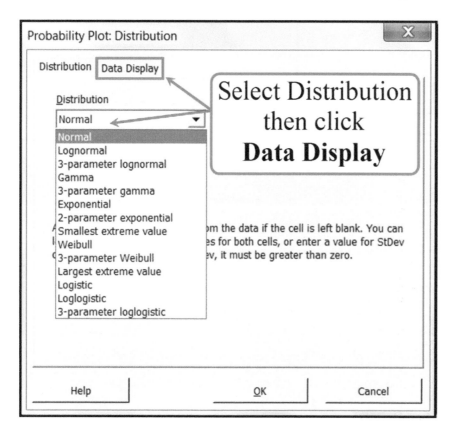

Select the desired distribution from the pull down menu. For this example, use the Normal distribution.

Input the distribution's parameters if known, (leave blank for this example).

Click the **Data Display** tab.

Remove the **Show confidence interval** option.

Click

OK (twice).

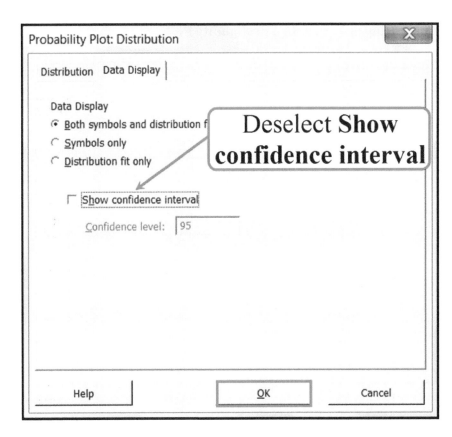

Probability Plot Output

The results are identical to the graph created by the *Stat > Basic Statistics > Normality Test option.* (This is expected since it's the same data.)

The high p-value indicates the idea that the sample originated from a normal distribution cannot be rejected.

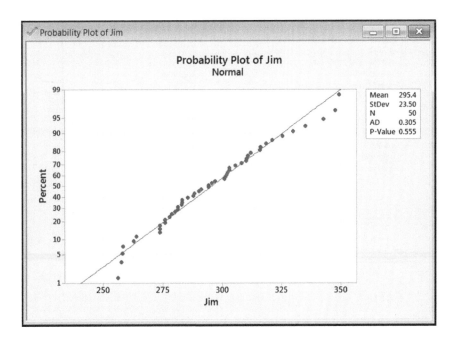

Comparing groups with a Probability Plot

Menu command: *Graph > Probability Plot>– Multiple*

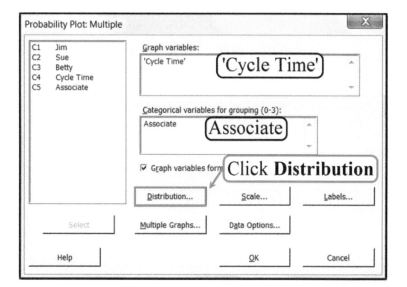

Input **Cycle Time** for the Graph variables:

Select **Associate** for the Categorical variables.

Click **Distribution**.

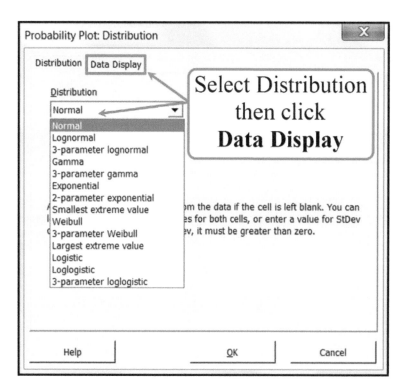

Select the **Normal** distribution.

Click the **Data Display** tab.

Deselect the **Show confidence interval** option.

Click **OK** twice.

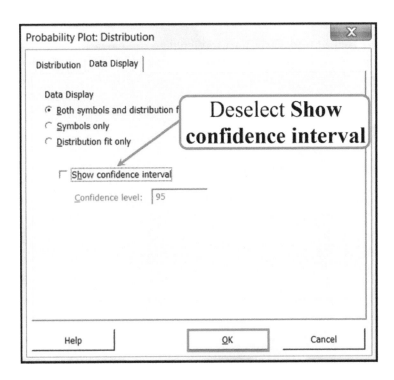

The graph shows all three associates' probability plots for the normal distribution.

Anderson – Darling statistics along with their p-values are shown to the right of the graphs.

Notice that the group with the smaller StDev (standard deviation) has a steeper slope to the line. (Group 2, red line, has the smaller standard deviation.)

Note: Care should be used when creating a graph containing a large number of groups; this will only create a mass of colors, making the graph unintelligible.

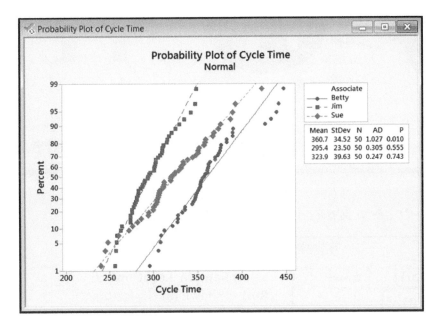

Multi-Vari Plot

Tool Use: Use a Multi-Vari Chart to visualize the variation within a nested study.

Note: Nested studies are discussed later in this chapter.

Data Type: The response requires numeric data; factors may be either numeric or attribute.

Minitab Project: **Nested.MPJ**

Worksheet: *Carpet*

Data originates from a test of carpet crushability. Five samples were measured from each of two locations per roll. The samples are nested within location and the location is nested within the roll. Seven rolls were used in the study.

Visual representation of the nested design.

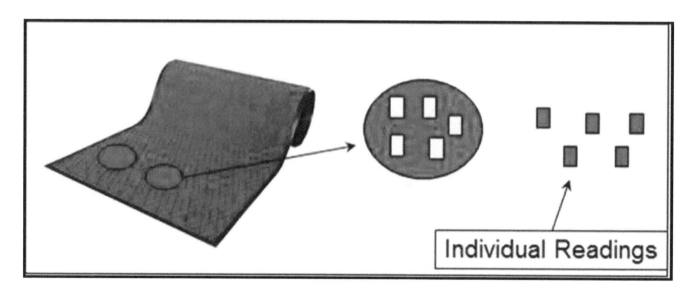

Menu command: *Stat > Quality Tools > Multi-Vari Chart*

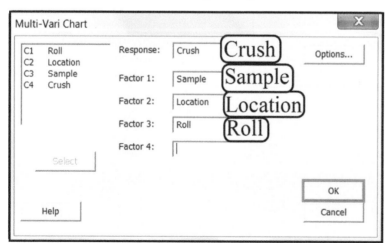

Select **Crush** as the Response.

Select **Sample**, **Location** and **Roll** as shown for the factors.

Click **OK**.

The sequence for factors is important to obtain a usable chart. Start with the lowest level of nesting; in this case, it is the sample. Move up from there until the top item (roll) is reached.

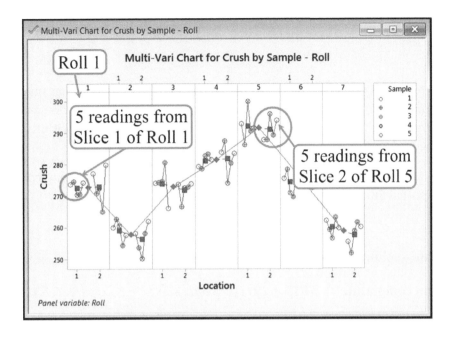

Each panel is one of the 7 rolls. Each panel contains the overall roll mean (diamond symbol), the mean of each location or slice (square symbol) and the five readings for each location (circles).

Now look at the chart produced when the order of factors is reversed.

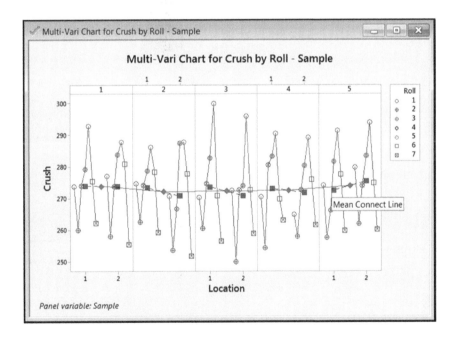

The line through the center is connecting the average of each reading location. So for all sample 1 readings in the seven rolls, the average is the diamond in the center of panel 1. Finding the average of all first readings for the samples within the rolls doesn't make sense.

Confidence Intervals

C1
Data
45
52
68
49
52
66
73
47
66
54

The team will often be concerned with estimating a population parameter such as the mean (μ) or standard deviation (σ). However, since the calculations use sample information, the estimates are not exact. This uncertainty requires an interval, within which the population value resides.

Minitab offers several methods to create confidence intervals; one common method is the **Graphical Summary** option under **Stat – Basic Statistics**.

Create a column of data in a Minitab worksheet as shown.

Menu command: *Stat > Basic Statistics > Graphical Summary*

Input **Data** as the Variables:

Click **OK**.

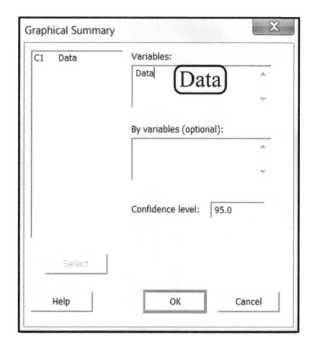

The Results appear in a separate Graph window.

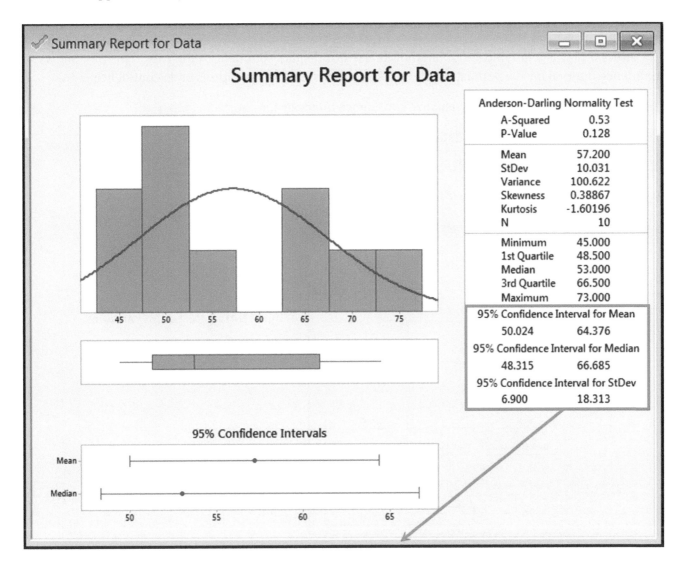

Based on sample data supplied, the population mean is between **50.024** and **64.376**, the population Median is between **48.315** and **66.685,** and the population Standard Deviation is between **6.900** and **18.313**.

95% Confidence Interval for Mean	
50.024	64.376
95% Confidence Interval for Median	
48.315	66.685
95% Confidence Interval for StDev	
6.900	18.313

Confidence Intervals – Graphical Display

The Interval Plot is a graphical tool in Minitab, used to display confidence intervals. This plot shows the confidence interval for the population mean using either standard deviations or % confidence.

Tool Use: Use an Interval Plot to visualize confidence intervals for data sets.

Data Type: Numeric continuous data is required for the interval plot.

Minitab Project: **QualityTools.MPJ**

Worksheet: *Check in Time*

Menu command: *Stat > ANOVA > Interval Plot > Simple*

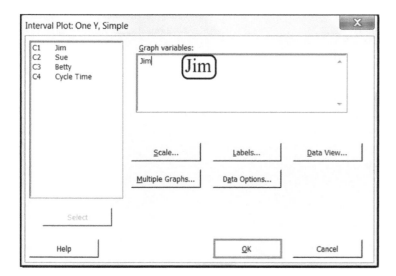

Input **Jim** as the Graph variables.

Click **OK**.

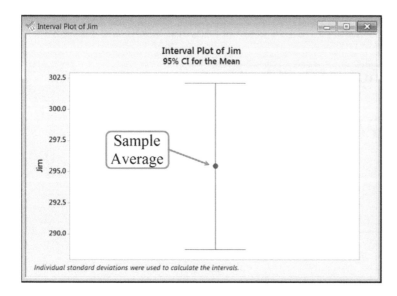

The circle is the sample average ($\overline{X}$), the point estimate of the population's mean (μ).

The bars indicate the confidence interval.

The default interval is a 95% interval.

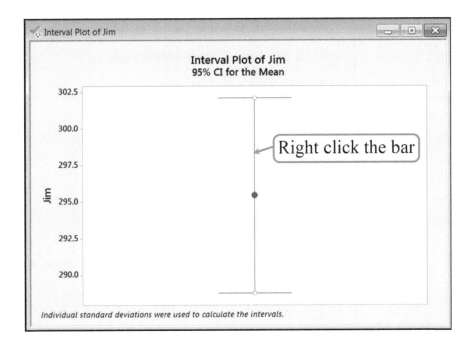

To change criteria for the interval, right click the bar.

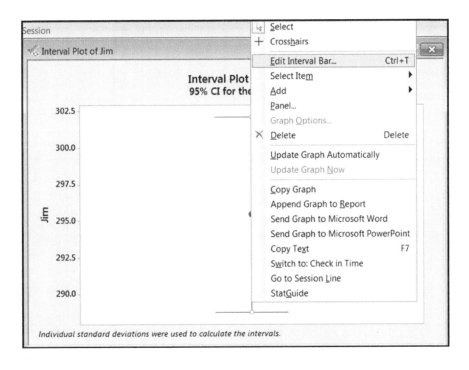

Select **Edit Interval Bar**.

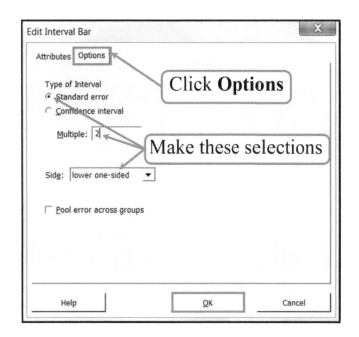

Click the **Options** tab.

Select the desired **Type of Interval**.

The Standard Error is based on the sample standard deviation divided by the square root of the sample size.

$$\left(\frac{s}{\sqrt{n}}\right)$$

The Confidence Interval is equal to (1-α).

Select the Multiples of the desired type of interval.

Decide on the type of interval; the choices are upper one-sided, lower one-sided and two-sided.

Click **OK**.

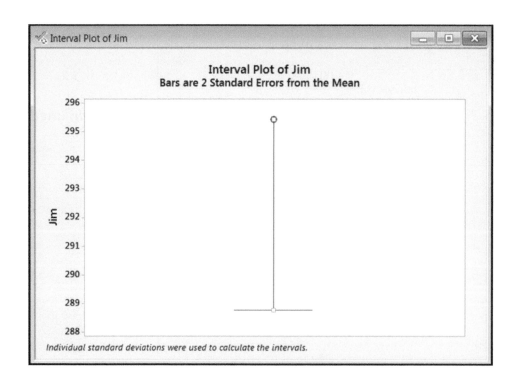

This is an example of a lower one-sided confidence interval based on 2 standard errors.

Note: At first glance, it may not be obvious what type of confidence interval is displayed, so always be sure what the interval represents before making any decisions.

Interval Plots with Groups

Menu command: *Stat > ANOVA > Interval Plot > With Groups*

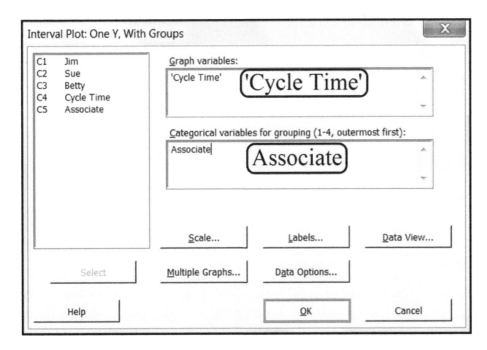

Input **Cycle Time** as the Graph variables.

Choose **Associate** as the Categorical variables.

Click **OK**.

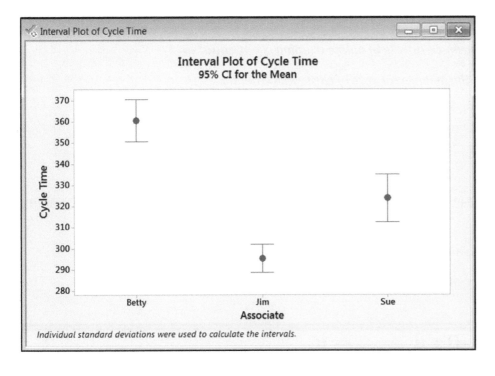

To edit the interval bars, use the same technique as shown with the single interval.

Hypothesis Testing

In the Analyze phase, use data obtained in the Measure phase and begin to 'dig' into it. The goal is to determine if differences exist between groups and whether there are significant relationships between X's and critical Y's. The technique used to make this determination is called hypothesis testing.

The steps in hypothesis testing are as follows:
1. Write the alternative hypothesis (H_a)
2. Write the null hypothesis (H_o)
3. Select a critical p-value
4. Choose the type of test to run
5. Plan and run the test
6. Based on the test results, reject H_o / fail to reject H_o and draw conclusions

Step 1: Write the alternative hypothesis

Experiments are performed with the intent of demonstrating a relationship (correlation) between factors, or a difference between the population parameter values of different groups. The alternative hypothesis is the statement used to explain which differences are being tested.

For example, suppose the team wishes to show that the input factor (Training) makes a difference in the number of errors produced in the invoice process. The team is investigating two different training methods – online training and classroom training.

If the team wishes to show only that there's a difference between the two methods and are not concerned about which one has the lower error rate, then the alternative hypothesis is:

*The mean error rate of online training is **not equal** to*

the mean error rate of classroom training.

This is written as:

$$H_a: \mu_{Error\ Online} \neq \mu_{Error\ Classroom}$$

Step 2: Write the null hypothesis

The null hypothesis comprises all other options not included in the alternative hypothesis. For the example above, the null hypothesis is:

*The mean error rate for online training is **equal** to*

the mean error rate of classroom training.

This is written as:

$$H_o: \mu_{Error\ Online} = \mu_{Error\ Classroom}$$

After performing the experiment, if evidence shows the alternative is correct then the team can make the statement:

**The training method makes a difference
in the mean number of errors for the invoice process.**

If the evidence does not support this then the team can make the statement:

**There is not enough evidence to show a difference
in the mean number of errors based on the training method.**

In some other situations, the team might expect the difference to favor one group over another. For example, suppose a drug company claims their diet pill (Mega Diet) produces greater weight loss compared to a rival diet pill (Mini Diet).

The proper alternative hypothesis is:

$$H_a: \mu_{\text{Weight loss Mega Diet}} > \mu_{\text{Weight loss Mini Diet}}$$

The null hypothesis is:

$$H_o: \mu_{\text{Weight loss Mega Diet}} \leq \mu_{\text{Weight loss Mini Diet}}$$

Minitab allows the team to select which type of alternative hypothesis to run. The team then runs and analyzes the experiment. The results determine if there is enough evidence to support the claim for the Mega Diet pill or if there is not enough evidence to support the claim for the Mega Diet pill.

Step 3: Select a p-value

The definition of p-value is:

The probability of obtaining the experimental data,
if the null hypothesis is true.

The key to this statement is the 'IF' portion. If the null hypothesis is not true, the p-value is meaningless.

Errors in Hypothesis Testing

The p-value indicates the risk the team us willing to accept in making a Type I error.

When running a test of hypothesis, there are four possible outcomes as shown in the following table:

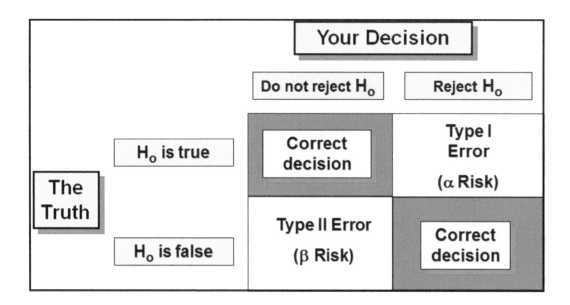

The table shows the true condition as 'The Truth'; this is what the experiment is trying to determine. The Truth may never actually be known. An experiment can be created that minimizes the two types of error, thus improving the chance of making a 'Correct Decision'.

Note: there are two situations where a correct decision is made:
1.   Reject the null hypothesis (H_o) and the null is in fact true.
2.   Reject H_o when it is in fact false.

There are also two boxes demonstrating potential errors:
1. H_o is the true condition, but the decision is to reject H_o. (This is called a Type I or Alpha error, also called the Alpha (α) risk.)
2.   Based on the data, the decision is to not reject H_o when it is in fact false. (This is called a Type II or Beta error, also called the Beta (β) risk.)

The critical p-value, then, is that value (calculated by Minitab during the analysis) below which the decision is to reject the Null hypothesis in favor of the Alternative hypothesis. So what is the correct critical p-value to use? The answer depends on the seriousness of making a Type I error.

Typically, if a Type I error is not serious a p-value of **.1** is used; if a Type I error is moderately serious a **.05** value is used; and if a Type I error is very serious a p-value of **.01** or less is used.

Step 4: Choose the type of test to run

Testing the hypothesis may involve several different statistical tests. These tests depend upon the data type of the inputs and the output. The following table is designed to help determine the best statistical test based on the type of data. Use it as follows:
1.   Determine the input data type, discrete for count data, and continuous for variables data.
2.   Determine the output data type.
3.   Find the intersection of the two data types to deter-
     mine the correct statistical analysis to perform.

Below are some examples of how this works.

EXAMPLE #1

Input: Associate (discrete data).

Output: Thickness of paint (a continuous factor).

Test: t-Test or ANOVA.

EXAMPLE #2

Input: Smoking (Y/N) – Discrete

Output: Cancer (Has cancer / cancer freer) – Discrete

Test: Chi-Square

EXAMPLE #3

Input: Hours of overtime – Continuous

Output: Hours missed for illness – Continuous

Test: Regression

EXAMPLE #4A

Input: Weight of Truck – Continuous

Output: Severity of Injury in accident (Mild, Moderate or Severe) – Discrete

Test: Logistic Regression

EXAMPLE #4B

An alternative for this example is to classify the trucks into groups (Light Duty, Medium Duty and Heavy Duty). In that situation, the results are as follows:

Input: Truck Group – Discrete

Output: Severity of Injury in accident (Mild, Moderate or Severe) – Discrete

Test: Chi-Square

There are several hypotheses for each test. The following table shows the commonly used hypotheses.

Test	Null Hypothesis	Alternative Hypothesis
One Sample t-Test:	μ = **Specified value** The population mean is (specify value) $\mu \leq$ **Specified value** The population mean is less than or equal to (specify value) $\mu \geq$ **Specified value** The population mean is greater than or equal to (specify value)	$\mu \neq$ **Specified value** The population mean is not (specify value) $\mu >$ **Specified value** The population mean is greater than (specify value) $\mu <$ **Specified value** The population mean is less than (specify value)
Two Sample t-Test	$\mu_1 = \mu_2$ The mean of population 1 is equal to the mean of population 2 $\mu_1 \leq \mu_2$ The mean of population 1 is less than or equal to the mean of population 2 $\mu_1 \geq \mu_2$ The mean of population 1 is greater than or equal to the mean of population 2	$\mu_1 \neq \mu_2$ The mean of population 1 is not equal to the mean of population 2 $\mu_1 > \mu_2$ The mean of population 1 is greater than the mean of population 2 $\mu_1 < \mu_2$ The mean of population 1 is less than the mean of population 2
ANOVA	$\mu_1 = \mu_2 = \mu_3 \dots = \mu_n$ The population mean of all groups are equal	**At least one $\mu_i \neq \mu_j$** At least one of the population mean is not equal to another population mean
Regression	β **(coefficient) = 0** The factor's coefficient is equal to zero. (Factor X does not have an effect on the output.)	β **(coefficient) $\neq$ 0** The factor's coefficient is not equal to zero. (Factor X does have an effect on the output.)
Logistic Regression	**Model coefficient β = 0** Coefficient for model is equal to zero. (Factor X in model does not have an effect on output.)	$\beta \neq 0$ Coefficient for model is not equal to zero. (Factor X does have an effect on output.)
Chi-Square	**Factors are Independent** The factors are statistically independent.	**Factors are dependent** The factors are statistically dependent.

Comparative Studies

One Sample t-Test

Tool Use: Use a One Sample t-Test to determine if a sample originated from a population with a specified population mean, or to create a confidence interval for the population mean.

Data Type: Input - Discrete (1 group); Output – Continuous

Minitab Project: ANOVA.MPJ

Worksheet: *One Sample t-Test*

This worksheet contains paint thickness data from a single operator (Sue). Her manager wants to determine if Sue's population mean value of paint thickness is not equal to 25 mils.

Null Hypothesis: μ_{Sue} = 25 mils

Alternative Hypothesis: $\mu_{Sue} \neq 25$

Menu command: *Stat > Basic Statistics > 1 Sample t*

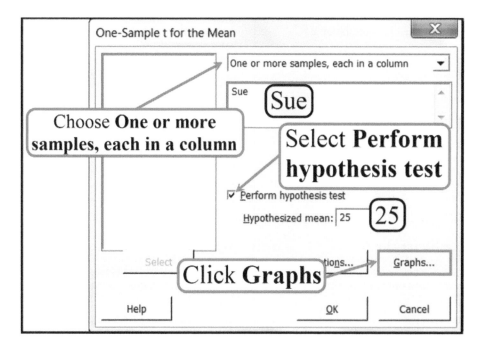

Select **One or more samples, each in a column.** Input **Sue** as the column to test.

To test the sample versus a specific population mean value, select **Perform hypothesis test**. This requires a **Hypothesized mean**; in this example use the value 25.

To create the summary graphs, (Box Plots, Histograms or Individual Value plot), click the **Graphs** button.

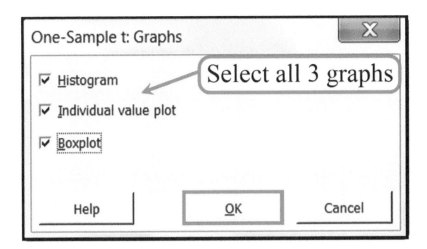

Select all three graphs.

Click **OK**.

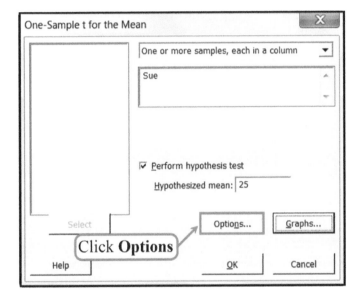

Select the **Options** button.

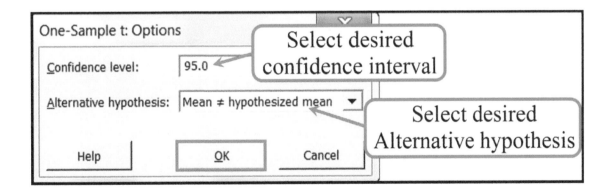

Select the desired Confidence level.

Select the alternative hypothesis (not equal).

Click **OK** (twice).

Graph Folder icon

Hint: *To create a window with all three graphs, click the graphs folder icon on the main menu bar.*

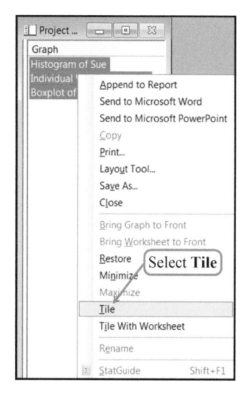

Select the three graphs.

Right click on one of the selected graphs.

Click '**Tile**'.

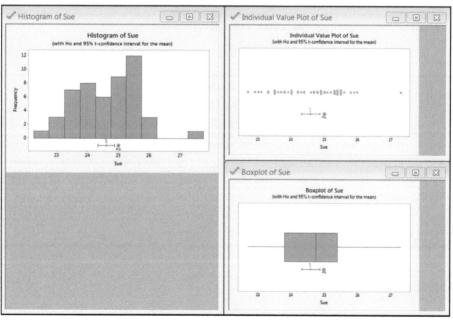

The three graphs appear.

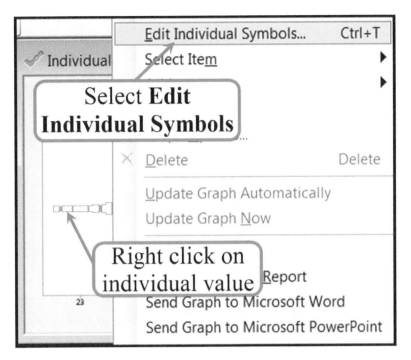

Looking at the **Individual Value Plot of Sue**, it's difficult to observe the individual values. To resolve this issue, right click on the individual symbols and select '**Edit individual Symbols**'.

Select **Identical Points**, then select **Jitter**. Click **OK**.

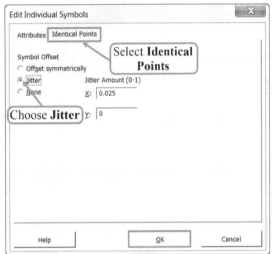

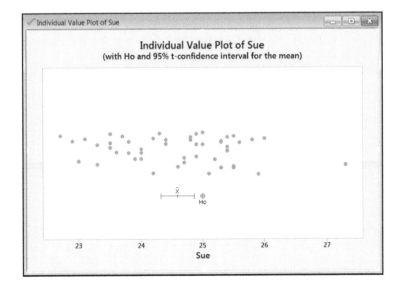

It is now easier to see the individual points.

Session window output:

```
One-Sample T: Sue

Test of μ = 25 vs ≠ 25

Variable   N    Mean   StDev  SE Mean        95% CI          T      P
Sue        50  24.596  0.963   0.136   (24.322, 24.870)  -2.97  0.005
```

The results show the **95% confidence interval** for the population mean; it indicates Sue's population mean is between the values 24.322 and 24.870.

The **p-value** references the specified hypothesized population mean. With the low p-value, reject the null hypothesis (H_o: Population mean for Sue equals 25, in favor of the alternative hypothesis, H_a: Population mean for Sue not equal to 25.)

Notice the p-value indicates the conclusion should be to reject the null hypothesis. This corresponds with the confidence interval that shows 25 is not part of the interval.

For a specified Type I (α) error, if the p-value is less than the specified value, the $(1 - \alpha)$ confidence interval will not contain the specified value. In the example above, the specified p-value (acceptable Type I error) is .05. The corresponding confidence interval is $(1 - \alpha)$ or .95, a 95% confidence interval.

Since the Minitab output has a p-value of .005 (less than .05), the corresponding 95% confidence interval does not contain the tested value of 25.

Assumptions for One Sample t-Test: The confidence interval calculation assumes the data is from a stable, normally distributed population. Both of these assumptions need verification.

Stability: To check stability, an I-MR control chart is used. The graph should resemble that of a stable in-control process.

Menu command:

Stat > Control Charts > Variables Charts for Individuals > I-MR

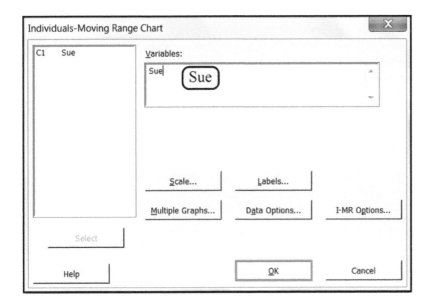

Select **Sue** as the variable.

Click **OK**.

For more information on control charts, see the Measure chapter and Control chapter.

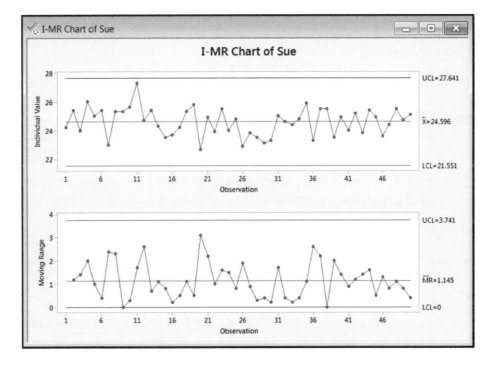

Normal Distribution: To check normality, use either the *Stat > Basic Statistics > Normality Test* or the *Graph > Probability Plot* option.

These options have been shown previously.

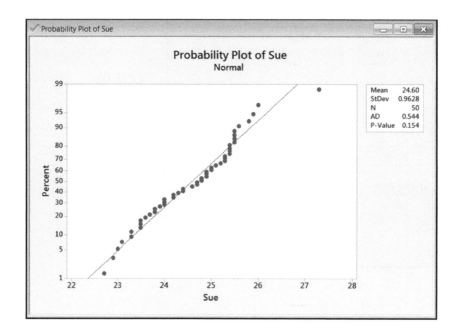

Here is the normality graph:

The high p-value shown here indicates the assumption of normality is not violated.

Two Sample t-Test

Tool Use: Use the Two Sample t-Test to determine if two samples originated from populations with equal mean values or from populations with mean values that are not equal.

Data Type: Input - Discrete (2 groups); Output – Continuous

Minitab Project: **ANOVA.MPJ**

Worksheet: **Two Sample t-Test.mtw**

Data was collected from two associates to determine if it is reasonable to believe their population means are not equal.

Assumptions for Two-Sample t-Test: The samples originate from two stable, normally distributed populations with equal variances. Both of these assumptions need verification.

Test for Stability: Use the I-MR control chart to check stability of each population.

Menu command: *Stat > Control Charts > Variables Charts for Individuals > I-MR*

Input **Sue** and **Fred** as the variables.

Click **OK**.

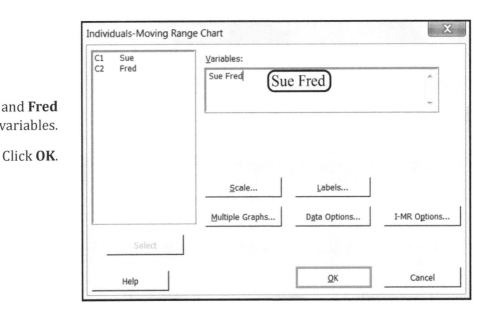

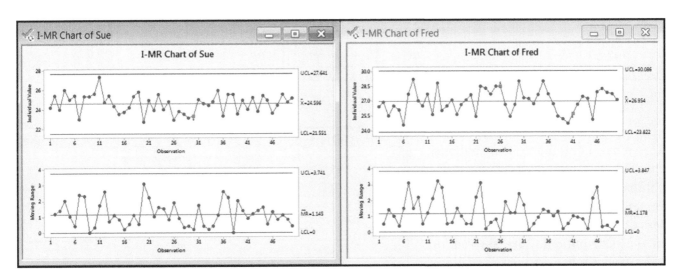

Nothing abnormal appears in either operator's chart. For more information on control charts, see the Measure and Control chapters.

Equal Variance

Menu command: *Stat > Basic Statistics > 2 Variances*

Null Hypothesis: H_o: $\sigma^2_{Sue} = \sigma^2_{Fred}$

Alternative Hypothesis: H_a: $\sigma^2_{Sue} \neq \sigma^2_{Fred}$

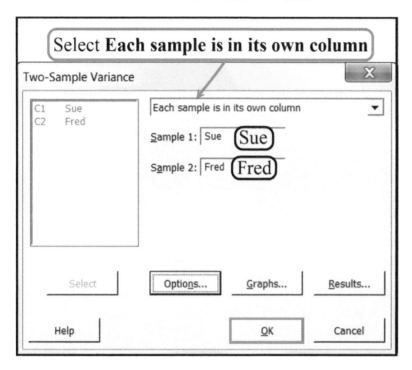

The data in the worksheet exists in two columns. Select **Each sample is in its own column**.

For the first column select **Sue**. For the second select **Fred**.

Click **OK**.

For most continuous distributions, the Bonett's test is more powerful compared to the Levene's tests, unless the following situations exist. There's less than 20 data points, or one or both of the distribution(s) are skewed, or have heavy tails. In these situations the Levene's test is preferred.

The high p-values indicate no evidence to reject the null hypothesis.

The Two Sample t-Test is run assuming equal variances.

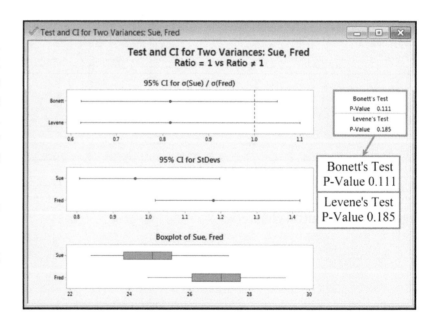

Menu command: *Stat > Basic Statistics > 2 Sample t*

Null Hypothesis: $\mu_{Sue} = \mu_{Fred}$

Alternative Hypothesis: $\mu_{Sue} \neq \mu_{Fred}$

The worksheet contains two columns of data, one for Sue and one for Fred.

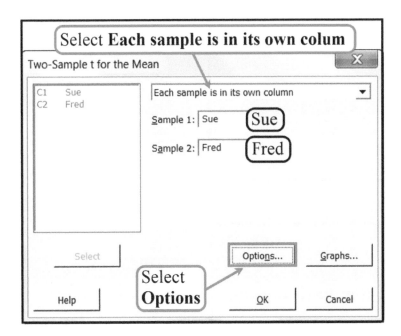

Select '**Each sample is in its own column**'.

Select **Sue** as the first sample and **Fred** as the second.

Click **Options.**

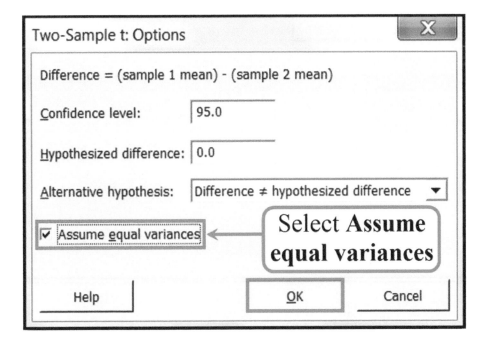

The **2 Variances** test could not reject the idea of the samples having equal variances, so select the box for **Assume equal variances**.

Click **OK.**

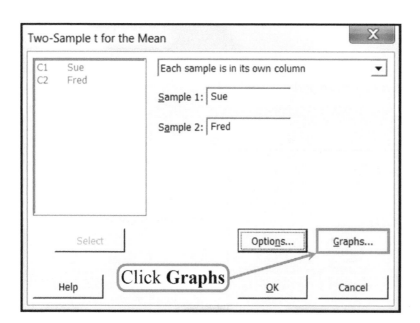

Click **Graphs**.

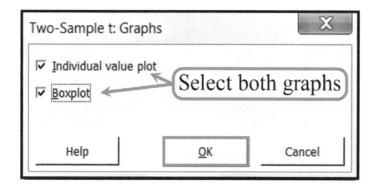

Select both types of graphs.

Click **OK** (twice).

The graphs display both Sue's and Fred's data with their sample mean values connected.

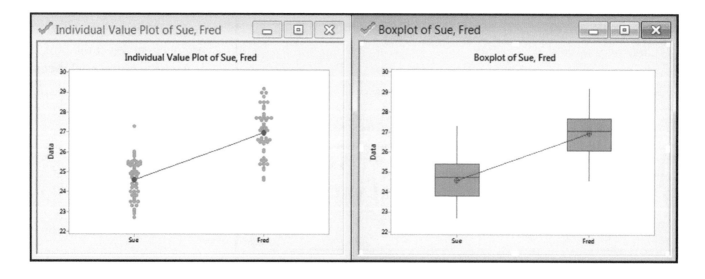

The Session window shows the results of the Two-Sample t-Test analysis.

```
Two-sample T for Sue vs Fred

N     Mean   StDev   SE Mean
Sue   50   24.596   0.963     0.14
Fred  50    26.95   1.18      0.17


Difference = μ (Sue) - μ (Fred)
Estimate for difference:   -2.358
95% CI for difference:   (-2.785, -1.931)
T-Test of difference = 0 (vs ≠): T-Value = -10.96
P-Value = 0.000  DF = 98

Both use Pooled StDev = 1.0759
```

The low **P-Value** (0.000) indicates the data supports a finding of two populations with different mean values.

The true difference between population means is shown under the **95% CI for differences**. Notice the interval (-2.785, -1.931) does not contain the value zero. This indicates, that at the 95% confidence, the two populations do not have equal means, ($\mu_{Sue} \neq \mu_{Fred}$).

Note: An advantage of the Two Sample t-Test is that it allows for an assumption of equal variances. If two groups do not have equal variances, simply leave the box unchecked.

ANOVA Analysis

Tool Use: Use the ANOVA technique to test two (or more) levels of a factor.

Data Type: Input - Discrete (2 or more groups); Output – Continuous

Minitab project ANOVA.MPJ,

Worksheet: *3LevelANOVA*.

Next compare the abilities of three operators: Sue, Fred and Jerry.

Assumptions for the ANOVA analysis are an extension of the Two Sample t-Test. Check stability and normality of each group (the three operators), then check for equal variance. Refer to the Two Sample t-Test for Stability and Normality checks.

C1	C2	C3
Sue	Fred	Jerry
24.2	26.4	24.3
25.4	26.9	24.8
24.0	25.5	26.2
26.0	26.5	25.3
25.0	26.1	26.7
25.4	24.6	24.9
23.0	27.7	23.6
25.3	29.2	24.4
25.3	27.0	24.6
25.6	26.5	25.0

Test of Equal Variance

One assumption for the ANOVA analysis is the groups have equal population variances. To test this assumption use the Test of Equal Variance in Minitab.

Tool Use: Use the Test for Equal Variance to test two or more groups to determine if there's evidence that at least one of their population's variances is not equal to the others.

Data Type: Input – Discrete; Output – Continuous

Menu command: *Stat > ANOVA > Test for Equal Variances*

Null Hypothesis: $H_o: \sigma^2_{Sue} = \sigma^2_{Fred} = \sigma^2_{Jerry}$

Alternate Hypothesis: Ha: At least one $\sigma 2i \neq \sigma 2j$

Select **Response data are in a separate column for each factor level**.

Input **Sue Fred Jerry** for Responses.

Click **OK**.

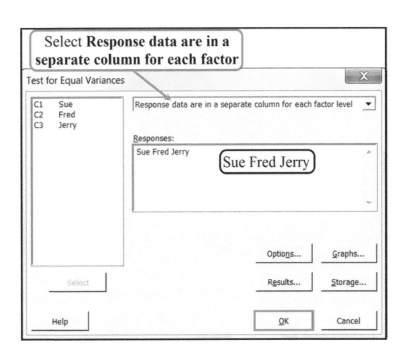

The resulting graph shows the multiple comparison intervals for each operator's population standard deviation.

As indicated at the bottom of the graph, 'if intervals do not overlap, the corresponding standard deviations are significantly different.

Use the Levene's Test with small samples from very skewed or heavy tailed distributions. Here the Multiple Comparison has a low p-value so the conclusion is that at least one of the Standard Deviations is different from another Standard Deviation.

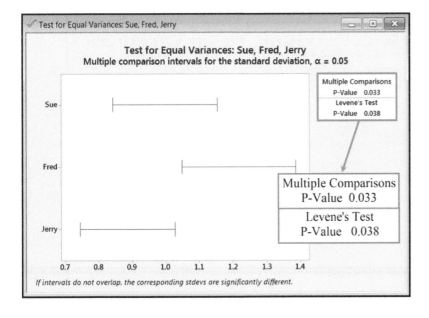

ANOVA Analysis

Null Hypothesis: $H_o: \mu_{Sue} = \mu_{Fred} = \mu_{Jerry}$

Alternative Hypothesis: $H_a:$ At least one $\mu_i \neq \mu_j$

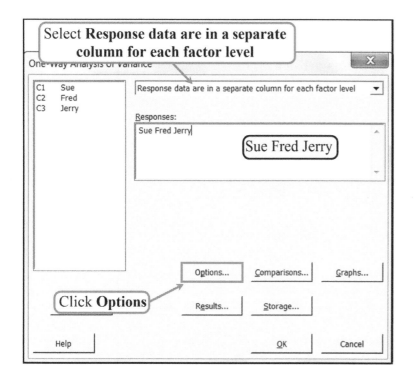

Menu command: *Stat > ANOVA Oneway.*

Select **Response data are in a separate column for each factor level**.

Input **Sue, Fred** and **Jerry** as Responses.

Click **Options**.

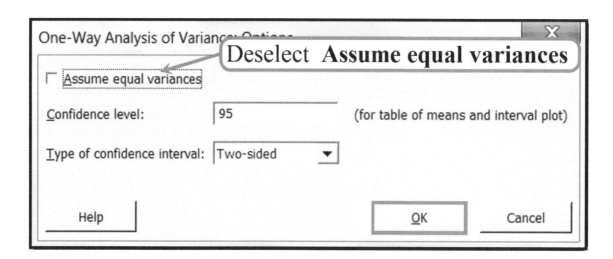

Since the Test for Equal Variance indicated the Standard Deviations were not all equal, deselect the option **Assume equal variances**.

Click **OK** (twice).

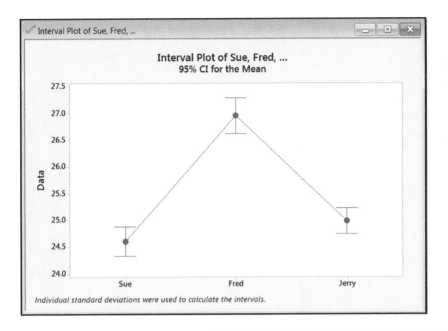

The **Interval Plot** is generated. This graphs shows the 95% confidence interval for each operators population mean. If the intervals do not overlap, it suggests that the population mean for those groups are not equal.

Session window output.

Welch's Test

Source	DF Num	DF Den	F-Value	P-Value
Factor	2	96.4680	65.69	0.000

Model Summary

R-sq	R-sq(adj)	R-sq(pred)
51.76%	51.11%	49.77%

Means

Factor	N	Mean	StDev	95% CI
Sue	50	24.596	0.963	(24.322, 24.870)
Fred	50	26.954	1.178	(26.619, 27.289)
Jerry	50	24.980	0.854	(24.737, 25.223)

The low **P-Value** indicates the null hypothesis should be rejected and conclude that at least one of the population means is different.

The **R-sq** value indicates the percent of the overall variation of the data explained by the group differences.

The **R-sq(adj)** takes into account the number of factors in the final model. With a single factor ANOVA the two values are similar.

To determine which factor levels have different population means, return to the input screen using the shortcut option **Ctrl+e**.

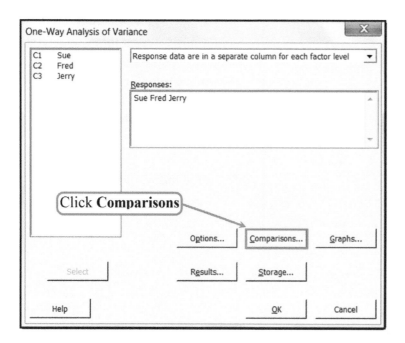

Keep the same Responses.

Click the **Comparisons** option.

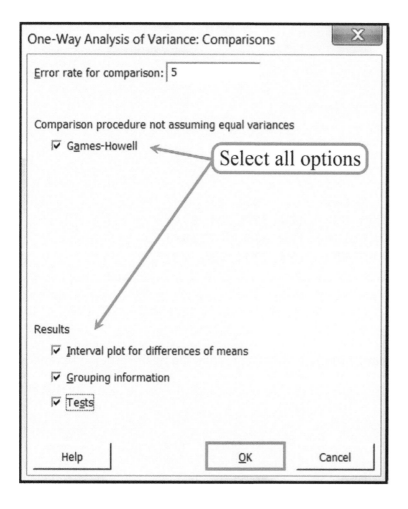

Select **Games-Howell**

Select all of the 'Results' options.

Click **OK** (twice).

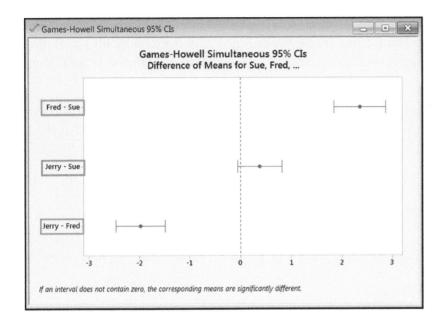

The results show the difference between all two factor (operator) levels.

Intervals with values that **do not** include zero are those where a difference between populations' means exist.

Sue and Fred are different, because their lower and upper interval values do not include zero. Since zero is **not** part of this interval, they cannot have equal population means.

Sue and Jerry are not different because this interval contains zero; Fred and Jerry are different because their interval does not contain zero.

Games-Howell Pairwise Comparisons

Grouping Information Using the Games-Howell Method and 95% Confidence

Factor	N	Mean	Grouping
Fred	50	26.954	A
Jerry	50	24.980	B
Sue	50	24.596	B

Means that do not share a letter are significantly different.

Games-Howell Simultaneous Tests for Differences of Means

Difference of Levels	Difference of Means	SE of Difference	95% CI	T-Value	Adjusted P-Value
Fred - Sue	2.358	0.215	(1.845, 2.871)	10.96	0.000
Jerry - Sue	0.384	0.182	(-0.050, 0.818)	2.11	0.093
Jerry - Fred	-1.974	0.206	(-2.464, -1.484)	-9.59	0.000

The **Grouping** output indicates which factor levels (operators) have population means that are **not** statistically different at the 95% confidence level. Since Fred is the only one with the letter A, his population mean is statistically different compared to Jerry and Sue. Since Sue and Jerry both contain the letter B, their population means could be equal.

The **95% CI** is the 95% confidence interval for the difference between the population means. For the first line, the difference between Fred and Sue's (Fred – Sue) population mean is between *1.845 and 2.871*. Notice the difference between Jerry and Sue includes the value zero, therefore they could have the same population mean.

Chi–Square Analysis

Tool Use: Use the Chi-Square analysis to determine if there is a relationship between two factors.

Data Types: Input – Discrete; Output – Discrete

Null Hypothesis H_o: The factors are statistically independent

Alternative Hypothesis H_a: The factors are statistically dependent

Minitab Project: Chi-Square.mpj

Worksheet: *Delivery*

The table consists of shipping location and whether the delivery was Early, On Time or Late.

The team wants to determine if a relationship exists between Location (X) and whether shipments (Y) are Early, On-Time or Late.

C1-D	C2	C3-T	C4-T
Date	Class	Origin	Delivery
2/21/2002	1	St Louis	On Time
2/22/2002	1	Miami	Late
2/23/2002	1	St Louis	On Time
2/24/2002	1	Reading	On Time
2/25/2002	1	Reading	Early
2/26/2002	1	St Louis	Early
2/27/2002	1	Reading	Early
2/28/2002	1	Reading	On Time
3/1/2002	1	St Louis	Early
3/2/2002	1	Reading	Early
3/3/2002	1	St Louis	On Time
3/4/2002	1	St Louis	On Time

Pareto Chart of Delivery Issues

Menu Command: *Stat > Quality Tools > Pareto Chart*

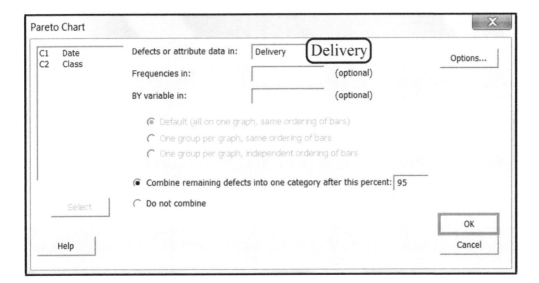

Input **Delivery** for the Defects or attribute data in:

Click **OK**.

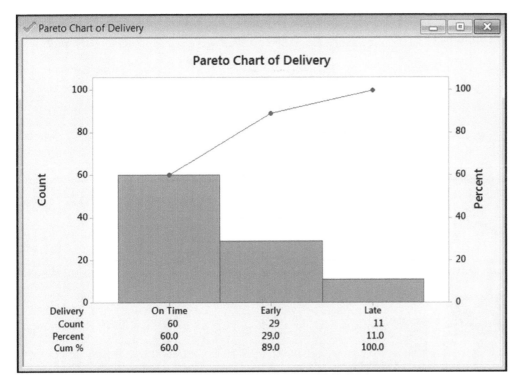

A Pareto Chart of all delivery conditions is shown.

Three categories exist; On Time, Early and Late.

The worksheet also contains information on where the delivery originated. To determine if there's an issue with delivery based on location, run a Pareto chart of delivery issues by location.

Menu Command: *Stat > Quality Tools > Pareto Chart*

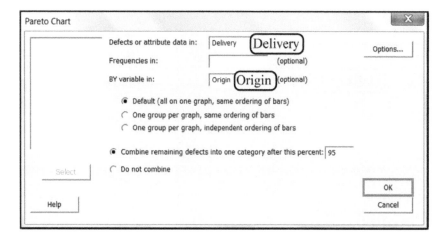

Input **Delivery** for 'Defects or attribute data in:

Input **Origin** for 'By variable in:'

Click **OK**.

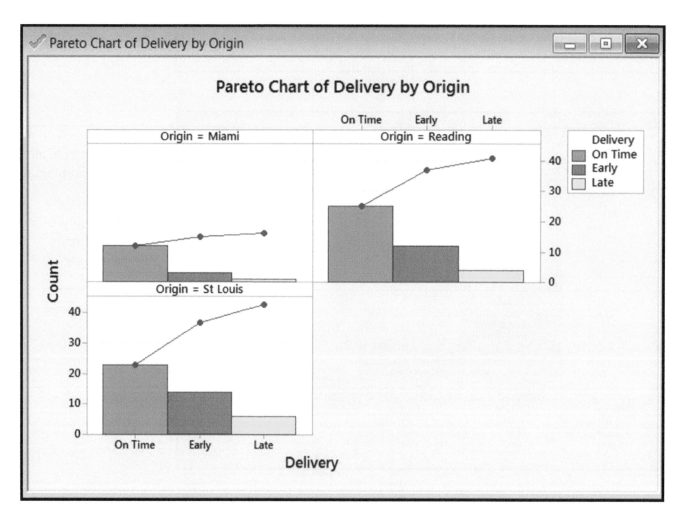

Ordering of bars is based on the original Pareto Chart without the By Variable. Use the Panel option to place all three locations on one row.

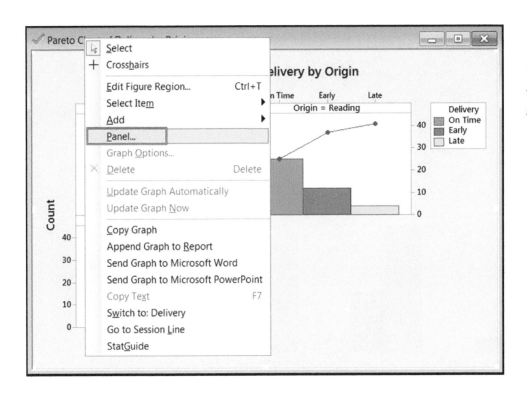

Right Click inside the graph window and select **Panel**.

Select the Arrangement tab.

Choose **Custom** for the 'Rows and Columns' option.

Change **Rows:** to **1**.

Change **Columns:** to **3**.

Click **OK**.

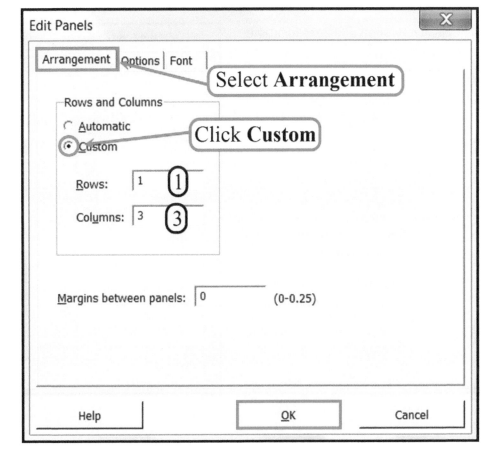

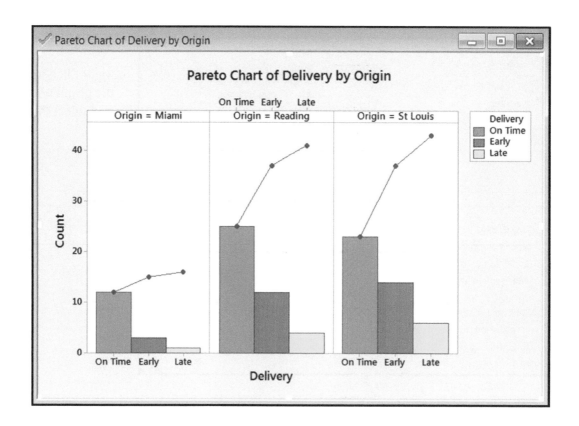

The chart now shows all three locations in one row.

Hint: To change the graph ratio, double click in the window to open the Edit Graph and Figure Region dialog box.

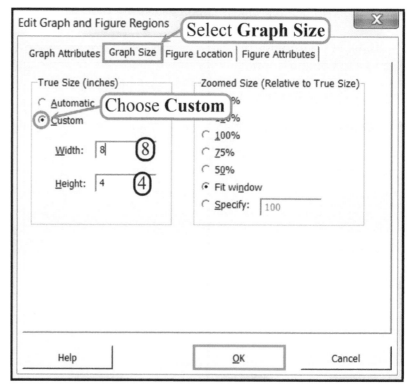

Select the **Graph Size** tab.

Choose the **Custom** button for 'True Size (inches)'.

Input **8** for the width and **4** for the Height.

Click **OK**.

This is the final graph window with the new aspect ratio.

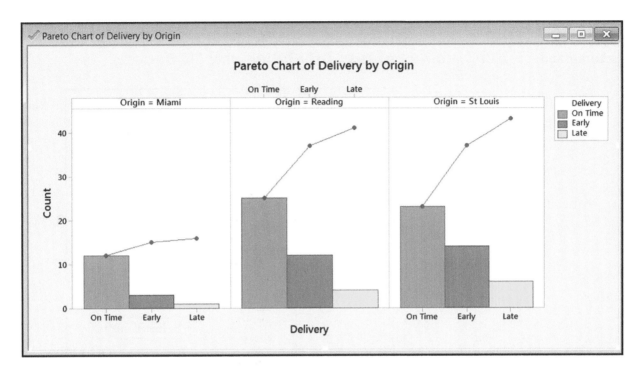

The Pareto shows the same relation of issues for all three locations; On-Time is the highest, followed by Early and then by Late.

Minitab's Chi-Square Analysis

Menu command: *Stat > Tables > Cross Tabulation and Chi-Square*

Select **Raw data (categorical variables)**

For rows: input **Origin.**

For columns: input **Delivery.**

For Display, use **Counts.**

Click **Chi-Square.**

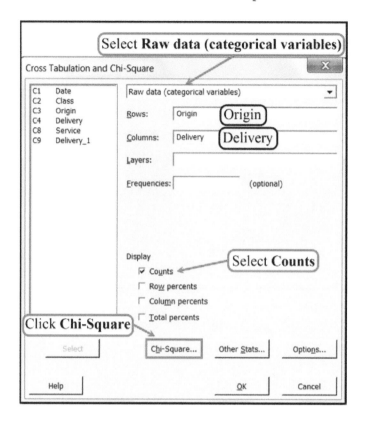

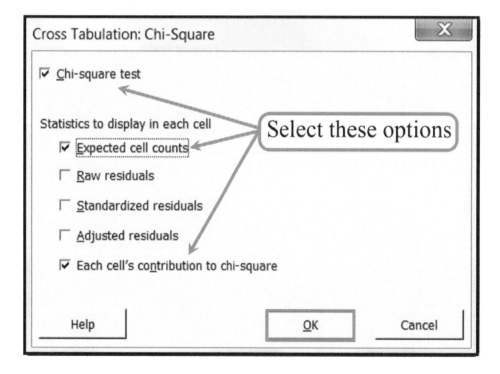

Select **Chi-Square test, Expected cell counts** and **Each cell's contribution to Chi-Square.**

Click **OK** (twice).

For each location:

```
Results for: Delivery

Tabulated Statistics: Origin, Delivery

Rows: Origin    Columns: Delivery

              Early      Late   On Time   All

Miami             3         1        12    16
              4.640     1.760     9.600
            0.57966   0.32818   0.60000

Reading          12         4        25    41
             11.890     4.510    24.600
            0.00102   0.05767   0.00650

St Louis         14         6        23    43
             12.470     4.730    25.800
            0.18772   0.34099   0.30388

All              29        11        60   100

Cell Contents:        Count
                      Expected count
                      Contribution to Chi-square

Pearson Chi-Square = 2.406, DF = 4, P-Value = 0.662
Likelihood Ratio Chi-Square = 2.486, DF = 4, P-Value = 0.647

* NOTE * 4 cells with expected counts less than 5
```

The first row represents the actual *cell count*.

The second row is the **expected count** based on the null hypothesis.

The third row is the individual contribution to the Chi-Square statistic.

The formula for each group's contribution to the overall Chi-Square statistic is:

$$\chi^2 = \frac{\left(f_o - f_e\right)^2}{f_e}$$

- f_o is the observed count in each cell of the table. This comes from observations or existing data.
- f_e is the expected count in each cell of the table, assuming H_o is true. This value is calculated by Minitab.
- The statistic will increase when there are large differences between observed and expected counts. (Chi-Sq)

The p-value of .662 indicates no evidence that the delivery category is related to location.

Summary Table Option

Worksheet: *Delivery*

Information may be presented as a summary table; use the columns **Service** and **Delivery_1** to create the table.

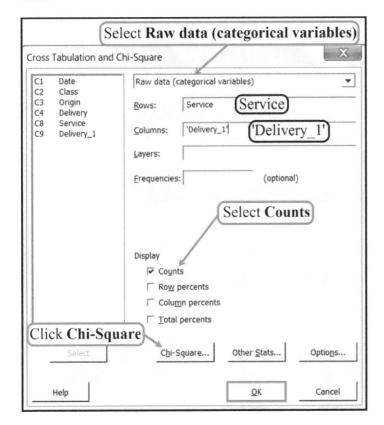

Menu command: *Stat > Tables > Cross Tabulation* and Chi-Square

Select: **Raw data (categorical variables)**

Input **Service** for 'rows'.

Input **Delivery_1** for the 'columns'.

Select **Counts** for 'Display'.

Click **Chi-Square**.

Clear all options.

Click **OK**.

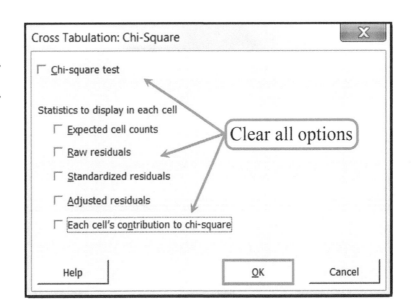

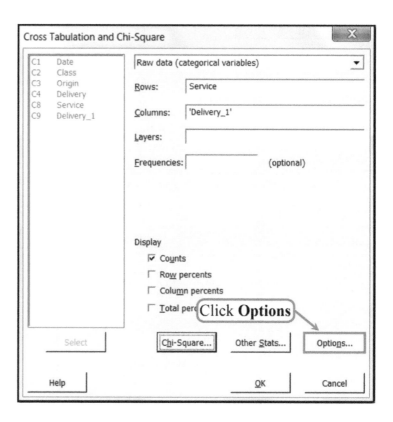

At the **Cross Tabulation and Chi-Square** window select **Options**.

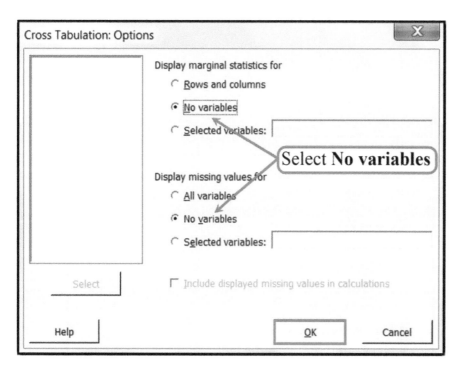

Select **No variables** for both '**Display marginal statistics for**' and '**Display missing values for**'.

Click **OK** twice.

This is the Session window output for cross tabulation.

	Early	Late	On Time
Fast Delivery	7	13	5
Friendly Delivery	9	5	22
Quick Delivery	14	2	23

The output must be modified before copying results into the worksheet because Minitab sees spaces as delimiters. Data will not be properly aligned if information from the session window was copied directly into the worksheet.

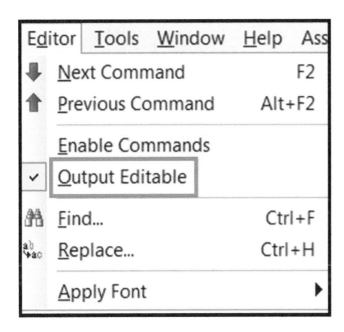

Hint: To modify the information, make the session window the active window and select the Editor option in the main menu.

Select **Output Editable**. (The check mark next to **Output** indicates it is selected.)

Here is the modified Session window:

```
                      Early   Late   On_
Time

Fast_Delivery           7     13      5
Friendly_Delivery       9      5     22
Quick_Delivery         14      2     23
```

Place underscores to eliminate spaces. Type 'On_' next to Time to produce 'On_Time'. Next, copy the information from the session window into the worksheet.

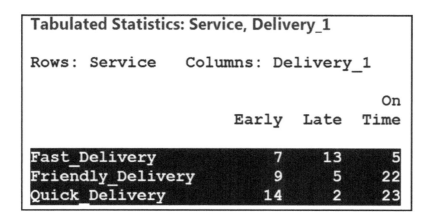

Hold down the left mouse button and select the three rows of information.

Do not highlight the column headings at this time.

Use the shortcut key (Ctrl +c) to copy the data; move to the appropriate location in the worksheet and use the shortcut key (Ctrl+v) to paste the information.

The following window will appear:

Select **Use space as a delimiter**.

Click **OK**.

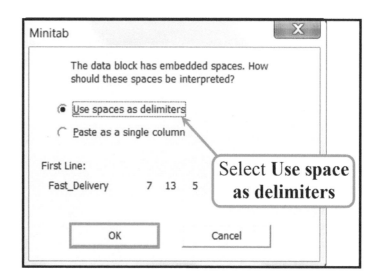

The information copies to the rows and columns starting with the highlighted cell.

C13-T	C14	C15	C16
Fast_Delivery	7	13	5
Friendly_Delivery	9	5	22
Quick_Delivery	14	2	23

Repeat the process to copy the column headings.

C13-T	C14	C15	C16
	Early	Late	On_Time
Fast_Delivery	7	13	5
Friendly_Delivery	9	5	22
Quick_Delivery	14	2	23

The information is now ready for analysis.

Menu command: *Stat > Tables > Chi-Square Test for Association*

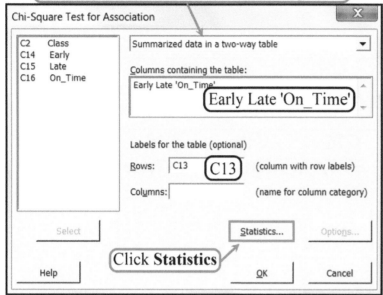

Select **Summarized data in a two-way table**

Select the columns containing the data, **Early**, **Late**, **On_Time**.

Click **Statistics**.

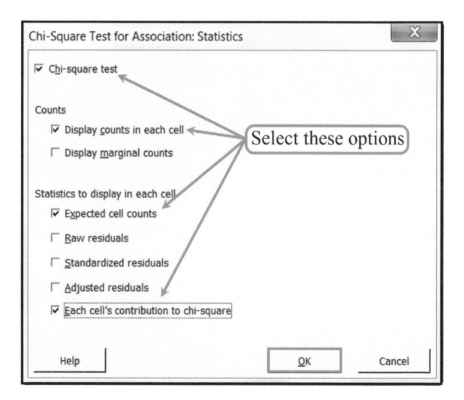

Select **Chi-square test**

For 'Counts' select **Display counts in each cell**.

For 'Statistics to display in each cell select: **Expected cell counts** and **Each cell's contribution to chi-square**.

Click **OK** (twice).

The results appear in the Session window.

```
Chi-Square Test for Association: C13, Worksheet columns

Rows: C13    Columns: Worksheet columns

                       Early     Late   On_Time

Fast_Delivery             7       13         5
                       7.50     5.00     12.50
                     0.0333  12.8000    4.5000

Friendly_Delivery         9        5        22
                      10.80     7.20     18.00
                     0.3000   0.6722    0.8889

Quick_Delivery           14        2        23
                      11.70     7.80     19.50
                     0.4521   4.3128    0.6282

Cell Contents:       Count
                     Expected count
                     Contribution to Chi-square


Pearson Chi-Square = 24.588, DF = 4, P-Value = 0.000
Likelihood Ratio Chi-Square = 23.791, DF = 4, P-Value = 0.000
```

The first row is the observed count found in the table and the second row is the expected count based on the null hypothesis. The last row is the individual Chi-Square value calculated from the equation:

$$\chi^2 = \frac{(f_o - f_e)^2}{f_e}$$

The low p-value indicates the null hypothesis should be rejected. There is evidence that Delivery Service (X) is related to delivery issue(s) (Y). A Pareto chart will show this relationship more clearly.

Create the Pareto chart as shown previously using the 'By variable' option. (Use the original worksheet, not the summarized table.)

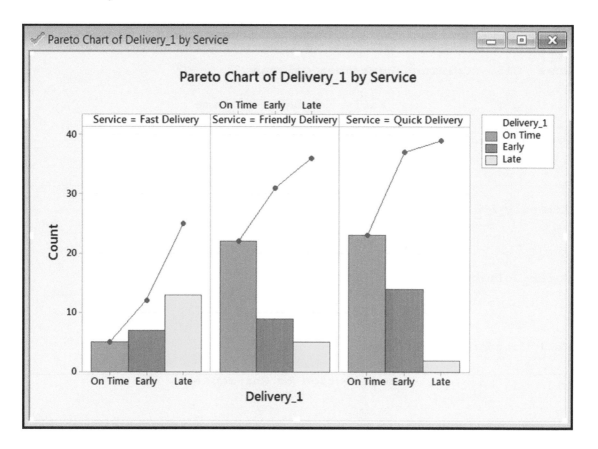

Friendly Service and Quick Service have On Time as the largest issue, followed by Early and then Late.

Fast Service has Late as the largest issue, followed by Early and On Time.

It is clear, that whether a delivery is On Time, Early or Late is dependent upon the service used.

Correlation

Tool Use: Use Correlation analysis to describe the degree of linear relationship between two factors. The Pearson product-moment coefficient measures the degree of this relationship.

The Correlation Coefficient (r)

Values lie between -1 and +1
A value of -1 depicts complete inverse (negative) dependence
A value of 0 depicts complete independence
A value of +1 depicts complete direct (positive) dependence

General Rules

Correlation Coefficient (r) > .75 or < -.75 is strong
Correlation Coefficient (r) between -.50 and .50 is not

Data Type: All factors (inputs and outputs) are **Continuous**

Null Hypothesis (H$_o$): Correlation coefficient (r) = 0

Alternative Hypothesis (H$_a$): Correlation coefficient (r) ≠ 0

Minitab Project: **Correlation - Regression.MPJ**

Worksheet: *Correlation*

It is best to visualize the relationship between the two variables before running the correlation calculation. This is accomplished with a scatter plot.

Menu command: *Graph > Scatter Plot > Simple*

Select **Y100** for the **Y** variable and **X** for the **X** variable.

Click **OK**.

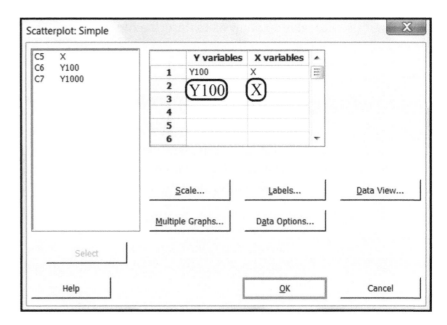

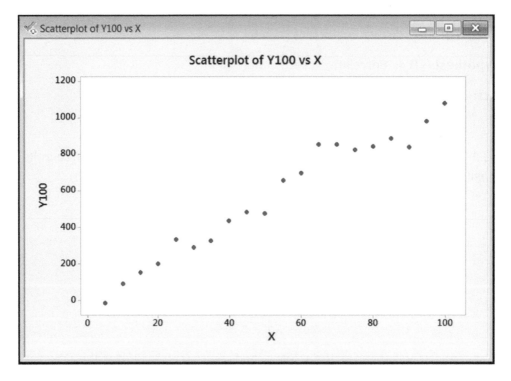

There appears to be a relation between the X and Y100 values; as X increases, Y100 increases.

Quantify this relationship further using Minitab's Correlation function.

Menu command: *Stat > Basic Statistics > Correlation*

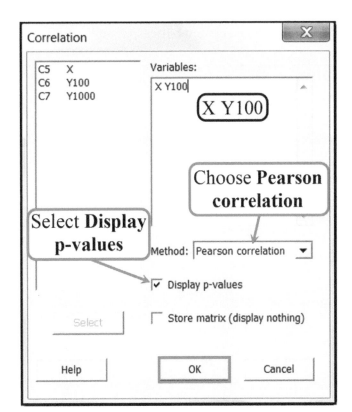

Select the factors **X** and **Y100**.

Choose **Display p-values**.

Select **Person correlation**.

Click **OK**.

Correlation: X, Y100

Pearson correlation of X and Y100 = .981

P-Value = 0.000

The correlation coefficient (r) is .981, with the corresponding p-value of .000.

Based on this information, reject H_o in favor of H_a; a linear correlation between the two factors is statistically significant.

Note: Remember, a significant correlation does not indicate a cause-effect relationship between the two factors.

Repeating this process with **X** and **Y100** produces the following graphs and Pearson correlation values result:

This graph shows almost no relation between X and Y1000.

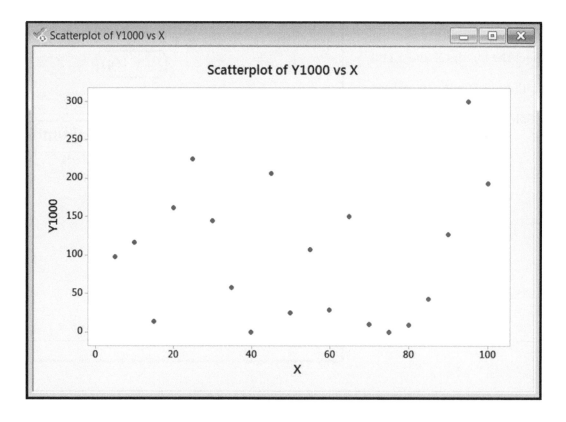

The low Pearson correlation value supports these findings.

Correlation X, Y1000

Person correlation of X and Y100 = 0.069
P-Value = 0.773

The correlation coefficient (r) is .069, with the corresponding p-value of .773.

Based on this information, do not reject H_o in favor of H_a; a linear correlation between the two factors is not statistically significant.

Simple Linear Regression Analysis

Tool Use: Use Simple Linear Regression analysis to determine the relationship between a single continuous X and a single continuous Y. The equation is:

$$Y = b_0 + b_1 X_1$$

For this example, a company compared the age of propellant used in a manufacturing process to the resultant shear strength of the material produced. Based on the data returned, the organization further requested creation of a predictive model to estimate shear strength based on age of the propellant.

Null Hypothesis (H$_0$): b$_0$ = 0

Alternative Hypothesis (H$_a$): b$_0$ ≠ 0

Second hypothesis:

Null Hypothesis (H$_0$): b$_1$ = 0

Alternative Hypothesis (H$_a$): b$_1$ ≠ 0

Data Type: Input – Continuous; Output - Continuous

Minitab Project: **Correlation - Regression.MPJ**

Worksheet: *Propellant*

Note: This example is taken from Introduction to Linear Regression Analysis by Montgomery and Peck 1992© p. 10.

Menu command: *Stat > Regression > Fitted Line Plot*

Input **Shear Strength (psi)** as the Response (Y).

Input **Age of Propellant (weeks)** as the Predictor (X).

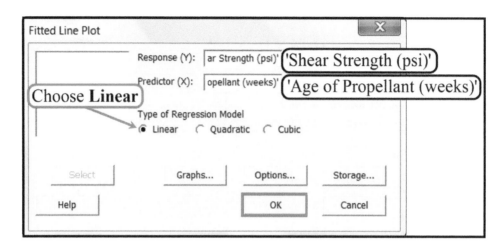

Choose **Linear** as the type of Regression. Click **OK**.

The results indicate the equation for the fitted line is:

Shear Strength (psi) = 26.28 - 37.15 Age of Propellant (weeks).

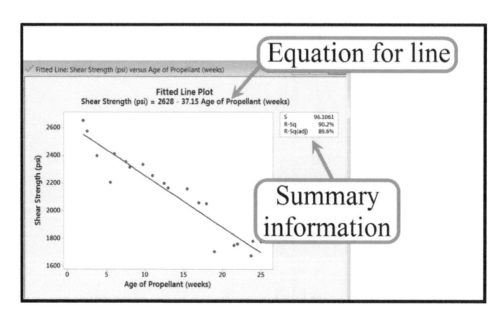

R-Sq indicates the percent of variation explained by the equation; in this example, R-Sq is 90.2%. Therefore, the equation above explains 90.2% of the variation observed in the Shear Strength. **S** is the standard deviation of the model's error term.

R-Sq (adj) is explained in the Multiple Regression section.

Session window output:

Regression Analysis: Shear Strength (psi) versus Age of Propellant (weeks) The regression equation is

Shear Strength (psi) = 2628 - 37.15 Age of Propellant (weeks)

S = 96.1061   **R-Sq = 90.2%**   R-Sq(adj) = 89.6%

Analysis of Variance

Source	DF	SS	MS	F	P
Regression	1	*1527483*	1527483	165.38	0.000
Error	18	166255	9236		
Total	19	1693738			

The session window includes the equation, R-Sq, R-Sq(adj) and S.

It also includes an Analysis of Variance table.

The Analysis of Variance table tests the regression equation to determine if at least one of the coefficients is not equal to zero. Since there is only one predictor variable, the low p-value indicates the coefficient (slope) for that predictor is not zero. Therefore, knowing the propellant's age helps to predict the resulting shear strength.

The SS column determines the R-Sq value:

$$\text{R-Sq} = SS_{Regression} / SS_{Total} = 1527483 / 1693738 = .902 \text{ or } \textbf{90.2\%}.$$

An important feature of any regression equation is its predictive abilities. Knowing the equation is not an exact fit, it may make sense to determine what Shear Strengths can be expected from a specific age of propellant. Minitab offers a confidence interval around the estimated equation to provide a range of values.

Return to the Fitted Line Plot window (ctrl + e) and select **Options**.

Select **Display prediction interval**.

Click **OK** (twice).

The **confidence interval** option provides an interval for the fitted line. While this is informative, it doesn't help with determining an individual run's shear strength. If an interval for the fitted line is desired, select the confidence interval option.

The fitted line graph with the Prediction Interval is shown:

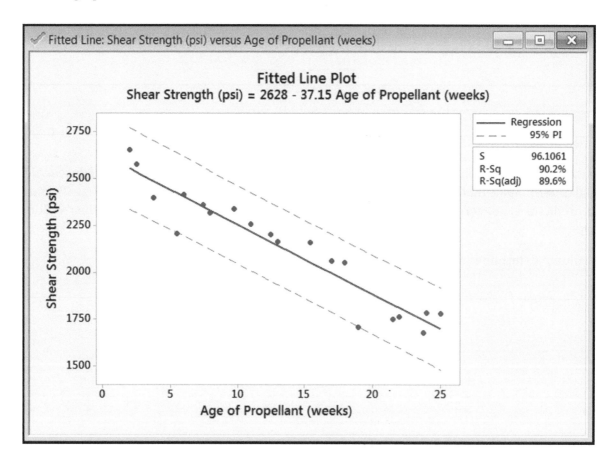

The 95% predictive interval (PI) displays the range within which 95% of the individual values are expected for a given value of the predictor.

Note: Use these results to interpolate between sample values for the Age of Propellant, but do not extrapolate beyond these values. In other words, do not extend the equation beyond the upper and lower X values used to determine the equation.

Hint: Use the crosshairs to determine the expected range of values for a given propellant age.

Place the cursor in the graph and **Click the Right mouse button.**

Select **Crosshairs**.

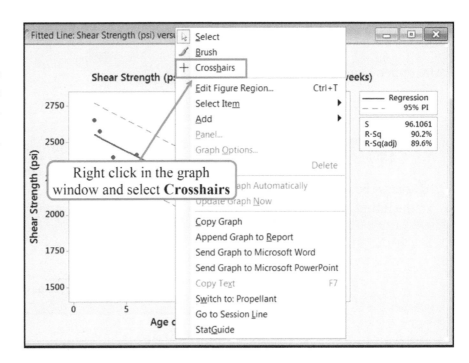

Move the cross-hairs to obtain the X and Y values at a specific location.

The results appear in the upper left corner of the Graph window.

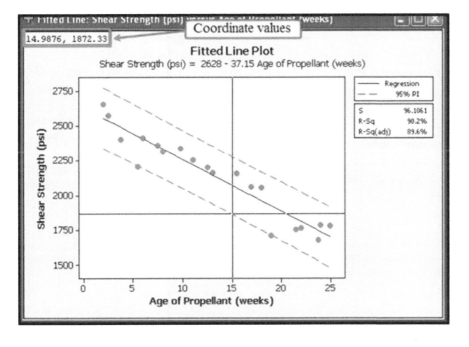

The X value is approximately 15, (14.9876) and the value for lower shear strength is 1872.33 psi. To obtain the upper value of shear strength at 15 weeks, move the cross hairs to the upper 95% PI line.

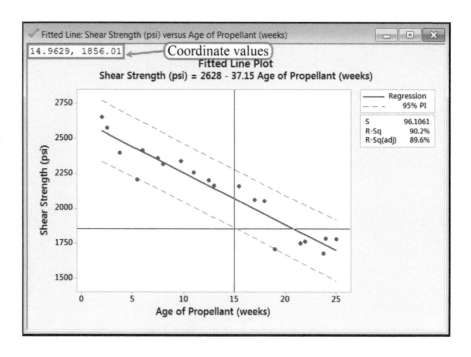

The upper value is 2276.65 psi.

For a propellant age of 15 weeks 95% of the shear strengths will range from 1872.33 to 2276.65 psi.

To access the residuals, return to the Fitted Line Plot screen;

(*Stat > Regression > Fitted Line Plot*) and select **Graphs**.

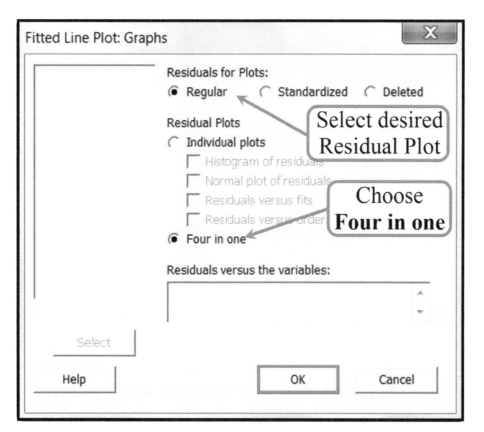

Select the desired type of residual to plot.

Choose **Four in one** for the residual plots.

Click **OK** (twice).

The residuals demonstrate the appropriateness of the model. The residual equals the fitted (or predicted) value minus the actual value. Residuals may be positive or negative.

With the Lease Squares analysis, an adequate model is demonstrated by residuals with the following characteristics:
- Residuals have a mean value equal to zero.
- Residuals have a constant variance.
- Residuals are normally distributed.
- Residuals are independent.

The Four in One Residual plot evaluates the residuals for these characteristics.

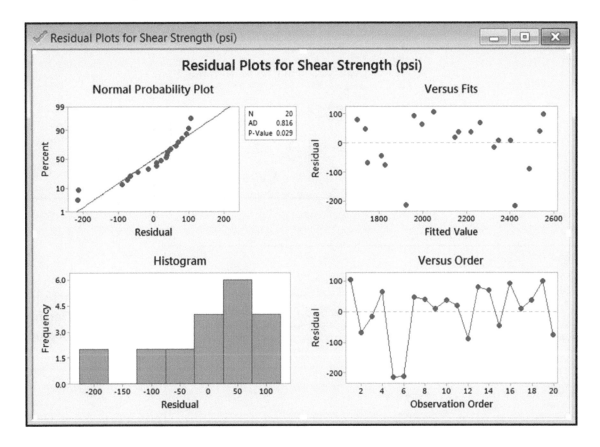

The Normal Probability Plot and Histogram are used to demonstrate the residual's distribution.

Note: To have the Anderson – Darling statistic displayed on the Residual plots, select: *Tools > Options > Linear Models > Residual Plots*

Open the **Linear Models** heading. (The minus sign next to the heading indicates the selection is open.)

Click the **Residual Plots**. The right side of the screen changes.

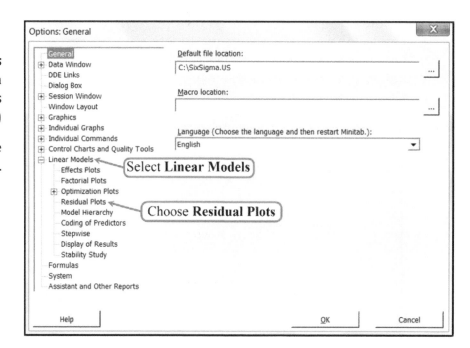

Check the **Include Anderson-Darling test with normal plot** option.

Click **OK**.

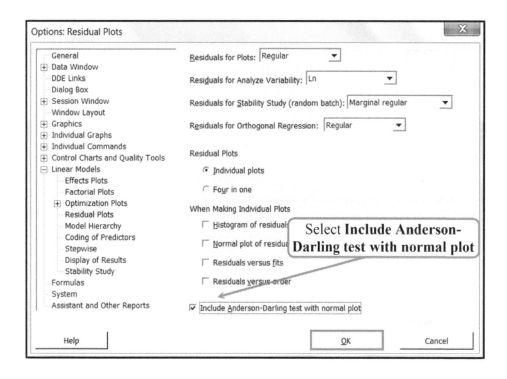

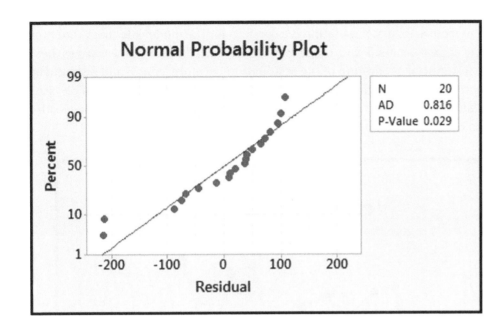

Rerun the Fitted Line Plot with the Residual Plots.

The Normal Probability plot and the associated p-value are checks for normality.

Low p-values indicate there is enough evidence to reject the idea that the residuals result from a population with a normal distribution. With a p-value of .029 the normality assumption is rejected.

The Histogram shows a couple of values on the low end that are removed from the rest of the values.

These should be investigated for either errors in recording or special cause effects.

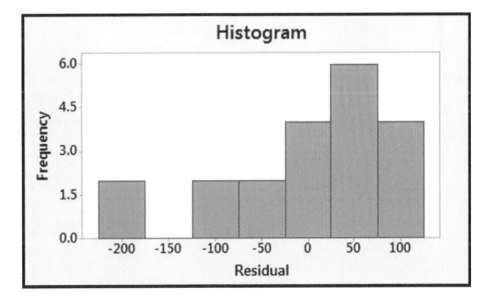

The Histogram is a visual display to show the general shape of the distribution. This, along with the Normal Probability Plot, produces evidence for the normality assumption.

The indication that residuals are not from a normal population is a concern for the model adequacy. Looking at the Four in One residual plot, it appears runs 5 and 6 are a bit removed from the other values; these readings could be the cause of the non-normal condition of the residuals. Therefore, runs 5 and 6 should be investigated to verify there was nothing abnormal about the run or the recording of the results. If an issue is found with those runs, they should be either re-run or eliminated. If no issue is found with those runs, additional experimentation should occur before accepting a final model.

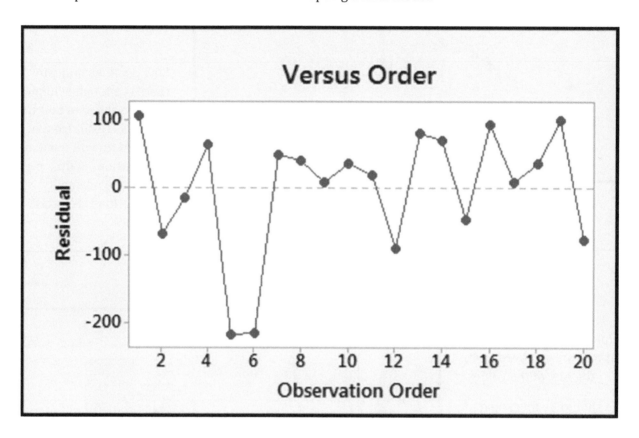

Residuals versus Fits

The Residuals versus Fits plot checks the constant variance assumption and looks for patterns in the residuals. If the scatter of points shows a constant spread throughout the range of Fitted values, the assumption of constant variance is upheld. Abnormal patterns may demonstrate the need for either a transformation or higher order terms.

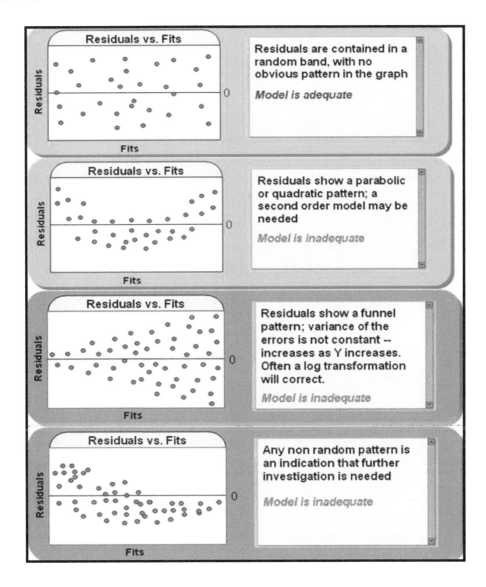

Residuals versus Run Order

Plotting the residuals versus run order demonstrates the residuals stability. If patterns exist, it may indicate the model is inadequate. However, this graph has meaning only if the worksheet is listed in the experiment's random order. If the worksheet has been sorted for any reason, this graph is no longer valid.

Another method to determine stability of residuals is to treat them as a process. Use the Individuals and Moving Range graph to make this determination.

To use the Individuals and Moving Range Control Chart, residuals must first be saved in the worksheet.

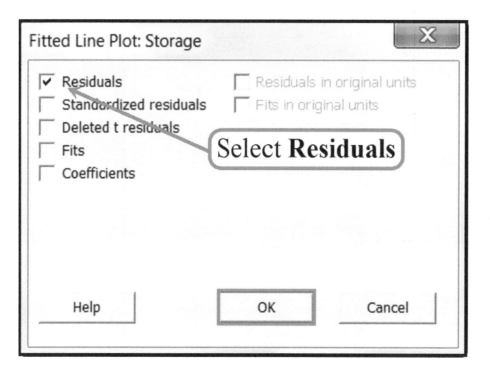

Return to the Fitted Line Plot window and select Storage.

Select **Residuals**.

Click **OK**.

The residuals appear in the worksheet under the column **RESI1**.

Menu command:

Stat > Control Charts > Variables Charts for Individuals > I-MR

Look for shifts, trends or points outside the red lines. These may indicate an inadequate model. (For detailed explanation of Control Charts, see the Control chapter.)

Select **RESI1** as the variable.

Click **OK**.

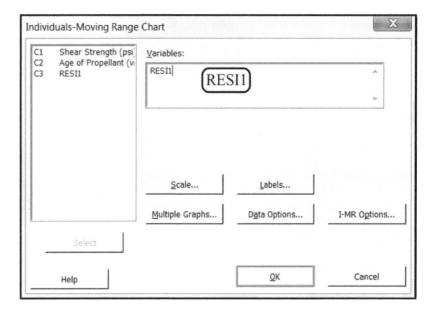

The resulting graphs show nothing abnormal.

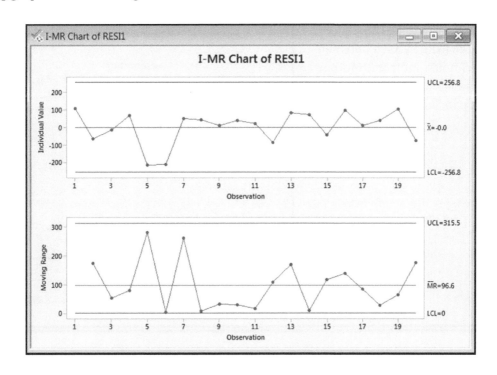

Multiple Regression

Tool Use: Use the Minitab Regression analysis to determine the relationship between several continuous inputs and a single continuous output variable. This creates the following equation:

$$Y = b_0 + b_1X_1 + b_2X_2 + b_3X_3 + \ldots + b_nX_n$$

Null Hypothesis (H$_o$): $b_i = 0$

Alternative Hypothesis (H$_a$): $b_i \neq 0$

A separate hypothesis test is performed for each X.

Data Type: Input – Numeric; Output – Continuous

Minitab Project; *Multiple Regression.MPJ*

Worksheet; *Longevity*

Best Subsets Regression

Menu command:

Stat > Regression > Regression > Best Subsets

Input **Longevity** as the Response.

Select all of the factors to be considered for the model. (The hyphen between Mother and Smoker indicates Mother and Smoker as well as all factors between these two are included in the model.)

Click **OK**.

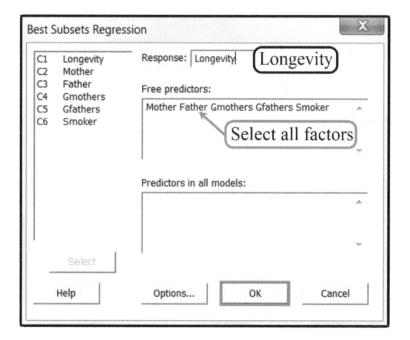

```
Best Subsets Regression: Longevity versus Mother, Father, ...

Response is Longevity

                                                    G G
                                                    m f
                                                M F o a S
                                                o a t t m
                                                t t h h o
                                                h h e e k
                  R-Sq   R-Sq  Mallows          e e r r e
  Vars   R-Sq    (adj)  (pred)     Cp      S    r r s s r
     1   59.5     59.1    57.8    99.1  3.2787             X
     1   49.8     49.3    47.5   146.2  3.6525  X
     2   73.6     73.1    71.9    33.2  2.6608  X X
     2   69.8     69.2    68.0    51.5  2.8453    X       X
     3   80.1     79.5    78.3     3.9  2.3220  X X       X
     3   74.1     73.3    72.0    33.0  2.6510  X X   X
     4   80.4     79.6    78.3     4.3  2.3149  X X   X X
     4   80.1     79.3    78.0     5.8  2.3338  X X X     X
     5   80.5     79.5    78.0     6.0  2.3235  X X X X X
```

The output shows the best and second best 1, 2, 3, 4 and 5 factor models.

The R-Sq, R-Sq (adj), Mallows Cp, and S values are used to determine which model to use.

Look for the model with a high R-Sq, a high R-Sq(adj), a high R-Sq(pred), low s, and a Mallows Cp close to the number of predictors (Vars) plus one (for the constant term).

The **R-Sq** value indicates the percent of variation explained by the model. Higher values of R-Sq are preferred; however, the R-Sq value will increase by adding factors whether they are significant or not.

The **R-Sq (adj)** metric is the R-Sq value adjusted for the number of factors. If factors are added to the model and they don't improve understanding of the variation, the R-Sq (adj) value will begin to decrease.

The **R-Sq(pred)** shows how well the model will predict the value for a new observation.

Mallows Cp is another method of determining how well the model fits the data. Typically look for values equal to the number of factors in the model plus.1. So for a model with 3 factors, a Mallow Cp value of 4 is sought.

The last value **S** is the standard deviation of the model's error. Smaller values are desired.

Overall, when comparing models with an equal number of parameters, use the one with the highest R-Sq value. For models that differ in the number of factors, look for the highest R-Sq(adj) and a Mallow's Cp equal to 1 more than the number of factors. Finally, if everything else is equal, look for the model with the smallest S value.

Based on the desired outcome for each criterion, the first three variables model is the best option; the factors should be 'Mother, Father and Smoker'. Although there might be a slight improvement in values going to the 4 factor model, the amount of improvement does not justify the increased model complexity.

In the example above, the three factor model is selected because overall it provides the best values with the fewest number of factors.

Creating the Regression Equation

Once the critical regression factors have been selected, the next step is to create the regression equation.

Menu command: *Stat > Regression > Regression > Fit Regression Model*

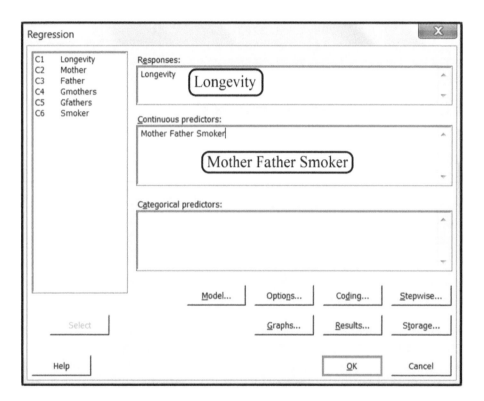

Select the Response: **Longevity**

Using the results for the Best Subset, the Continuous Predictors are **Mother**, **Father**, and **Smoker**.

Click **OK**.

Session window output shows the equation with additional information.

Analysis of Variance table:

Low p-value for Regression indicates that at least one of the coefficients is not equal to zero.

The factors (Mother, Father, and Smoker) all have low p-values. This should be expected since the Best Subset options suggested these were important factors.

The Lack-of-fit having a large p-value suggests this model fits the data well.

```
Analysis of Variance

Source          DF    Adj SS    Adj MS   F-Value   P-Value
Regression       3   2086.16   695.385    128.97     0.000
  Mother         1    267.67   267.668     49.64     0.000
  Father         1    281.19   281.192     52.15     0.000
  Smoker         1    169.15   169.151     31.37     0.000
Error           96    517.60     5.392
  Lack-of-Fit   87    487.94     5.608      1.70     0.196
  Pure Error     9     29.67     3.296
Total           99   2603.76


Model Summary

      S     R-sq   R-sq(adj)   R-sq(pred)
2.32200   80.12%      79.50%       78.32%
```

The high R-sq and R-sq(adj) shows about 80% of the variation in the data is explained using these 3 factors.

R-Sq(pred) is used to define predictability of the model. The higher the R-Sq(pred), the better the model is at predicting future responses.

For more information on the output, look in the Help menu of Minitab.

Coefficients

Term	Coef	SE Coef	T-Value	P-Value	VIF
Constant	27.23	5.10	5.34	0.000	
Mother	0.3344	0.0475	7.05	0.000	1.52
Father	0.3238	0.0448	7.22	0.000	1.34
Smoker	-3.738	0.667	-5.60	0.000	1.88

Regression Equation

Longevity = 27.23 + 0.3344 Mother + 0.3238 Father - 3.738 Smoker

The coefficients for each factor is displayed.

Notice the effect of smoking. A smoker (Smoker = 0 is a non-smoker. Smoker = 1 is a smoker), will have their longevity reduced by 3.738 years.

The VIF (Variance Inflation Factor) is an indication of multi-colinearity between inputs; values less than 5 are considered acceptable. Multi-colinearity indicates inputs are correlated, which can lead to erroneous results.

The final equation is shown at the bottom.

Finally, the session window displays unusual observations. The list is based on standardized residual values greater than 2.0, or for high leverage values.

Fits and Diagnostics for Unusual Observations

Obs	Longevity	Fit	Resid	Std Resid	
14	63.000	67.600	-4.600	-2.01	R
43	84.000	83.121	0.879	0.41	X
60	89.000	80.919	8.081	3.57	R
71	64.000	68.927	-4.927	-2.14	R
87	68.000	73.815	-5.815	-2.60	R
88	66.000	70.642	-4.642	-2.04	R

R   Large residual
X   Unusual X

Another option to determine which factors should be in the Regression model would be to go directly to the Stepwise Regression without using the Best Subset function.

Menu command:

Stat > Regression > Regression > Fit Regression Model

For the Response, select **Longevity.** For Continuous predictors, select **Mother**, **Father**, **Gmother**, **Gfather**, **Smoker**.

Click **Stepwise**.

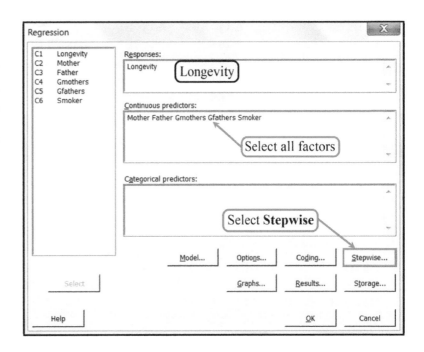

For Method, select **Stepwise**.

Click **OK**.

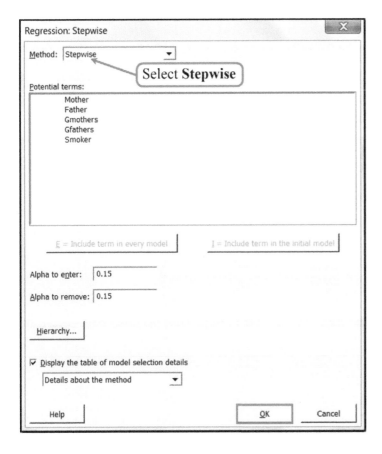

The session window displays the results. The Stepwise method selected Mother, Father, and Smoker. These are the same results as the Best Subset method produced.

Analysis of Variance

Source	DF	Adj SS	Adj MS	F-Value	P-Value
Regression	3	2086.2	695.385	128.97	0.000
Mother	1	267.7	267.668	49.64	0.000
Father	1	281.2	281.192	52.15	0.000
Smoker	1	169.2	169.151	31.37	0.000
Error	96	517.6	5.392		
Total	99	2603.8			

Coefficients

Term	Coef	SE Coef	T-Value	P-Value	VIF
Constant	27.23	5.10	5.34	0.000	
Mother	0.3344	0.0475	7.05	0.000	1.52
Father	0.3238	0.0448	7.22	0.000	1.34
Smoker	-3.738	0.667	-5.60	0.000	1.88

Regression Equation

Longevity = 27.23 + 0.3344 Mother + 0.3238 Father - 3.738 Smoker

An advantage of using the Stepwise method over the Best Subset occurs with categorical predictors. Suppose instead of having the Smoker data as 1 and 0, the data was presented as Yes, and No.

The Best Subset would not allow the use of the categorical data in the list of predictors.

Minitab Project; Multiple Regression.MPJ

Worksheet; *Longevity_code*

Menu command: *Stat > Regression > Regression > Fit Regression Model*

For Response select **Longevity**.

For Continuous predictors select **Mother**, **Father**, **Gmother**, and **Gfather**.

For Categorical predictors select **Smoke**.

Click **Coding**.

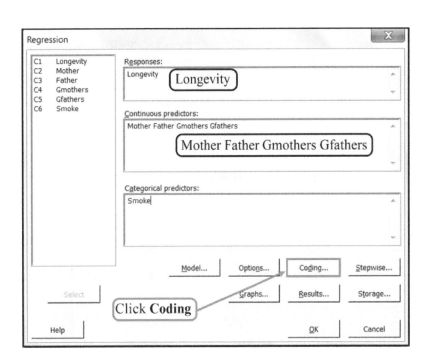

For Coding for categorical predictors select **(1, 0)**.

For Reference level select **No**.

Click **OK** (twice).

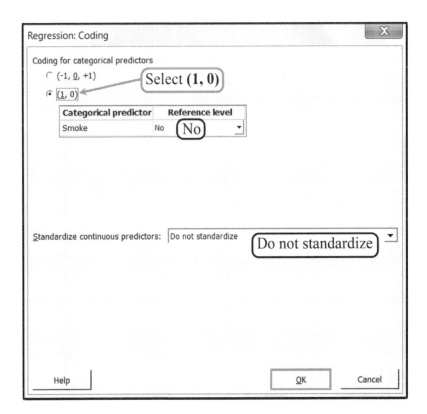

The session window output again recommends the same factors (Mother, Father, and Smoker). However, there's a slight difference in the Coefficients table and the Regression Equation.

Coefficients

Term	Coef	SE Coef	T-Value	P-Value	VIF
Constant	27.23	5.10	5.34	0.000	
Mother	0.3344	0.0475	7.05	0.000	1.52
Father	0.3238	0.0448	7.22	0.000	1.34
Smoke					
Yes	-3.738	0.667	-5.60	0.000	1.88

Regression Equation

Smoke
No   Longevity = 27.23 + 0.3344 Mother + 0.3238 Father

Yes   Longevity = 23.49 + 0.3344 Mother + 0.3238 Father

In this output the Smoke category is listed as Yes. This is the reference value of 1.

The Equations are listed for Smoke No and Smoke Yes. The difference between the two conditions appears in the Constant term. For Smoker No the value is 27.23, for Smoke Yes the value is 23.49. So, again it indicates the Longevity is reduced for Smoke Yes by 3.74 years.

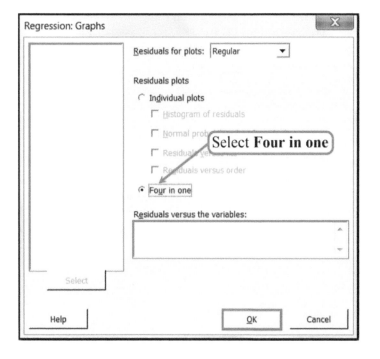

Once the final equation is determined, check the Residuals.

In the Regression window, (use Cntrl+e), click Graphs.

Select **Four in one**.

Click **OK** (twice).

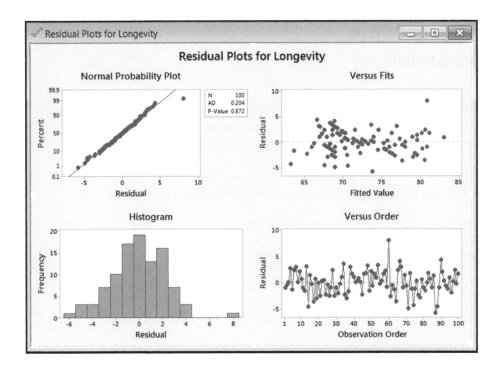

Nothing looks abnormal in the residual analysis.

Finally, the session window displays unusual observations. The list is based on standardized residual values greater than 2.0, or for high leverage values.

Fits and Diagnostics for Unusual Observations

Obs	Longevity	Fit	Resid	Std Resid	
14	63.000	67.600	-4.600	-2.01	R
43	84.000	83.121	0.879	0.41	X
60	89.000	80.919	8.081	3.57	R
71	64.000	68.927	-4.927	-2.14	R
87	68.000	73.815	-5.815	-2.60	R
88	66.000	70.642	-4.642	-2.04	R

R   Large residual
X   Unusual X

These values should be investigated to ensure no errors occurred in data collection. It should also be investigated for special causes of variation.

Factorial Experiments

General Factorial Designs

Tool Use: Use General Factorial Designs to investigate several levels of X's versus Y in a designed experiment. Minitab's General Factorial Design allows a set up with two or more factors, each with 2 to 100 levels. The factors may be numeric or text. These experiments are designed to determine the effect X's have on the Y's.

Null Hypothesis (H₀): The Designed Experiments have null hypotheses similar to the Regression tool. Interaction of factors can only be determined with the Designed Experiment.

Alternative Hypothesis (Hₐ): Same as for Regression.

Data Type: Input - Numeric or Discrete; Output – Continuous

Experiment: Study the effects of wording and type of image used in Sunday newspaper ads.

Output: Sales volume of product advertised for one week after the sale.

Inputs: Wording (Simple, Moderate, Advanced); Type of Image (None, Person, Cartoon)

Creating the General Factorial Design

Menu command: *Stat > DOE > Factorial > Create Factorial Design*

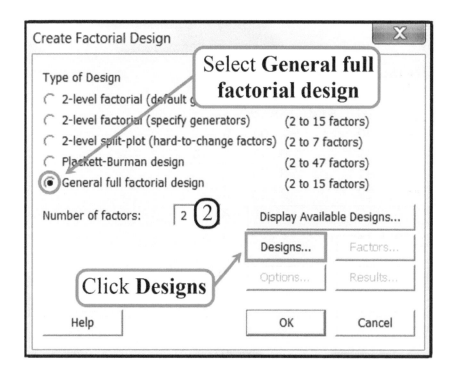

Choose the **General full factorial design** option.

Select **2** for the number of factors.

Click **Designs**.

Input the factor names, **Wording** and **Image**.

Input **3** for the number of levels of each factor.

Select **2** for number of replicates.

Click **OK**.

In the Create Factorial Design window, select Factors.

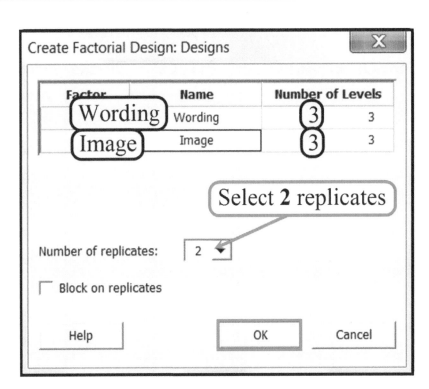

The inputs are text values. For type select **Text**. Input the category names.

For Wording input **Simple**, **Moderate** and **Advanced**.

For Image input **None**, **Person**, and **Cartoon**.

Click **OK** twice.

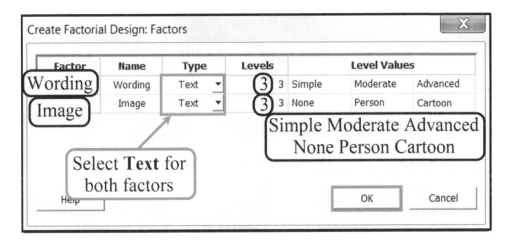

Multilevel Factorial Design

```
Factors:        2      Replicates:       2
Base runs:      9      Total runs:      18
Base blocks:    1      Total blocks:     1

Number of levels: 3, 3
```

The Session window shows summary information explaining the number of factors, the number of replicates, total runs and number of levels for each factor.

C1	C2	C3	C4	C5-T	C6-T
StdOrder	RunOrder	PtType	Blocks	Wording	Image
17	1	1	1	Advanced	Person
3	2	1	1	Simple	Cartoon
14	3	1	1	Moderate	Person
12	4	1	1	Simple	Cartoon
6	5	1	1	Moderate	Cartoon
18	6	1	1	Advanced	Cartoon
8	7	1	1	Advanced	Person
9	8	1	1	Advanced	Cartoon
4	9	1	1	Moderate	None
15	10	1	1	Moderate	Cartoon
1	11	1	1	Simple	None
2	12	1	1	Simple	Person
13	13	1	1	Moderate	None
10	14	1	1	Simple	None
7	15	1	1	Advanced	None
11	16	1	1	Simple	Person
5	17	1	1	Moderate	Person
16	18	1	1	Advanced	None

The worksheet is displayed in a random order.

General Full Factorial Design Analysis

Minitab Project: **GeneralFactorial.MPJ**

Worksheet: *GeneralFactorial*

Menu command: *Stat > DOE > Factorial > Analyze Factorial Design*

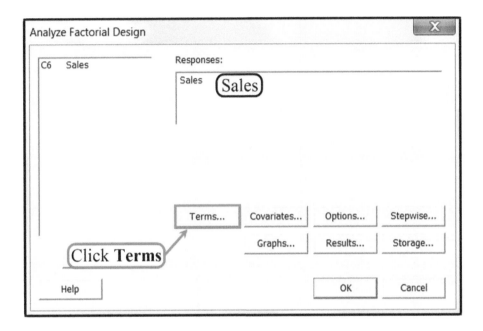

Input the response **Sales**.

Click **Terms**.

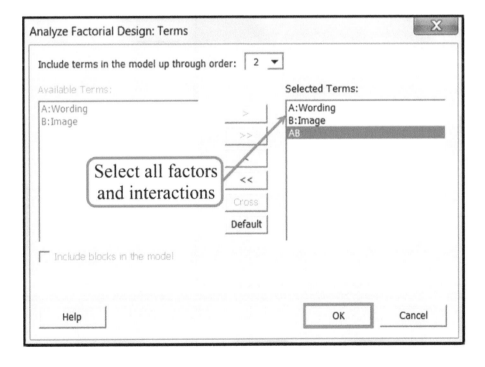

Select all factors and interactions.

Click **OK**.

In the Analyze Factorial Design window, click the **Graphs** button.

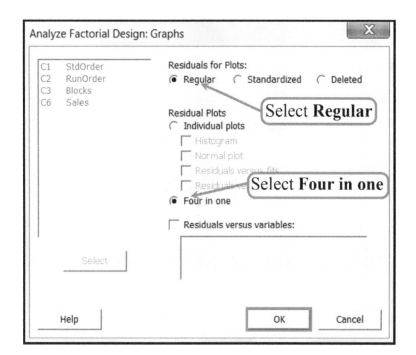

Select the desired Residuals.

Select **Four in one** for the Residual plots.

Click **OK** twice.

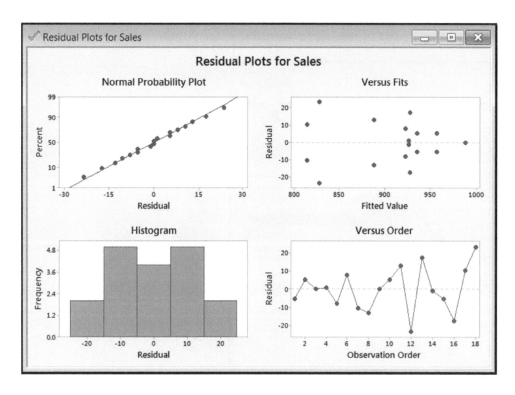

Analyze the residuals as shown previously.

The Analysis of Variance for Sales output shows the results of multiple hypothesis tests: one for the Wording factor, one for the Image factor, and one for the interaction between Wording and Image.

Analysis of Variance

Source	DF	Adj SS	Adj MS	F-Value	P-Value
Model	8	52074	6509.2	23.19	0.000
Linear	4	47024	11756.1	41.88	0.000
Wording	2	4937	2468.7	8.79	0.008
Image	2	42087	21043.4	74.96	0.000
2-Way Interactions	4	5050	1262.4	4.50	0.029
Wording*Image	4	5050	1262.4	4.50	0.029
Error	9	2526	280.7		
Total	17	54600			

Model Summary

S	R-sq	R-sq(adj)	R-sq(pred)
16.7548	95.37%	91.26%	81.49%

All three tests produce low p-values. This indicates all three are statistically significant in explaining Sales. For more information on interactions, see the Improve chapter.

Graphs of Factors

Minitab constructs graphs showing factor levels and interaction.

Menu command: *Stat > DOE > Factorial > Factorial Plots*

Select both **Sales** as the Response.

Select **Wording** and **Image** as the variables.

Click the **Graphs** button.

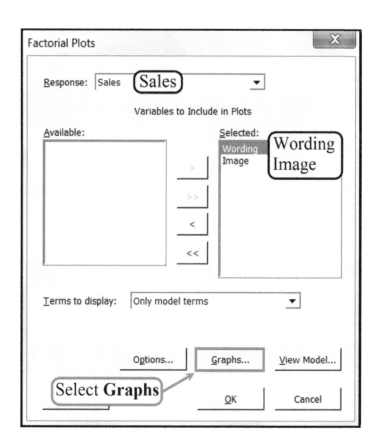

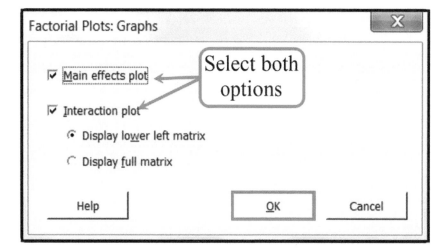

Select both options (**Main effects plot** and **Interaction plot**).

Click **OK** (twice).

The resulting graphs show average values for all factor settings.

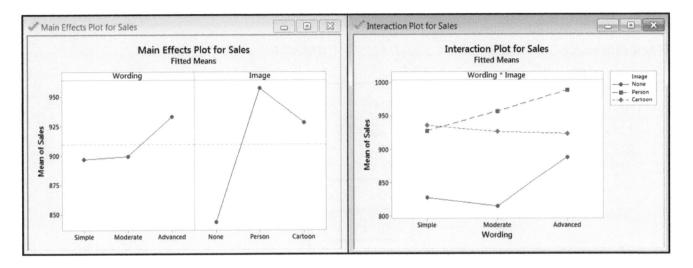

The main effects show the difference between the sample averages of each level. In the interaction plot, non-parallel lines indicate a potential interaction.

Paired t-Test

Tool Use: Use the Paired t-Test to determine if a difference exists between two groups where a natural pairing of information exists. Examples of natural pairings include the measure of a student's before and after scores for a class or standardized test, and matching the two associates' output when working on the same items.

Null Hypothesis: (H_o): $d_i = 0$

The difference between population means of the two groups is zero.

Alternative Hypothesis: (H_a): $d_i \neq 0$

The difference between population means of the two groups is not zero.

Data Type: Input – Discrete; Output – Continuous

A pre-test was administered to a group of students at the beginning of a unit. Students were then given a post-test after the unit was taught. The question to answer is: are post-test scores higher than pre-test scores?

Minitab Project:	***ANOVA.MPJ***
Worksheet:	***Paired Data***
Menu command:	***Stat > Basic Statistics > Paired t***

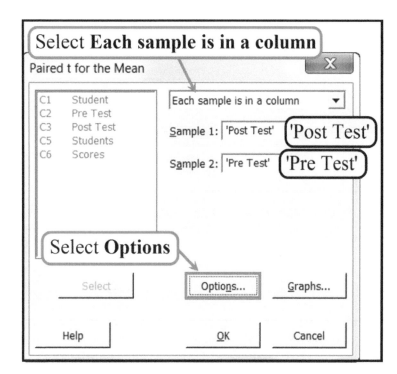

Select **Each sample is in a column**.

Input **'Post Test'** as Sample 1.

Input **'Pre Test'** as Sample 2.

Click **Options**.

Select **0** for the Hypothesized difference.

Post-test scores are expected to be higher than pre-test stores, so the alternative is **Difference > hypothesized difference (0)**.

Click **OK**.

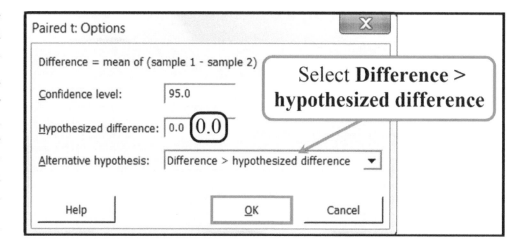

The Session window contains the results.

The minimal difference between the pre and post test values is 1.41.

Paired T-Test and CI: Post Test, Pre Test

```
Paired T for Post Test - Pre Test

              N    Mean   StDev  SE Mean
Post Test    10   81.50   10.19     3.22
Pre Test     10   78.00   12.68     4.01
Difference   10    3.50    3.60     1.14


95% lower bound for mean difference: 1.41
T-Test of mean difference = 0 (vs > 0): T-Value = 3.08  P-Value = 0.007
```

Balanced ANOVA

Tool Use: Use the Balanced ANOVA to determine the effect of two or more factors. The worksheet must have an equal number of readings for each unique factor combination.

Null Hypothesis: (H$_o$): $\mu_i = \mu_j$ (for each factor and interaction)

Alternative Hypothesis: (H$_a$): At least one $\mu_i \neq \mu_j$ (for each level within each factor or interaction)

Data Type: Input – Discrete; Output – Continuous

Minitab Project: **ANOVA.MPJ**

Worksheet: *Balanced ANOVA*

Menu command: *Stat > ANOVA > Balanced ANOVA*

Input **Cycle Time** as the Response.

Use **Location**, **Department** and **Level** as the Model.

The vertical bar (referred to as a pipe) between the factors tells Minitab to include all possible interactions between the factors.

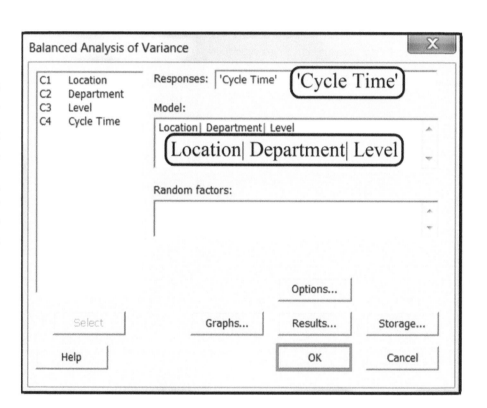

Another format for inputting the model is to list all factors and interactions separately. In this case, input the factors and interactions as: **Location Department Level Location*Department Location*Level Department*Level Location*Department*Level**

Click **OK**.

The analysis appears as follows:

ANOVA: Cycle Time versus Location, Department, Level

```
Factor        Type    Levels  Values
Location      fixed       2   Chicago, New York
Department    fixed       3   Engineering, HR, Legal
Level         fixed       2   Exempt, Non-Exempt
```

Analysis of Variance for Cycle Time

Source	DF	SS	MS	F	P
Location	1	7.042	7.042	1.99	0.184
Department	2	105.583	52.792	14.91	0.001
Level	1	513.375	513.375	144.95	0.000
Location*Department	2	3.083	1.542	0.44	0.657
Location*Level	1	18.375	18.375	5.19	0.042
Department*Level	2	9.750	4.875	1.38	0.290
Location*Department*Level	2	14.250	7.125	2.01	0.176
Error	12	42.500	3.542		
Total	23	713.958			

```
S = 1.88193   R-Sq = 94.05%   R-Sq(adj) = 88.59%
```

The top part consists of summary information. The Analysis of Variance for Cycle Time produces a table with the information required to decide which factors or interactions are significant. Remember, the low p-value indicates at least one of the factor level's population mean is not equal to at least one other level's population mean. The R-Sq and R-Sq(adj) values were discussed earlier.

GLM

Tool Use: Use the GLM tool to determine the effect of two or more X's on the Y's. The worksheet for the GLM does not require an equal number of readings for each unique factor combination. (A balanced worksheet is not required for the **GLM** procedure.)

Null Hypothesis: (H_o): $\mu_i = \mu_j$ (for each factor and interaction)

Alternative Hypothesis: (H_a): At least one $\mu_i \neq \mu_j$ (for each level within each factor or interaction)

Data Type: Input – Discrete; Output – Continuous

Minitab Project: **ANOVA.MPJ**

Worksheet: *GLM*

Menu command: *Stat > ANOVA > General Linear Model > Fit General Linear Model*

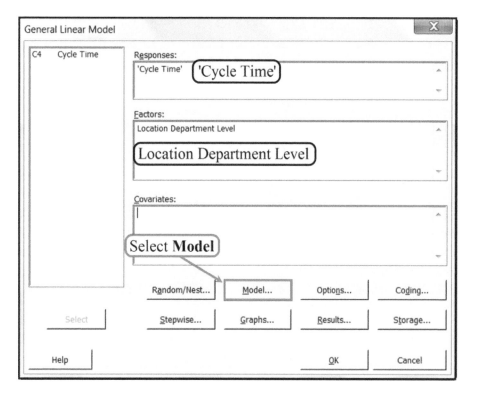

Input **'Cycle Time'** for the Response.

For Factors, input

Location Department Level.

Click **Model**.

Highlight all the factors for the model.

Choose **3** for Interactions through order:

Click **Add**.

The 2 factor and 3 factor interactions are added to the model.

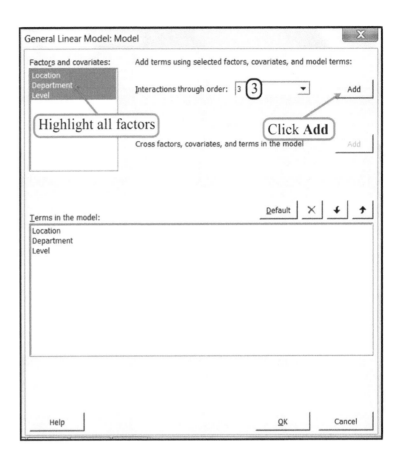

To eliminate one of the terms, select the term and click the red X button.

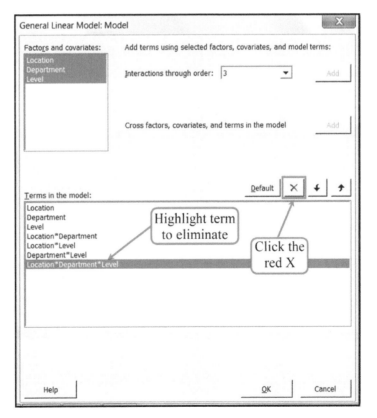

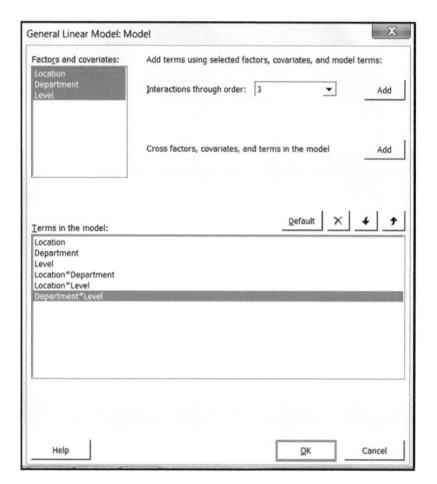

Once the final model
is created, click **OK**

At the General Linear Model screen select Stepwise.

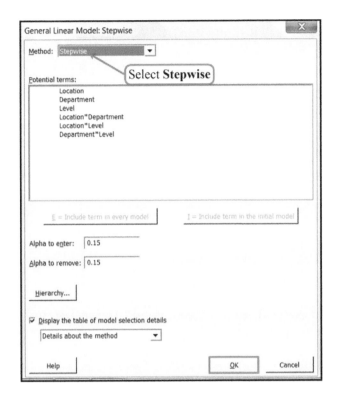

For 'Method:' select **Stepwise**.

Click **OK**.

Analysis of Variance

Source	DF	Adj SS	Adj MS	F-Value	P-Value
Location	1	7.042	7.042	1.82	0.194
Department	2	105.583	52.792	13.66	0.000
Level	1	513.375	513.375	132.80	0.000
Location*Level	1	18.375	18.375	4.75	0.043
Error	18	69.583	3.866		
Lack-of-Fit	6	27.083	4.514	1.27	0.338
Pure Error	12	42.500	3.542		
Total	23	713.958			

The Stepwise Regression procedure shows the factors it determined to be statistically significant at the levels determined by the criteria in the Stepwise window.

Analyze the output for the **GLM** in a similar manner to the **Balanced ANOVA**.

```
Model Summary

        S     R-sq   R-sq(adj)   R-sq(pred)
  1.96615   90.25%      87.55%       82.67%
```

Summary information for the model is provided. Explanations for these metrics have been shown previously.

Additional actions in the GLM module.

To analyze the residuals of the model, select the **Graphs** button found in the **General Linear Model** screen. Then select the desired **Residual plots**.

For factor and interaction plots, select:

Stat > ANOVA > General Linear Model > Factorial Plots.

Inputs and results are the same as described in the General Full Factorial analysis.

Covariates: A Covariate is a continuous factor that is not controlled in an experiment. Measuring these factors during the experiment and introducing them into the model helps reduce the error variance.

Covariates are listed for the model in the **General Linear Regression** window.

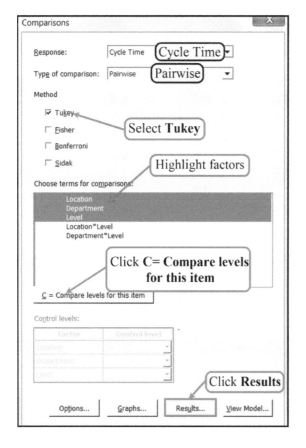

Comparisons:

To perform all pairwise comparisons for the discrete factor levels, select:

Stat > ANOVA > General Linear Model > Comparisons

Select the response (**Cycle Time**), and **Pairwise** as the 'Type of comparison'.

Choose **Tukey** as the Method.

Highlight the desired factors, then click the '**C = Compare levels for this item**' button. Click **Results**.

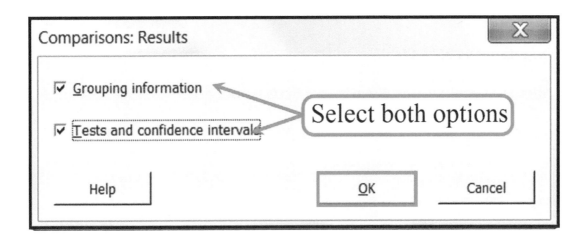

Select both options (Grouping information and Tests and confidence intervals).

Click **OK**.

```
Tukey Simultaneous 95% CIs

Tukey Pairwise Comparisons: Response = Cycle Time, Term = Level

Grouping Information Using the Tukey Method and 95% Confidence

Level          N    Mean   Grouping
Exempt        12  35.1667  A
Non-Exempt    12  25.9167           B


Means that do not share a letter are significantly different.

Tukey Simultaneous Tests for Differences of Means

Difference of Level  Difference      SE of      Simultaneous
Levels                of Means   Difference       95% CI          T-Value
Non-Exempt - Exempt    -9.250       0.803    (-10.936, -7.564)    -11.52

Difference of Level  Adjusted
Levels               P-Value
Non-Exempt - Exempt    0.000

Individual confidence level = 95.00%
```

For Grouping, factor levels that do not share the same letter can be considered statistically different at the specified significance level.

The Simultaneous 95% CI indicates where the difference between the population's mean of the two levels reside.

For this example, the difference between the population mean of the Non-Exempt minus the population mean of the Exempt is between the values of:

-11.280 and *-7.615*. Since zero is not part of that interval, then there's a difference between the two population means at a 95% confidence level.

Fully Nested ANOVA

Tool Use: Use the Fully Nested ANOVA to determine the effect of two or more factors in a situation where one or more factors are **Nested** within other factors.

Null Hypothesis: (H_o): $\mu_i = \mu_j$ (for each factor and interaction)

Alternative Hypothesis: (H_a): At least one $\mu_i \neq \mu_j$ (for each level within each factor or interaction)

Data Type: Input – Discrete; Output - Continuous

Minitab Project: Nested.MPJ

Worksheet: *Carpet*

Menu command: *Stat > ANOVA > Fully Nested ANOVA*

Data originates from a test of carpet crushability. Five samples were measured from each of two locations per roll. The samples are nested within location and the location is nested within the roll. Seven rolls were used in the study.

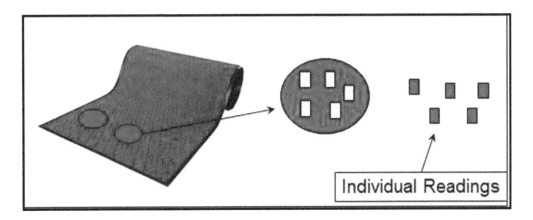

The nesting occurs because the five readings in location 1 are not the same as the five readings in location 2. Also, location 1 in roll 1 is not the same as location 1 in roll 2. Therefore, the samples are nested in location, the location is nested in rolls.

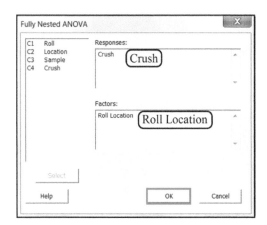

Input **Crush** as the Response, select **Roll** and **Location** as the Factors.

Click **OK**.

```
Nested ANOVA: Crush versus Roll, Location

Analysis of Variance for Crush

Source      DF         SS         MS        F       P
Roll         6  8599.1149  1433.1858  167.507   0.000
Location     7    59.8920     8.5560    0.543   0.798
Error       56   881.9840    15.7497
Total       69  9540.9909
```

The low p-value (**0.000**) for Roll indicates there's evidence that at least one Roll has a population mean that differs from another Roll's population mean. The high p-value (*0.798*) for Location shows that there's not enough evidence to indicate any of the Locations have a population mean that differs from another.

The variance components show the percent of variation resulting from each factor and the error term.

```
Variance Components

                              % of
Source      Var Comp.     Total    StDev

Roll          142.463     90.05   11.936

Location       -1.439*     0.00    0.000

Error          15.750      9.95    3.969

Total         158.213             12.578


* Value is negative, and is estimated by zero.
```

In this case, 90% of the variation is caused by a Roll to Roll variation, while essentially 0% is caused by the variation in location. The remaining 10% is caused by the variation in sites. This is labeled as the error term. To determine the Variance components, Minitab uses the Analysis of Variance table (the MS column) along with the Expected Mean Squares.

The terms in parenthesis indicate the term from the Analysis of Variance table.

```
Expected Mean Squares

1   Roll        1.00(3) +  5.00(2) + 10.00(1)
2   Location    1.00(3) +  5.00(2)
3   Error       1.00(3)
```

Calculation of Variance Components:

For the Error term, the MSError = 1*(Error Variance Component), or 1*(15.75).

The Mean Square for Location (8.556) = 1*(Error Variance) + 5*(Location Variance).

Rearranging; (Location Variance) = (8.556 – 15.75)/5, or Location variance = -1.439.

Analyzing Roll 1433.1858 = 15.75 + 5*(0) +10*(Variance Roll), or

Variance Component for Roll = (1433.1858 – 5(-1.439) – 15.75)/10 = 142.463

Multi-Vari Graph

The Multi-Vari graph for this example was shown in the beginning of this chapter.

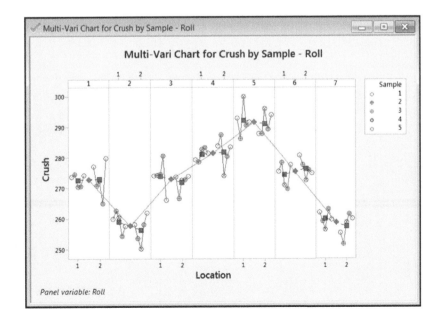

Improve Phase

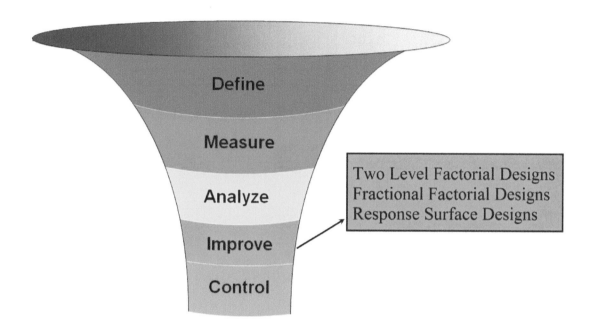

Define

Measure

Analyze

Improve

Control

Two Level Factorial Designs
Fractional Factorial Designs
Response Surface Designs

Improve Phase

The Improve phase of a Six Sigma process builds on previous phases, focusing on investigation and examination of which factors (X's) have the largest effect on critical Y's. By the end of this phase, teams have clearly identified and quantified the relationship between critical inputs and critical outputs.

Tools And Outcomes

During the Improve phase teams use a variety of tools, including:
- Two Level Factorial Designs
- Fractional Factorial Designs
- Response Surface Designs

These tools help teams come to a clear understanding of which factors are critical to the output, and then use this information to create an improvement plan. The primary goal of an improvement plan is to determine the best way(s) to control inputs (X's) for the purpose of improving critical outputs (Y's).

It is not unusual for the Improve phase to uncover several different options for creating improvement; when this occurs, teams generally conduct pilot studies to determine which option has the best chance for long term success.

Background for Design of Experiments (DOE)

The primary goal of a designed experiment is to understand and quantify the relationship of inputs (X's) with critical outputs (Y's). A good DOE explores the relationship of individual factors and factor interactions, creating quantifiable results.

Keep in mind that experimentation, while both efficient and powerful, is an iterative process. In other words, no single experiment will result in a complete understanding of a situation; many times, the results of an experiment produce more questions than answers.

Teams control the amount of variation in X's during an experiment by changing inputs in a purposeful manner. If too much change occurs, the effect of a single factor may overshadow all other factors; if too little change occurs, the effect of a single factor may not be seen. Because of this, a critical part of every Designed Experiment is planning which factors will be manipulated and at what levels those manipulations will occur.

The Interactive Nature of Experimentation

The experimental process begins with a conjecture, which may or may not be the result of previous experiments. Based on this conjecture, teams specify a design, conduct the experiment, and analyze the results. Results of analysis may or may not support the original conjecture, which often leads to additional questions. When this occurs, the experimental process is repeated (perhaps several times) until a truer conjecture and associated answers emerge.

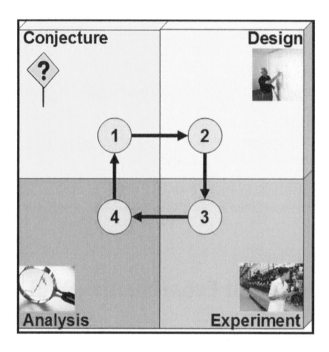

This chapter will discuss the benefits of designed experiments and show how to construct, run and analyze those experiments using Minitab.

Two Level Factorial Designs

Two Level Factorial Designs are the basic building blocks for more advanced designs. As the name implies, each factor is run at two levels; the Full Factorial Design includes all possible combinations of the factors' two levels.

Here is an example:

A medical school wants to determine the causes of misdiagnosis attributable to Physician Assistants (PAs). Factors to be studied are Time Allocated Per Patient; Experience Of The PA; and Complexity Of The Diagnosis. The levels for each factor are as follows:

Time/Patient	Experience	Complexity
5 Minutes	1 Year	Simple
15 Minutes	5 Years	Complex

At this point some definitions are required regarding the important terminology associated with Two Level Factorial Designs.

Factorial Points

Factorial points are the experimental runs consisting of either a high or low condition of each factor. Looking at the medical school example, the eight unique factorial points are as follows:

Time/Patient	Experience	Complexity
5 Minutes	1 Year	Simple
15 Minutes	1 Year	Simple
5 Minutes	5 Years	Simple
15 Minutes	5 Years	Simple
5 Minutes	1 Year	Complex
15 Minutes	1 Year	Complex
5 Minutes	5 Years	Complex
15 Minutes	5 Years	Complex

Replicates

The eight runs identified constitute a replicate of the experiment; these eight runs can be repeated if a second replicate is desired. Teams use replicates to improve the precision of the error term.

Randomization

Experiments should run in random order to prevent unknown factors from affecting output. If experiments are run in blocks, runs within each block should run in random order.

Design of Experiments (DOE)

Tool Use: Use designed experiments to determine relationships between input factors (X's) and response(s) (Y's). If an experiment uses qualitative X's, use a coding system to solve the response equation. For instance, if the experiment included three factors it will determine coefficients for the following equation:

$$Y = \beta_0 + \beta_1 X_1 + \beta_2 X_2 + \beta_3 X_3 + \beta_{12} X_1 X_2 + \beta_{13} X_1 X_3 + \beta_{23} X_2 X_3 + \beta_{123} X_1 X_2 X_3$$

Each coefficient (β) is tested using a Test of Hypothesis. Therefore, designed experiments will test multiple hypotheses, one for each coefficient. For each coefficient, the hypotheses tested are:

Null Hypothesis: (H$_o$): $\beta_i = 0$

Alternative Hypothesis: (H$_a$): $\beta_i \neq 0$

Data Type: Input – Discrete or Continuous; Output - Numeric

The following steps will create an experiment in Minitab using the above example.

Menu command: *Stat > DOE > Factorial > Create Factorial Design*

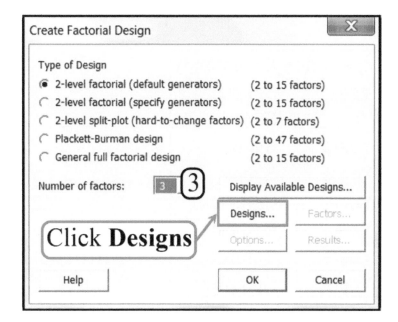

Select **3** for the Number of factors.

Click **Designs**.

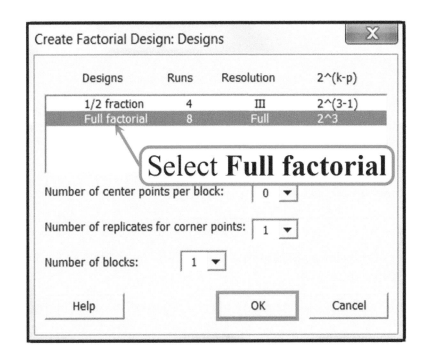

Select the **Full factorial** design

Maintain the defaults for the other options.

Click **OK**.

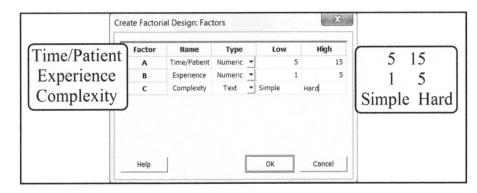

Select the Factors tab in the Create Factorial Design screen.

Input the factors and settings as shown.

Change the Type from Numeric to Text for Complexity.

Click **OK** (twice).

Minitab creates the experimental design in a new worksheet.

C1	C2	C3	C4	C5	C6	C7-T
StdOrder	RunOrder	CenterPt	Blocks	Time/Patient	Experience	Complexity
6	1	1	1	15	1	Hard
2	2	1	1	15	1	Simple
1	3	1	1	5	1	Simple
7	4	1	1	5	5	Hard
5	5	1	1	5	1	Hard
8	6	1	1	15	5	Hard
3	7	1	1	5	5	Simple
4	8	1	1	15	5	Simple

The design is listed in a random order.

The session window provides a summary of the design.

```
Full Factorial Design

Factors:   3    Base Design:        3, 8
Runs:      8    Replicates:            1
Blocks:    1    Center pts (total):    0


All terms are free from aliasing.
```

It shows the number of factors (3), the number of runs for a full replicate (8), the number of blocks (1), the number of replicates (1), and the number of Center Points (0).

The base design is a short hand method of listing the number of factors and runs required for one replicate.

The experiment's worksheet with the result column (Percent Errors) is found in the following Minitab project and worksheet.

C1	C2	C3	C4	C5	C6	C7-T	C8
StdOrder	RunOrder	CenterPt	Blocks	Time/Patient	Experience	Complexity	Percent Error
6	1	1	1	15	1 Hard	3
2	2	1	1	15	1 Simple	6
1	3	1	1	5	1 Simple	19
7	4	1	1	5	5 Hard	5
5	5	1	1	5	1 Hard	6
8	6	1	1	15	5 Hard	3
3	7	1	1	5	5 Simple	18
4	8	1	1	15	5 Simple	8

Minitab Project: FullFactorial

Worksheet: *Patient Diagnosis*

Analysis of the Full Factorial Experiment

Analysis of the Full Factorial Experiment proceeds as follows:
1. Create the Full Model (all factors and interactions)
2. Determine significant factors based on a predetermined alpha level
3. Run Factorial Plots to visualize significant factors
4. Run a new model with significant factors; this is called the Reduced Model
5. Check the model using ANOVA and Coefficients Session window outputs
6. Check the final model using residual analysis (graphs).

Menu command: *Stat > DOE > Factorial > Analyze Factorial Design*

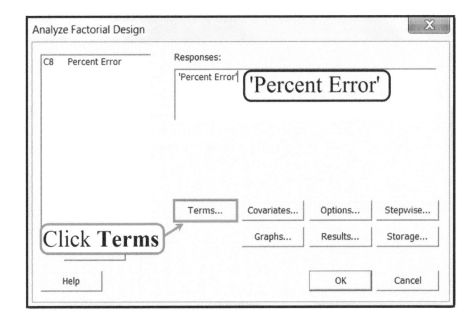

Input **Percent Errors** as the Responses.

Click **Terms**.

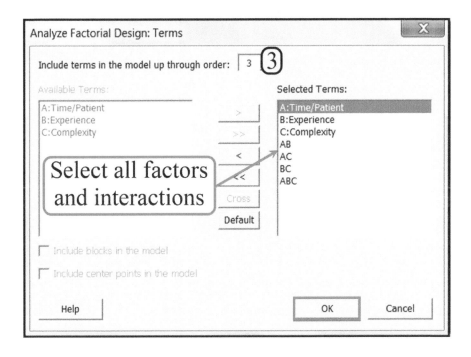

Choose **3** for the terms to include in the model. This will create a model with all three main factors (effects) along with all two factor interactions and the single three factor interaction.

All factors and interactions should be listed under 'Selected Terms:'. If they aren't, select them by highlighting the desired factor in the left column and clicking the single arrow (>) pointing to the right.

Click **OK**.

In the Analyze Factorial Design window, click **Graphs**.

Select all three 'Effects Plots'.

Choose 'Display only model terms'.

Click **OK**.

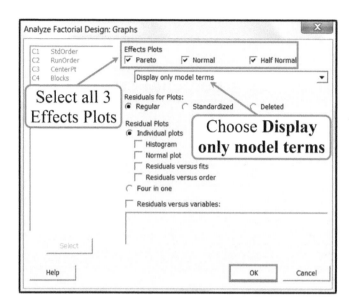

The Effects Plots appear in separate Graph windows.

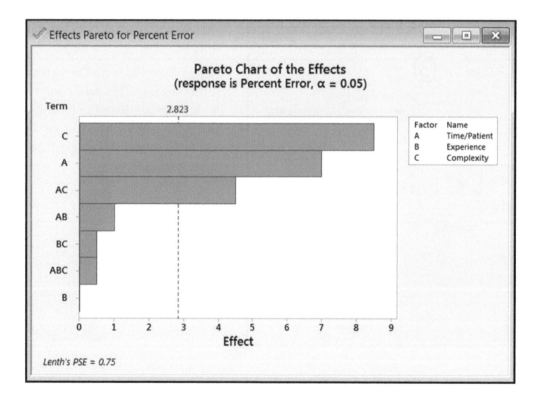

In the Pareto Chart the significant factors are those factors with bars extending to the right of the red line.

Here factors A, C, and AC interactions are significant.

In the Normal Plot, the significant factors are displayed as red squares with the factor listed. Again, A, C and the AC interaction are significant.

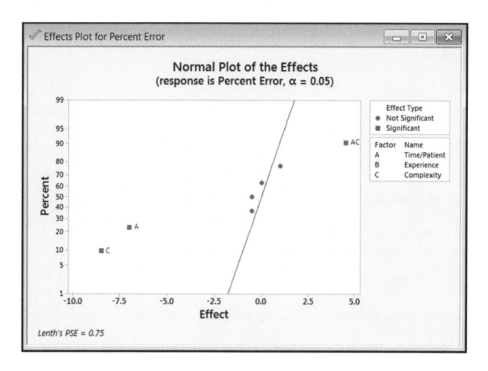

The half normal plot contains the same information as the Normal plot, except the values are listed as their absolute values.

The same terms appear significant.

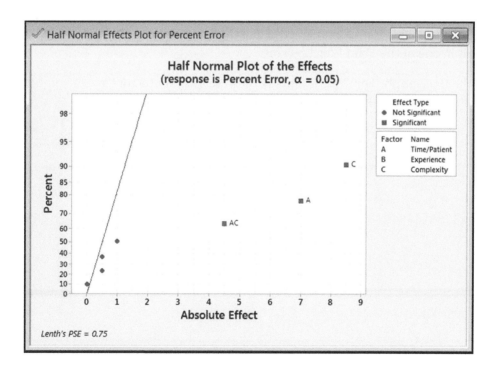

Users determine which chart to use.

The session window provides analytical information on the effects. The **Effect** is defined as the change in output as the factor changes from its low to high condition.

Coded Coefficients

Term	Effect	Coef	SE Coef	T-Value
Constant		8.500	*	*
Time/Patient	-7.000	-3.500	*	*
Experience	-0.000000	-0.000000	*	*
Complexity	-8.500	-4.250	*	*
Time/Patient*Experience	1.0000	0.5000	*	*
Time/Patient*Complexity	4.500	2.250	*	*
Experience*Complexity	-0.5000	-0.2500	*	*
Time/Patient*Experience*Complexity	-0.5000	-0.2500	*	*

The effect values are the same as those found in the normal and half normal plots (the X-axis values).

The session window notes the coefficients are for 'coded' units; this coding lists the low condition of a factor as -1 and the high condition as +1. Using this coding scheme, all factors (numeric or text) are on the same relative scale, (-1, +1). So the effect is covering the same relative X scale, 2 units.

A series of Factorial Plots are available to display the calculated effects. The first is for Main Effects; it shows changes in output that occur as each factor is moved from the low to high condition.

The Interaction Plot displays all possible two factor interactions. If an interaction is present, visualize it first (before the Main Effects). This is important, because if the interaction is strong enough it could produce an insignificant result in one of the Main Effects terms.

The Cube Plot is the final graph. For experiments with three or more factors, a cube plot is an excellent way to show change in output. A cube plot can accept from two to eight factors.

Menu command: *Stat > DOE > Factorial > Factorial Plots*

Input the response **Percent Errors**.

Choose all 3 factors.

Select **Only model terms**.

Click **Graphs**.

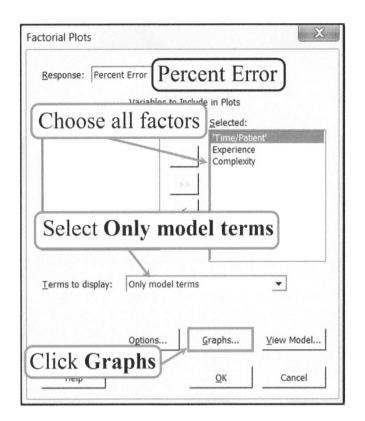

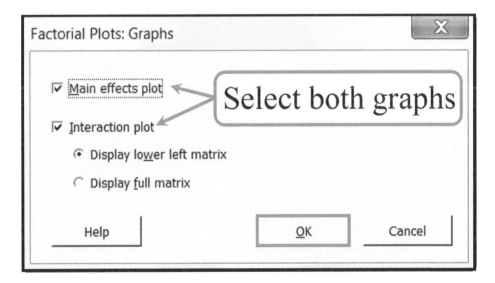

Select both the Main Effects and the Interaction graphs. Click **OK** (twice).

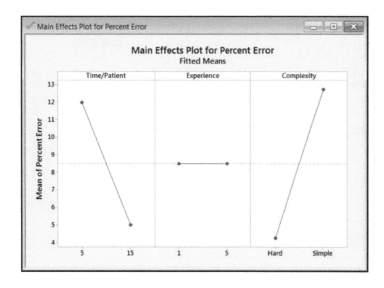

The Main Effects plot shows the Time/Patient Percent Errors decreases as the time per patient increases. This is called a negative effect.

The Experience level shows no effect, as the Percent Errors remains unchanged regardless of experience.

The Complexity level shows a positive effect, as the Percent Errors increases when the Simple situation (1) is compared to the Hard situation (10).

The Interaction plot shows all two factor interactions.

An interaction exists if the effect of one factor on the output changes based on the level of a second factor.

The interaction between Time/Patient and Complexity is significant. The change in the Percent Errors for a 5 minute visit (black solid line) is steeper than the change in the Percent Errors for a 15 minute visit (dashed red line).

When interactions are present they should be investigated first, because a significant interaction can cause one or both of the factors involved in the interaction to appear insignificant. If an interaction exists, the two factors involved in that interaction must remain in the final model.

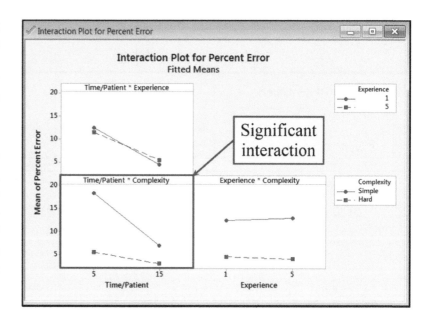

Menu command: *Stat > DOE > Factorial > Cube Plot*

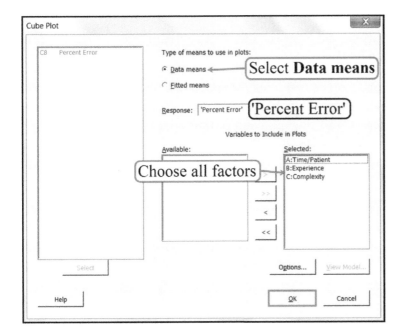

Select **Data means** for the type of means to use in plot.

Select the desired response, and input factors.

Click **OK**.

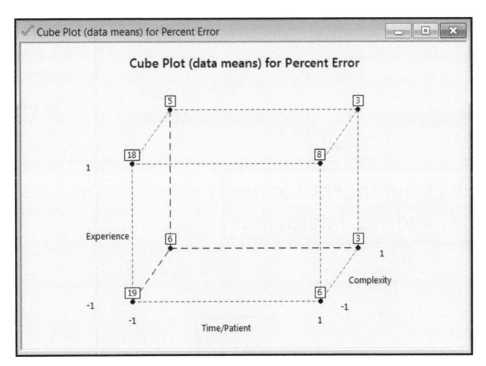

A Cube Plot shows the relationship between X's and a Y.

The values at the corners of the cube are the experiments output values for those conditions.

Cube plots with only two factors result in a square plot.

Reduced Model

After reviewing Effects Plots, Session Window output, and Factorial Plots, it is evident that factors A, C, and the AC interaction are important terms to use in a final model.

Re-run the analysis using these three terms and analyze the residuals. Remember, a residual is calculated as the difference between expected and actual values. Analysis of residuals demonstrates the appropriateness of the model. If the model is adequate, residuals will have the following characteristics:
- They have a normal distribution
- They have a mean value of zero
- They are independent
- They demonstrate a constant variance along the range of fitted values.

For more detailed discussion of residuals, review the regression section in the Analysis chapter.

Menu command: *Stat > DOE > Factorial > Analyze Factorial Design*

Select the **Terms** button.

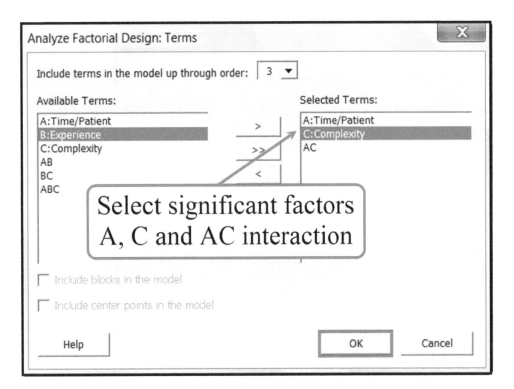

Select **A**, **C** and the **AC** interaction as terms.

Click **OK**.

At the Analyze Factorial Design window, select the **Graphs** button.

With the Reduced model there is no reason to re-run the Effects Plots.

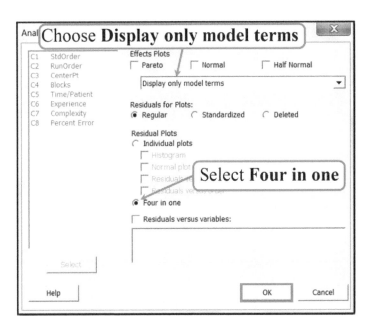

Choose **Display only model terms**.

For Residual Plots select **Four in one**.

Click **OK**.

At the Analyze Factorial Design window, select **Storage**.

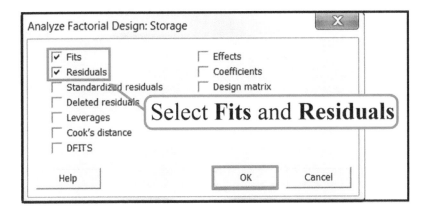

Select **Fits** and **Residuals**.

Click **OK** twice.

The residuals show nothing abnormal.

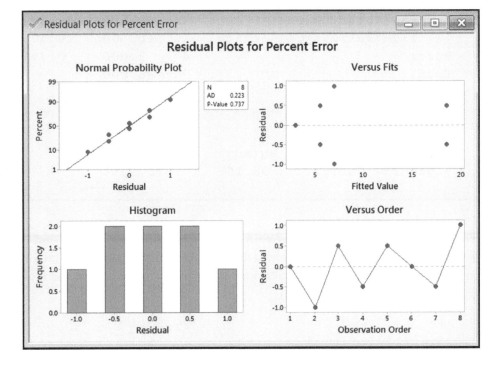

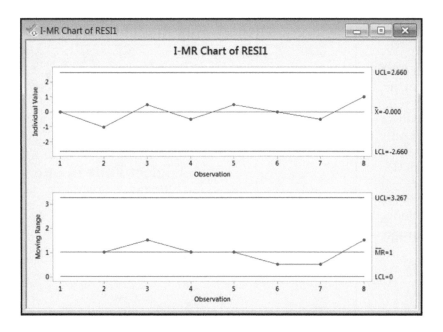

The I-MR chart of the residuals also looks good.

The Session window output begins with Estimated Effects and Coefficients for the Reduced model.

Factorial Regression: Percent Error versus Time/Patient, Complexity

Analysis of Variance

Source	DF	Adj SS	Adj MS	F-Value	P-Value
Model	3	283.000	94.333	125.78	0.000
Linear	2	242.500	121.250	161.67	0.000
Time/Patient	1	98.000	98.000	130.67	0.000
Complexity	1	144.500	144.500	192.67	0.000
2-Way Interactions	1	40.500	40.500	54.00	0.002
Time/Patient*Complexity	1	40.500	40.500	54.00	0.002
Error	4	3.000	0.750		
Total	7	286.000			

Model Summary

S	R-sq	R-sq(adj)	R-sq(pred)
0.866025	98.95%	98.16%	95.80%

The **Analysis of Variance**, along with the **Model Summary**, shows that by using the two main factors of Time/Patient, and Complexity along with the interaction of these two factors, 98.15% (R-sq) of the variation in the output can be explained. The high R-sq(pred) indicates that the model does a good job of predicting the response of new observations.

Coded Coefficients

Term	Effect	Coef	SE Coef	T-Value	P-Value	VIF
Constant		8.500	0.306	27.76	0.000	
Time/Patient	-7.000	-3.500	0.306	-11.43	0.000	1.00
Complexity	-8.500	-4.250	0.306	-13.88	0.000	1.00
Time/Patient*Complexity	4.500	2.250	0.306	7.35	0.002	1.00

```
Regression Equation in Uncoded Units

Percent Error = 15.500 - 0.7000 Time/Patient - 8.750 Complexity
              + 0.4500 Time/Patient*Complexity
```

The Effect for each term and interaction was described previously.

Notice that the Coefficients are equal to ½ the Effects.

This results from analyzing the experiment using coded values. Coding the factors places the low condition at a -1 value and the high condition at +1. Display the worksheet with coded values to view this more clearly.

VIF values above 5 are a concern. This indicates there's a correlation between input factors that can lead to unstable coefficients.

Some factors cannot be used in an equation due to the nature of their values; an example of this is Complexity, expressed with values of Simple and Hard. When this occurs, analyze the factor(s) in the coded condition.

The final equation, using uncoded input values, becomes:

Percent Errors = 15.50 – 0.70*Time/Patient - 8.750*Complexity + 0.450*(Time/Patient*Complexity)

For Time/Patient = 5 and a Complexity of Simple (-1) the equation is:

Percent Errors = 15.50 – 0.70*(5) - 8.750*(-1) + 0.450*(5*(-1)) = **18.5**

Menu command: *Stat > DOE > Display Design*

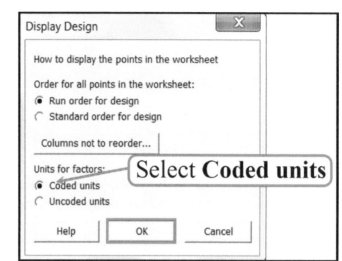

Select **Coded units**.

Click **OK**.

The factors have the low conditions as -1 and the high as 1. Even the term Complexity that had text values are listed with the -1, 1 code.

C1	C2	C3	C4	C5	C6	C7	C8
StdOrder	RunOrder	CenterPt	Blocks	Time/Patient	Experience	Complexity	Percent Error
6	1	1	1	1	-1	1	3
2	2	1	1	1	-1	-1	6
1	3	1	1	-1	-1	-1	19
7	4	1	1	-1	1	1	5
5	5	1	1	-1	-1	1	6
8	6	1	1	1	1	1	3
3	7	1	1	-1	1	-1	18
4	8	1	1	1	1	-1	8

Referring back to the Session window, the **Effect** was defined as the change in the output as the input factor went from the low to high condition. The **Coefficient** is defined as the change in the output (Y) per unit change in the input factor. The Effect is a change from -1 to 1 which is two units, so the coefficient will be ½ this amount. (The coefficient is a change of one unit.)

To display the worksheet with the original values, return to the Display Design window and select **Uncoded units**.

Design of Experiments (DOE) with Center Points

A company wants to reduce the number of man hours required to assemble a product. It decides to study the effects of three variables on Man-Hours per Unit assembly time, as follows:
- Number of Items per order
- Number of Subassemblies available
- Number of Associates on a team

The levels of variables investigated are as follows:

C1	C2	C3
Items per Order	Subassemblies	Associates
5	30	2
15	60	6

The Average Man-Hours per unit is calculated on a per shift basis.

Center Points and Blocks

Continuous factors have the ability to create a center value (the value midway between the high and low values in a two level design). A Center Point exists when **all** continuous factors are run at their center or middle condition simultaneously. The Center Point for the example above is as follows:

Items per Order	# Subassemblies	#Associates
10	45	4%

The Center Point has several purposes:
1. *Verify the assumption of a linear response.* If the response between the high and low condition of an X factor is linear, the center point falls on the line connecting the response at the high and low conditions.
   Note: The Center Point indicates if curvature exists, but does not indicate which factor or factors cause the curvature.
2. *Estimate the pure error of an experiment.* When there are multiple Center Points, the variation of results is an estimate of the experiment's pure error.
3. *Show process stability over time, when multiple Center Points are spaced throughout the experiment.* A stable process is required for reliable experimental results. An experiment run on an unstable process could produce results based on the effect of special cause variation, not the effect of factor(s) under consideration.

Blocks

Running experiments in blocks allows for proper distribution of runs to account for potential factors that are not part of the current experiment. These factors are called Noise factors.

For instance, if for logistical purposes the experiment must be split between two days, then day is a Noise variable. Simply dividing the random runs into two groups and running one group on day 1 and the other group on day 2 may not result in an even distribution of all factor settings. Running the experiment in two blocks, however, assures an equal number of high and low conditions for each factor in each block.

This type of situation is used for the example experiment.

Menu command: *Stat > DOE > Factorial > Create Factorial Design*

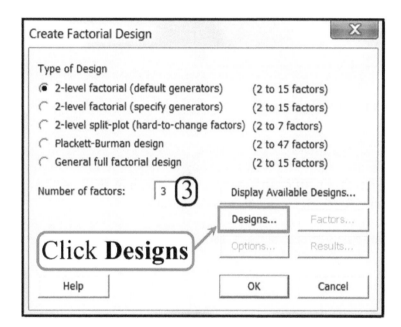

Select **3** for the number of factors.

Click **Designs**.

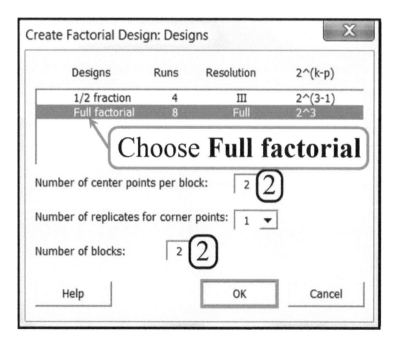

Choose **Full factorial**.

Select **2** Center Points per block.

Select **2** for blocks and leave the replicates at 1.

Click **OK**.

At the Create Factorial Design window, select **Factors.**

Input the Factor Names and the low and high conditions as shown.

Click **OK** twice.

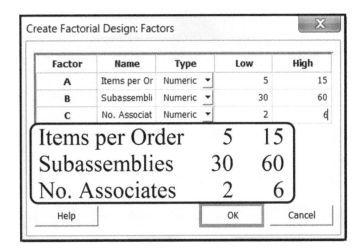

The Experimental Worksheet appears as follows:

C1	C2	C3	C4	C5	C6	C7
StdOrder	RunOrder	CenterPt	Blocks	Items per Order	Subassemblies	No. Associates
2	1	1	1	15	60	2
1	2	1	1	5	30	2
4	3	1	1	5	60	6
3	4	1	1	15	30	6
6	5	0	1	10	45	4
5	6	0	1	10	45	4
8	7	1	2	5	60	2
11	8	0	2	10	45	4
10	9	1	2	15	60	6
12	10	0	2	10	45	4
9	11	1	2	5	30	6
7	12	1	2	15	30	2

Note: The worksheet is arranged in random order. The CenterPt column shows the factorial points as a 1 and the Center Points as a 0. The Blocks contain an equal number of low and high settings for each factor.

For analysis, open the following worksheet:

Minitab Project: **FULLFACTORIAL**

Worksheet: *Cycle Time*

This is the experiment just created with the output in column C8, (Cycle Time).

C1	C2	C3	C4	C5	C6	C7	C8
StdOrder	RunOrder	CenterPt	Blocks	Items per Order	Subassemblies	No. Associates	Cycle Time
5	1	0	1	10	45	4	6
6	2	0	1	10	45	4	9
4	3	1	1	5	60	6	7
3	4	1	1	15	30	6	1
2	5	1	1	15	60	2	18
1	6	1	1	5	30	2	10
11	7	0	2	10	45	4	8
8	8	1	2	5	60	2	12
12	9	0	2	10	45	4	10
10	10	1	2	15	60	6	2
9	11	1	2	5	30	6	6
7	12	1	2	15	30	2	15

Analyze Full Factorial with Center Points and Blocks

Analysis of the Full Factorial design with Center Points and Blocks proceeds as follows:
1. Create the Full Model (all factors and interactions)
2. Determine significant factors based on a predetermined alpha level
3. Determine if the Center Points and or Blocks are significant
4. Run Factorial Plots to visualize significant factors
5. Run a new model with significant factors (the Reduced Model)
6. Check the model using ANOVA and Coefficients Session window outputs
7. Check the model using residual analysis (graphs)

Menu command: *Stat > DOE > Factorial > Analyze Factorial Design*

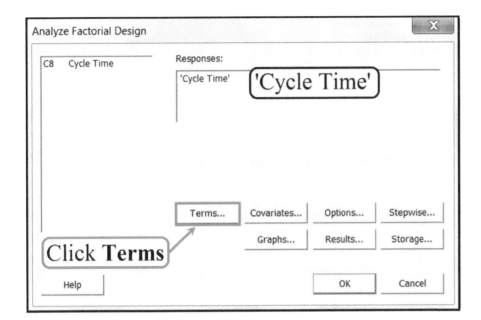

Select **Cycle Time** as the Response.

Click **Terms**.

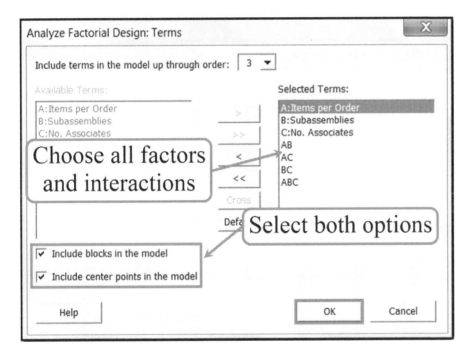

Select all terms for the Full Model.

Select 'Include blocks in the model' and 'Include center points in the model'.

Click **OK**.

In the Analyze Factorial Design window, click **Graphs**.

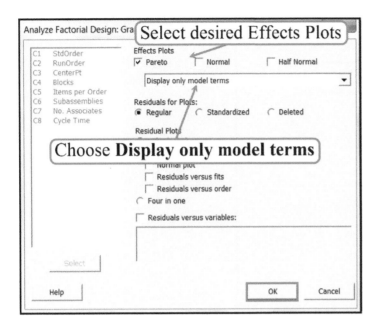

Select the desired **Effects Plots**. The Effects plots were explained previously, so only the Pareto plot will be presented.

Select **Display only model terms**.

Click **OK** (twice).

To change the confidence level (.95 is the default), at the Analyze Factorial Design window, select **Options**.

Select the Confidence level, click **OK** (twice).

Note: Only a portion of the window is shown here.

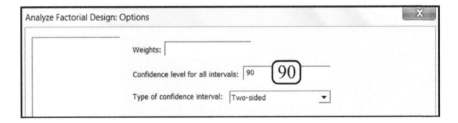

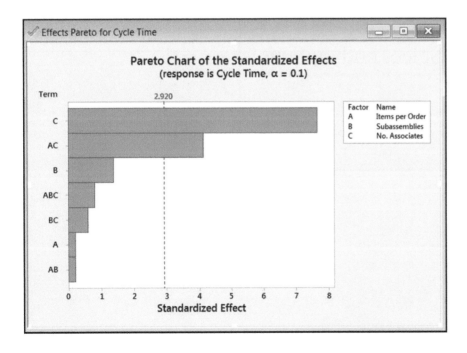

Factors C and the AC interaction are shown to be significant. (Number of Associates, and the Items on Order/Number of Associates interaction.)

Session Window Output

The Coded Coefficients show the main effect 'No. Associates' and the interaction 'Item per Order*No. Associate' as significant.

```
Coded Coefficients

Term                          Effect    Coef  SE Coef  T-Value  P-Value
Constant                                8.875   0.637    13.92    0.005
Blocks
  1                                    -0.750   0.901    -0.83    0.493
Items per Order                0.250    0.125   0.637     0.20    0.863
Subassemblies                  1.750    0.875   0.637     1.37    0.303
No. Associates                -9.750   -4.875   0.637    -7.65    0.017
Items per Order*Subassemblies  0.250    0.125   0.637     0.20    0.863
Items per Order*No. Associates -5.250  -2.625   0.637    -4.12    0.054
Subassemblies*No. Associates  -0.750   -0.375   0.637    -0.59    0.616
Items per Order               -1.75    -0.87    1.10     -0.79    0.511
   *Subassemblies*No. Associates
Ct Pt                                  -0.62    1.10     -0.57    0.628
```

```
Analysis of Variance

Source                          DF   Adj SS   Adj MS  F-Value  P-Value
Model                            9  256.167   28.463     8.76    0.107
  Blocks                         1    2.250    2.250     0.69    0.493
  Linear                         3  196.375   65.458    20.14    0.048
    Items per Order              1    0.125    0.125     0.04    0.863
    Subassemblies               1    6.125    6.125     1.88    0.303
    No. Associates               1  190.125  190.125    58.50    0.017
  2-Way Interactions             3   56.375   18.792     5.78    0.151
    Items per Order*Subassemblies 1   0.125    0.125     0.04    0.863
    Items per Order*No. Associates 1  55.125   55.125    16.96    0.054
    Subassemblies*No. Associates 1    1.125    1.125     0.35    0.616
  3-Way Interactions             1    2.042    2.042     0.63    0.511
    Items per Order*Subassemblies
             *No. Associates      1    2.042    2.042     0.63    0.511
  Curvature                      1    1.042    1.042     0.32    0.628
Error                            2    6.500    3.250
Total                           11  262.667
```

The Analysis of Variance shows both Blocks and Center Points (Curvature) are not significant. This information will be used to produce the Reduced Model.

Factorial Plots

Create the Factorial plots as shown previously. Again, these plots help identify significant factors.

Menu command: *Stat > DOE > Factorial > Factorial Plots*

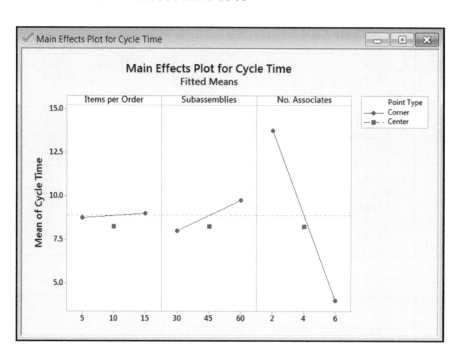

The Main Effects plot shows the strong effect caused by 'Number of Associates'. Notice the Center Point (red square) is almost on the lines. This confirms the Session window output indicating that no curvature exists in the response.

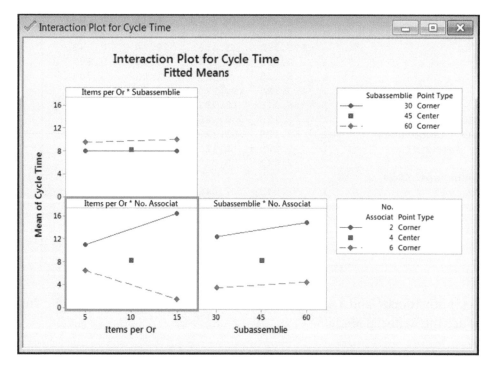

The Interaction Plots show the 'Items per Order * No. Associates' interaction.

Menu command: *Stat > DOE > Factorial > Cube Plot*

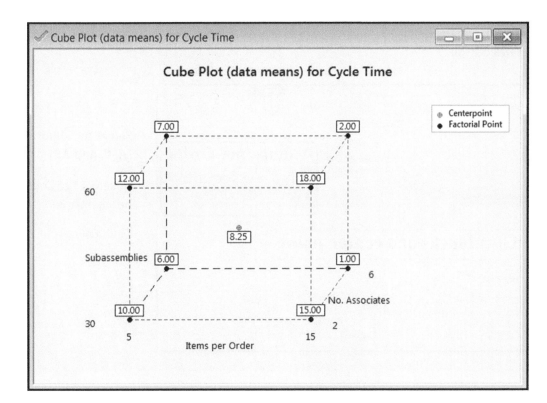

The Cube Plot shows values for each Factorial point and the average of the Center Points.

The Reduced Model

As shown before, the Reduced Model is created and analyzed using the significant factors. Re-run the analysis using the following factors:
- No. Associates
- Items per Order
- Items per Order * No. Associates

Note: *Items per Order* is not significant, but it must be included in the model because it is a factor of the interaction.

Create the Reduced Model

Return to the Terms window.

Menu command: *Stat > DOE > Factorial > Analyze Factorial Design*

Select the **Terms** button

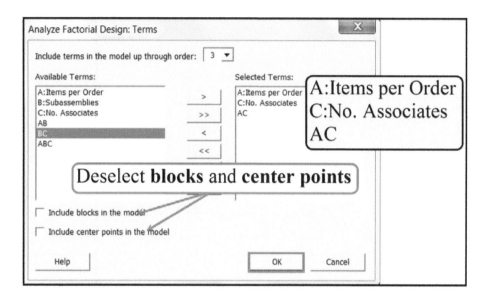

Select the significant terms. (**A, C,** and **AC**)

Deselect the Center Point and Block options.

Click **OK**.

At the Analyze Factorial Design window click the Storage button.

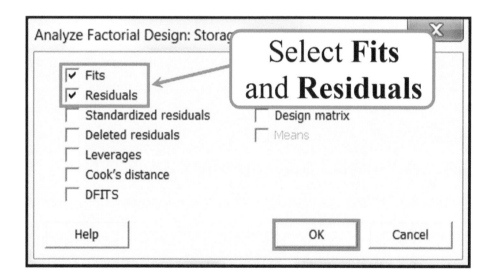

Select both **Fits** and **Residuals**.

Click **OK**.

At the Analyze Factorial Design window click the **Graphs** button.

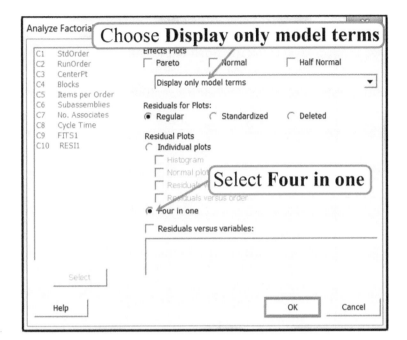

Select the **Four in one** Residual Plots.

Click **OK** (twice).

It is not necessary to have the Effects Plots selected.

Residual plots

Residuals were discussed in the Simple Linear Regression section of the Analyze chapter.

Four In One Graph

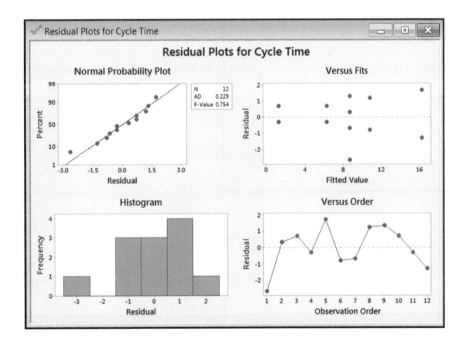

The Four in One Residual plot evaluates residuals for the reduced model.

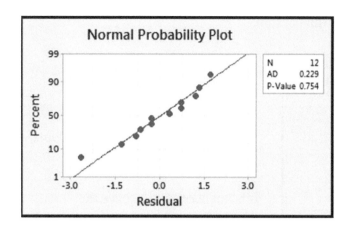

Normal Probability Plot

Observing the Normal Probability Plot, the p-value of .754 indicates the normality assumption is upheld.

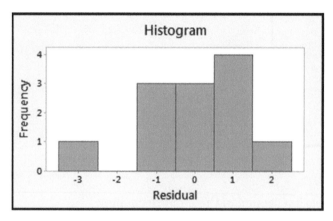

Histogram

The Histogram shows nothing abnormal regarding the normality assumption. This is a visual display showing the general shape of distribution.

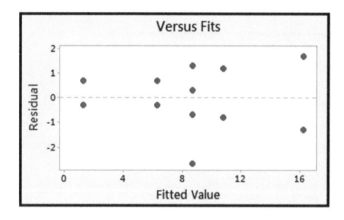

Residuals versus Fits

The Residuals versus Fits plot shows the general width of residuals. No evidence exists to reject the constant variance assumption.

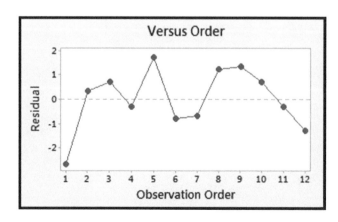

Residuals versus Run Order

No patterns exist in the Residual versus Run Order plot. The pattern appears to resemble a stable process.

To provide additional support for this assumption, an I-MR chart is created.

Menu command:

Stat > Control Charts > Variables Charts for Individuals > I-MR

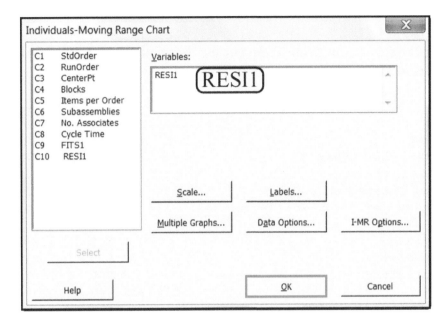

Select **RESI1**.

Click **OK**.

No shifts, trends or points outside the red lines (control limits) exist.

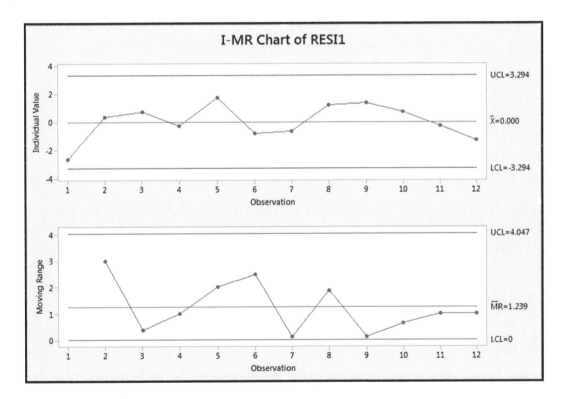

Session window output

The Session window output has the same explanation as before.

Factorial Regression: Cycle Time versus Items per Order, No. Associates
Analysis of Variance

Source	DF	Adj SS	Adj MS	F-Value	P-Value
Model	3	245.375	81.792	37.84	0.000
Linear	2	190.250	95.125	44.01	0.000
Items per Order	1	0.125	0.125	0.06	0.816
No. Associates	1	190.125	190.125	87.96	0.000
2-Way Interactions	1	55.125	55.125	25.50	0.001
Items per Order*No. Associates	1	55.125	55.125	25.50	0.001
Error	8	17.292	2.161		
Curvature	1	1.042	1.042	0.45	0.524
Lack-of-Fit	4	7.500	1.875	0.64	0.669
Pure Error	3	8.750	2.917		
Total	11	262.667			

One additional metric is the R-Sq(adj) value. This is related to the R-Sq value.

Model Summary

S	R-sq	R-sq(adj)	R-sq(pred)
1.47019	93.42%	90.95%	85.54%

The *R-Sq (93.42%)* value indicates the percent of variation of output explained by the model. The **R-Sq(adj) (90.95%)** value displays the percent of variation explained by the model, adjusted for the number of terms in the model. Both values are at or above 90%. The R-sq (pred) value shows how well the model predicts the output based on new input value.

The model for Cycle Time is developed using the coefficients for the uncoded units.

Regression Equation in Uncoded Units

```
Cycle Time = 7.67 + 1.075 Items per Order + 0.187 No. Associates
           - 0.2625 Items per Order*No. Associates
```

Fractional Factorial Designs

Tool Use: Use a Fractional Factorial Design in the same way as a Full Factorial when resources are a concern. With this approach the number of runs are reduced by deciding beforehand which interaction coefficients are not important.

The equation for a Fractional Factorial depends upon the degree of fractionation.

The hypothesis is the same - determining if the coefficients are zero or not equal to zero.

Understanding the compromises made with Fractional Factorial designs is assumed throughout this section.

Null Hypothesis: (H_o): $\beta_i = 0$

Alternative Hypothesis: (H_a): $\beta_i \neq 0$

Data Type: Input – Discrete or Continuous; Output - Numeric

Creating a Fractional Factorial Design

Menu command: *Stat > DOE > Factorial > Create Factorial Design*

Maintain the default value for Type of Design.

Select **5** factors, click **Designs**.

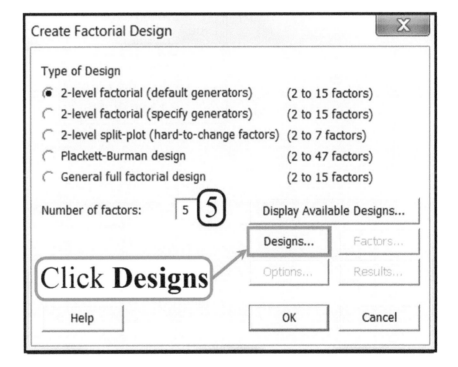

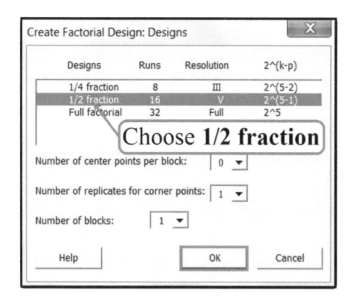

Select the ½ fraction options.

The default is the ¼ fraction, so be sure to select the ½ fraction.

Click **OK**.

At the Create Factorial Design window, select **Factors**.

Input the factor names and values as shown.

Click **OK** (twice).

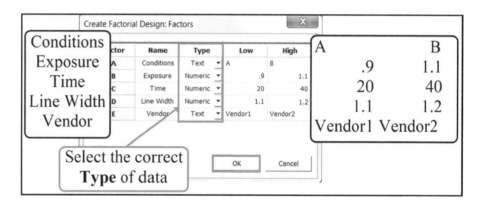

Here is the final DOE worksheet.

↓	C1	C2	C3	C4	C5-T	C6	C7	C8	C9-T
	StdOrder	RunOrder	CenterPt	Blocks	Conditions	Exposure	Time	Line Width	Vendor
1	7	1	1	1	A	1.1	40	1.1	Vendor2
2	1	2	1	1	A	0.9	20	1.1	Vendor2
3	6	3	1	1	B	0.9	40	1.1	Vendor2
4	15	4	1	1	A	1.1	40	1.2	Vendor1
5	5	5	1	1	A	0.9	40	1.1	Vendor1
6	3	6	1	1	A	1.1	20	1.1	Vendor1
7	16	7	1	1	B	1.1	40	1.2	Vendor2
8	10	8	1	1	B	0.9	20	1.2	Vendor2
9	11	9	1	1	A	1.1	20	1.2	Vendor2
10	12	10	1	1	B	1.1	20	1.2	Vendor1
11	2	11	1	1	B	0.9	20	1.1	Vendor1
12	8	12	1	1	B	1.1	40	1.1	Vendor1
13	14	13	1	1	B	0.9	40	1.2	Vendor1
14	13	14	1	1	A	0.9	40	1.2	Vendor2
15	4	15	1	1	B	1.1	20	1.1	Vendor2
16	9	16	1	1	A	0.9	20	1.2	Vendor1

Session window Output

This is the Upper portion. It shows a summary of the design.

The design contains 5 factors, with 16 runs. This creates a ½ fraction with only 1 replicate.

Fractional Factorial Design

```
Factors:   5   Base Design:        5, 16   Resolution:    V
Runs:     16   Replicates:             1   Fraction:    1/2
Blocks:    1   Center pts (total):     0
```

Design Generators: E = ABCD

Alias Structure

```
I + ABCDE

A + BCDE
B + ACDE
C + ABDE
D + ABCE
E + ABCD
AB + CDE
AC + BDE
AD + BCE
AE + BCD
BC + ADE
BD + ACE
BE + ACD
CD + ABE
CE + ABD
DE + ABC
```

The lower portion shows the Generator used to create the design along with the Alias structure.

Analyze Fractional Factorial Designs

To demonstrate analysis, the Yield worksheet in the Fractional Factorial project contains the design created with the response (Yield).

Minitab Project: **FractionalFactorial**

Worksheet: *Yield*

♦	C1	C2	C3	C4	C5-T	C6	C7	C8	C9-T	C10
	StdOrder	RunOrder	CenterPt	Blocks	Conditions	Exposure	Time	Line Width	Vendor	Yield
1	6	1	1	1	B	0.9	40	1.1	Vendor 2	22
2	15	2	1	1	A	1.1	40	1.2	Vendor 1	44
3	5	3	1	1	A	0.9	40	1.1	Vendor 1	16
4	16	4	1	1	B	1.1	40	1.2	Vendor 2	53
5	12	5	1	1	B	1.1	20	1.2	Vendor 1	40
6	11	6	1	1	A	1.1	20	1.2	Vendor 2	30
7	8	7	1	1	B	1.1	40	1.1	Vendor 1	50
8	10	8	1	1	B	0.9	20	1.2	Vendor 2	10
9	9	9	1	1	A	0.9	20	1.2	Vendor 1	6
10	4	10	1	1	B	1.1	20	1.1	Vendor 2	42
11	14	11	1	1	B	0.9	40	1.2	Vendor 1	21
12	1	12	1	1	A	0.9	20	1.1	Vendor 2	8
13	7	13	1	1	A	1.1	40	1.1	Vendor 2	45
14	13	14	1	1	A	0.9	40	1.2	Vendor 2	15
15	3	15	1	1	A	1.1	20	1.1	Vendor 1	34
16	2	16	1	1	B	0.9	20	1.1	Vendor 1	9

Yield worksheet

Menu command: *Stat > DOE > Factorial > Analyze Factorial Design*

Input **Yield** for the Responses.

Click **Terms**.

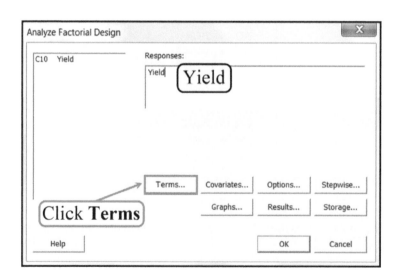

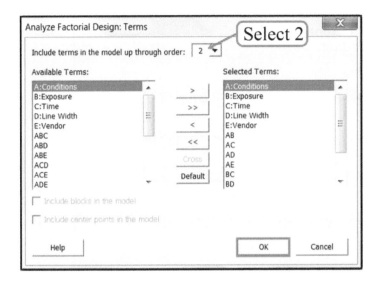

Select **2** for 'Include terms in the model up through order': This will include the main factors and all two factor interactions in the model. (Even though the 2 may be the default, use the pull down option and reselect 2.)

Click **OK**.

In the Analyze Factorial Design window, select **Graphs**.

Input the desired Effects Plots.

Select **Display only model terms**.

Click **OK**.

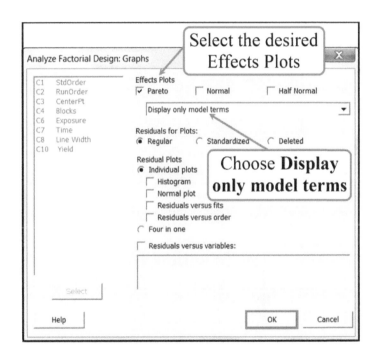

To change the Confidence Level for the analysis, select **Options** in the **Analyze Factorial Design** window.

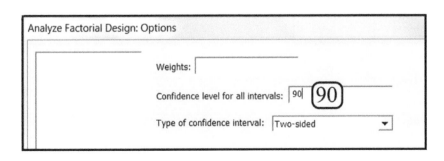

Change the Confidence level to **90**. Click **OK** (twice).

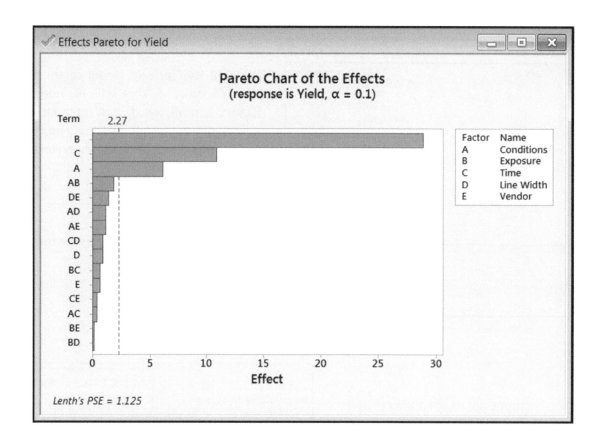

The Pareto plot show factors A, B, and C are significant.

Note: Follow previous examples to view Main Effects and Interaction Plots.

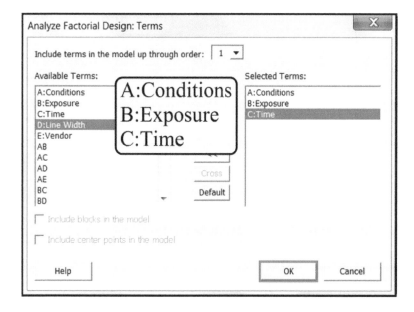

Next, create the reduced model.

In the **Terms** window, select **A**, **B**, and **C**.

Click **OK**.

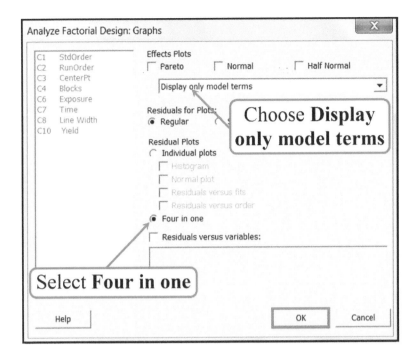

Choose Display only model terms.

Select the **Four in one** plot of residuals.

Click **OK**.

There's no need for Effects Plots since the factors selected were deemed significant.

Analysis of the Reduced Model for the Fractional Factorial experiment proceeds along the line of the Full Factorial.

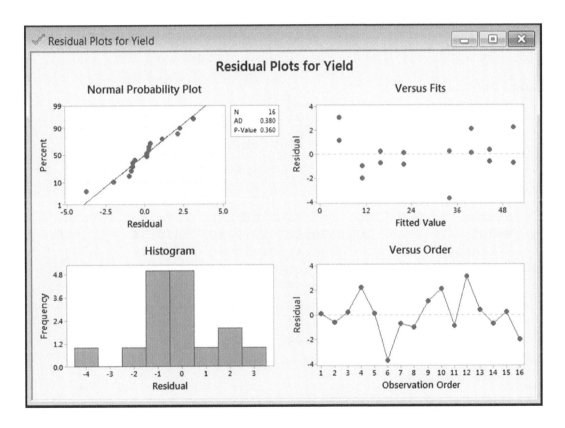

Residual plots were explained previously; in this example, no issues exist with residuals.

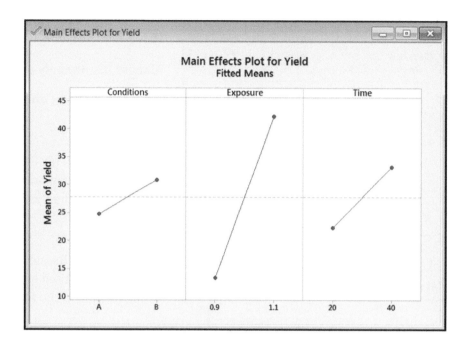

Factorial Plots are again used to visualize results; create them in the same manner as in the Full Factorial analysis.

No interactions were significant so the Interaction Graphs are not displayed.

Session window outputs

Factorial Regression: Yield versus Conditions, Exposure, Time

Analysis of Variance

Source	DF	Adj SS	Adj MS	F-Value	P-Value
Model	3	3958.19	1319.40	374.74	0.000
Linear	3	3958.19	1319.40	374.74	0.000
Conditions	1	150.06	150.06	42.62	0.000
Exposure	1	3335.06	3335.06	947.24	0.000
Time	1	473.06	473.06	134.36	0.000
Error	12	42.25	3.52		
Total	15	4000.44			

Model Summary

S	R-sq	R-sq(adj)	R-sq(pred)
1.87639	98.94%	98.68%	98.12%

The R-Sq and R-Sq(adj) and R-sq (pred) values are all in the high 90% range.

All three factors show significance.

> **Regression Equation in Uncoded Units**
>
> ```
> Yield = -132.88 + 3.063 Conditions + 144.38 Exposure
> + 0.5437 Time
> ```

Remember, the 'Condition' will be either a -1 or 1 for Condition A and Condition B respectively.

> **Fits and Diagnostics for Unusual Observations**
>
> ```
> Obs    Yield      Fit    Resid  Std Resid
>   2   30.000   33.750   -3.750      -2.31  R
>
> R   Large residual
> ```

The unusual observation should be checked and if found to be in error, corrected.

To display this value on the Four in one plot, return to the Residual graph.

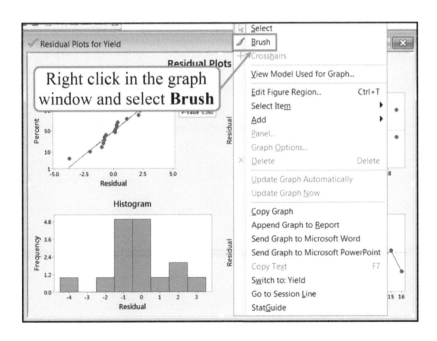

Right click inside the graph window and select **Brush**.

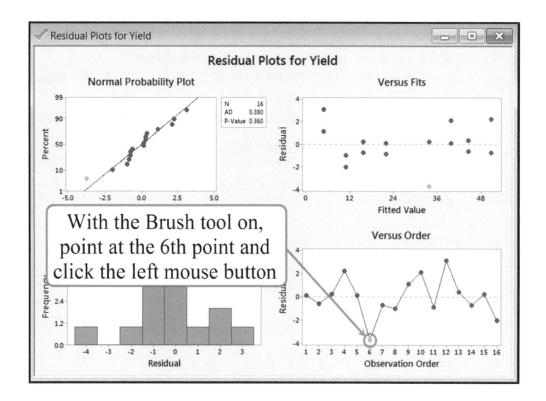

With the Brush option on, point at and click the sixth observation in the Versus Order graph.

All points corresponding to the sixth point will be highlighted.

Only the Histogram will not have a highlighted point.

Response Surface Designs

Tool Use: Use a Response Surface Design in the same way as a Full Factorial to model a nonlinear response. This approach creates a model with quadratic terms.

The equation for a two factor Response Surface design is:

$$Y = \beta_0 + \beta_1 X_1 + \beta_2 X_2 + \beta_{11} X_1{}^2 + \beta_{22} X_2{}^2 + \beta_{12} X_1 X_2$$

The hypothesis is the same - determining if the coefficients are zero or not equal to zero.

Null Hypothesis: (H$_o$): $\beta_i = 0$

Alternative Hypothesis: (H$_a$): $\beta_i \neq 0$

Data Type: Input – Continuous or categorical; Output - Numeric

Menu command:

Stat > DOE > Response Surface > Create Response Surface Design

A three factor Central Composite design will be created. This experiment is set up to determine the best settings for minimum clumping of candy while maintaining a desired taste level (as measured on a one to ten scale).

Select **Central composite** as the design.

Select **3** continuous factors.

Click **Designs**.

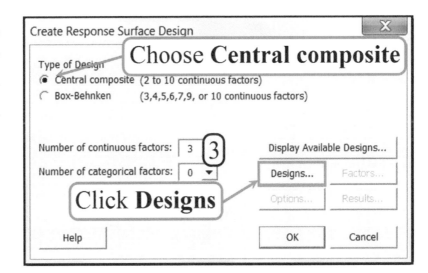

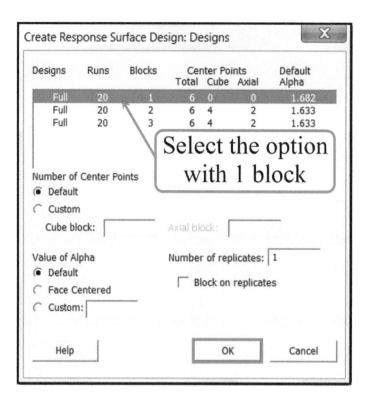

Select the first option, to run in 1 block.

Click **OK**.

In the Create Response Surface Design window select **Factors**.

Select **Cube points**.
Input the factor names
and settings as shown.

Click **OK** (twice).

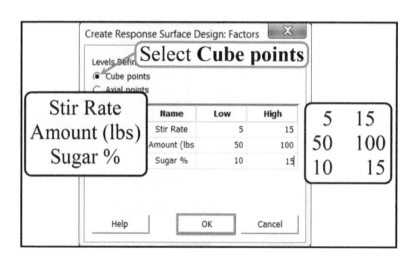

The final DOE worksheet. (Remember the table is in a random order.)

↓	C1	C2	C3	C4	C5	C6	C7
	StdOrder	RunOrder	PtType	Blocks	Stir Rate	Amount (lbs)	Sugar %
1	12	1	-1	1	10.0000	117.045	12.5000
2	10	2	-1	1	18.4090	75.000	12.5000
3	11	3	-1	1	10.0000	32.955	12.5000
4	3	4	1	1	5.0000	100.000	10.0000
5	14	5	-1	1	10.0000	75.000	16.7045
6	20	6	0	1	10.0000	75.000	12.5000
7	17	7	0	1	10.0000	75.000	12.5000
8	4	8	1	1	15.0000	100.000	10.0000
9	5	9	1	1	5.0000	50.000	15.0000
10	7	10	1	1	5.0000	100.000	15.0000
11	8	11	1	1	15.0000	100.000	15.0000
12	13	12	-1	1	10.0000	75.000	8.2955
13	19	13	0	1	10.0000	75.000	12.5000
14	9	14	-1	1	1.5910	75.000	12.5000
15	1	15	1	1	5.0000	50.000	10.0000
16	15	16	0	1	10.0000	75.000	12.5000
17	16	17	0	1	10.0000	75.000	12.5000
18	6	18	1	1	15.0000	50.000	15.0000
19	2	19	1	1	15.0000	50.000	10.0000
20	18	20	0	1	10.0000	75.000	12.5000

Session Window output

The Session window summarizes the design.

Central Composite Design

```
Factors:        3      Replicates:     1
Base runs:     20      Total runs:    20
Base blocks:    1      Total blocks:   1
```

Two-level factorial: Full factorial

```
Cube points:                 8
Center points in cube:       6
Axial points:                6
Center points in axial:      0


α: 1.68179
```

The type, number of factors, Replicates and the number of points for each type of design point are listed.

PtType

The PtType column (C3) defines the design point type. A one (1) represents a corner or cube point, a zero (0) is a center point and a minus one (-1) is a star or axial point.

Alpha represents the Star Point's distance from the center of the design.

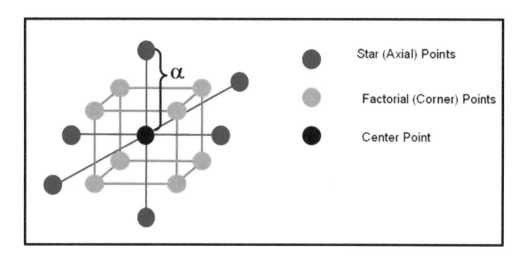

Switch to worksheet *Candy* in the RSM project. This is the same design as the one just created, with the addition of the response columns % Clump and Taste.

Minitab Project: **RSM**

Worksheet: *Candy*

	C1	C2	C3	C4	C5	C6	C7	C8	C9
	StdOrder	RunOrder	PtType	Blocks	Stir Rate	Amount (lbs)	Sugar %	% Clump	Taste
1	4	1	1	1	15.0000	100.000	10.0000	12	5
2	5	2	1	1	5.0000	50.000	15.0000	23	9
3	16	3	0	1	10.0000	75.000	12.5000	5	7
4	15	4	0	1	10.0000	75.000	12.5000	6	7
5	9	5	-1	1	1.5910	75.000	12.5000	33	8
6	17	6	0	1	10.0000	75.000	12.5000	5	8
7	18	7	0	1	10.0000	75.000	12.5000	4	7
8	7	8	1	1	5.0000	100.000	15.0000	16	9
9	10	9	-1	1	18.4090	75.000	12.5000	12	8
10	1	10	1	1	5.0000	50.000	10.0000	21	6

These are the first 10 rows of the worksheet.

Analyze RSM

Menu command:

Stat > DOE > Response Surface > Analyze Response Surface Design

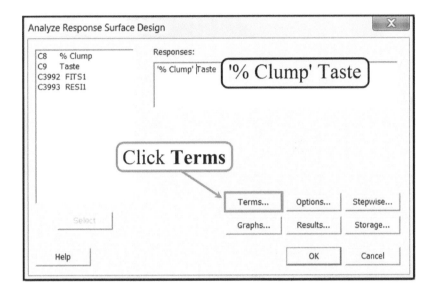

Input **% Clump** and **Taste** as the Responses.

Click **Terms**.

Select the **Full quadratic** model.

Click **OK** (twice).

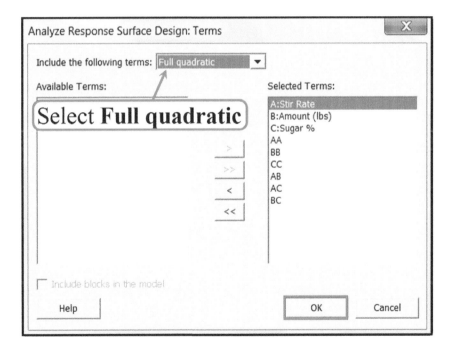

Interpret Session window output in the same way as for the Full and Fractional factorial experiments. The important output for this step is determining significant factors. .

Coded Coefficients

Term	Effect	Coef	SE Coef	T-Value	P-Value
Constant		5.63	1.10	5.12	0.000
Stir Rate	-8.833	-4.417	0.729	-6.06	0.000
Amount (lbs)	-1.704	-0.852	0.729	-1.17	0.270
Sugar %	0.592	0.296	0.729	0.41	0.693
Stir Rate*Stir Rate	12.394	6.197	0.710	8.73	0.000
Amount (lbs)*Amount (lbs)	3.555	1.777	0.710	2.50	0.031
Sugar %*Sugar %	4.615	2.308	0.710	3.25	0.009
Stir Rate*Amount (lbs)	1.250	0.625	0.953	0.66	0.527
Stir Rate*Sugar %	-0.250	-0.125	0.953	-0.13	0.898
Amount (lbs)*Sugar %	-0.750	-0.375	0.953	-0.39	0.702

For **% Clump** the following are significant factors:
- Stir Rate
- Stir Rate*Stir Rate
- Amount*Amount
- Sugar %*Sugar %

Coded Coefficients

Term	Effect	Coef	SE Coef	T-Value	P-Value
Constant		7.159	0.257	27.83	0.000
Stir Rate	-0.439	-0.220	0.171	-1.29	0.227
Amount (lbs)	0.100	0.050	0.171	0.29	0.776
Sugar %	2.643	1.321	0.171	7.74	0.000
Stir Rate*Stir Rate	0.690	0.345	0.166	2.08	0.065
Amount (lbs)*Amount (lbs)	0.336	0.168	0.166	1.01	0.335
Sugar %*Sugar %	-1.785	-0.892	0.166	-5.37	0.000
Stir Rate*Amount (lbs)	0.250	0.125	0.223	0.56	0.587
Stir Rate*Sugar %	-0.250	-0.125	0.223	-0.56	0.587
Amount (lbs)*Sugar %	0.250	0.125	0.223	0.56	0.587

For **Taste** the significant factors are:
- Sugar
- Stir Rate * Stir Rate
- Sugar*Sugar

Run the reduced model for both factors and check the residuals.

% Clump:

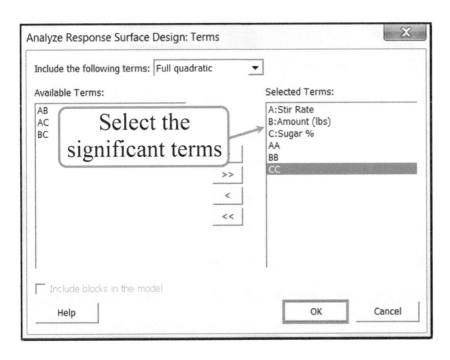

Select the significant factors.

Remember, if a quadratic or interaction term appears, the linear terms must also appear; therefore B:Amount (lbs) is selected.

Click **OK**.

In the Analyze Response Surface Design window, click **Graphs**.

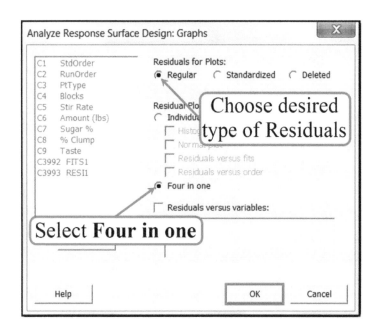

Choose the type of **Residual** to analyze.

Select the **Four in one** Residual Plots.

Click **OK** (twice).

Residual analysis is the same as presented previously.

No issues exist with
the residuals.

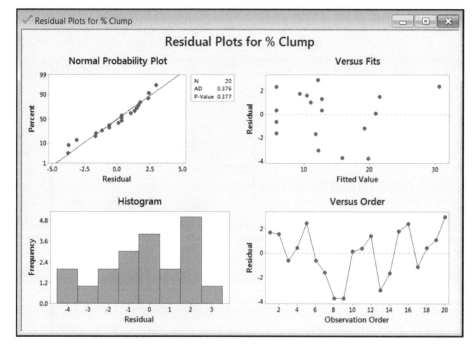

The Session window output shows estimated coefficients and their associated p-values.

Model Summary

```
      S    R-sq  R-sq(adj)  R-sq(pred)
2.43386  92.02%    88.33%      68.12%
```

Coded Coefficients

```
Term                       Effect    Coef  SE Coef  T-Value  P-Value
Constant                             5.629    0.993     5.67    0.000
Stir Rate                  -8.833   -4.417    0.659    -6.71    0.000
Amount (lbs)               -1.704   -0.852    0.659    -1.29    0.218
Sugar %                     0.592    0.296    0.659     0.45    0.660
Stir Rate*Stir Rate        12.394    6.197    0.641     9.67    0.000
Amount (lbs)*Amount (lbs)   3.555    1.777    0.641     2.77    0.016
Sugar %*Sugar %             4.615    2.308    0.641     3.60    0.003
```

The R-Sq and R-Sq(adj) are acceptable.

The equation for uncoded units.

Regression Equation in Uncoded Units

```
% Clump = 114.0 - 5.841 Stir Rate - 0.461 Amount (lbs) - 9.11 Sugar %
          + 0.2479 Stir Rate*Stir Rate + 0.00284 Amount (lbs)*Amount (lbs)
          + 0.369 Sugar %*Sugar %
```

The unusual observations show two points with high residuals. These points should be investigated.

Fits and Diagnostics for Unusual Observations

```
Obs  % Clump    Fit  Resid  Std Resid
  9    12.00  15.73  -3.73      -2.44  R
 13     9.00  12.09  -3.09      -2.03  R

R   Large residual
```

Run the reduced model for **Taste** in a similar manner.

Input the reduced model terms for **Taste** as shown.

Click **OK**.

In the Analyze Response Surface Design window, click **Graphs**.

Select the same options as for **%Clump**.

Click **OK** (twice).

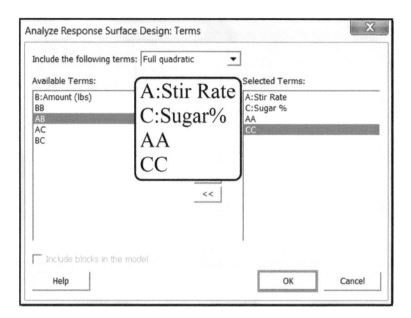

Analyze the residuals in the manner previously shown.

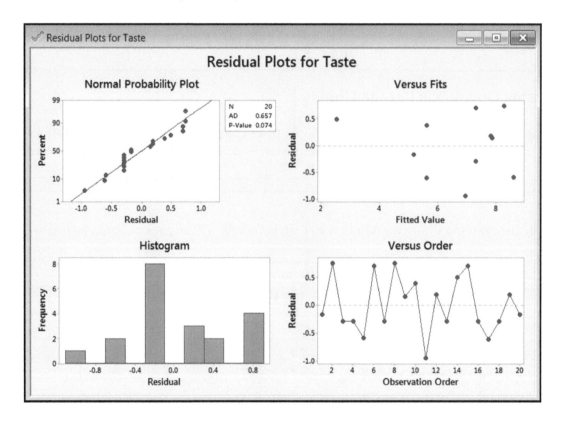

The Coefficients and associated p-values are shown. The R-Sq and R-Sq(adj) are acceptable.

```
Model Summary

        S      R-sq   R-sq(adj)   R-sq(pred)
0.565385   89.05%      86.13%        68.71%

Coded Coefficients

Term                 Effect    Coef   SE Coef   T-Value   P-Value
Constant                      7.297     0.196     37.28     0.000
Stir Rate            -0.439  -0.220     0.153     -1.44     0.172
Sugar %               2.643   1.321     0.153      8.64     0.000
Stir Rate*Stir Rate   0.657   0.328     0.148      2.22     0.043
Sugar %*Sugar %      -1.818  -0.909     0.148     -6.13     0.000
```

```
Analysis of Variance

Source                 DF    Adj SS    Adj MS   F-Value   P-Value
Model                   4   39.0051    9.7513     30.51     0.000
  Linear                2   24.5031   12.2516     38.33     0.000
    Stir Rate           1    0.6590    0.6590      2.06     0.172
    Sugar %             1   23.8441   23.8441     74.59     0.000
  Square                2   14.5020    7.2510     22.68     0.000
    Stir Rate*Stir Rate 1    1.5686    1.5686      4.91     0.043
    Sugar %*Sugar %     1   12.0303   12.0303     37.63     0.000
Error                  15    4.7949    0.3197
  Lack-of-Fit          10    3.9616    0.3962      2.38     0.176
  Pure Error            5    0.8333    0.1667
Total                  19   43.8000
```

The high p-value for Lack of Fit indicates there's no issue with this model. However, additional investigation is required before accepting the final model.

Check the unusual observation as described previously.

Fits and Diagnostics for Unusual Observations

Obs	Taste	Fit	Resid	Std Resid	
11	6.000	6.947	-0.947	-2.61	R

R Large residual

The Regression Equation provides the coefficients for Taste using uncoded units.

Regression Equation in Uncoded Units

Taste = -20.29 - 0.307 Stir Rate + 4.165 Sugar % 0.01313 Stir Rate*Stir Rate
    - 0.1455 Sugar %*Sugar %

Graphical Display

The Contour/Surface plots are used to display results. However, with 2 Y's it is more meaningful to display those combinations of factors that produce the desired outcome for both Y's.

Menu Command: *Stat > DOE > Response Surface > Overlaid Contour Plot*

Select the Y's (%Clump and Taste).

Choose **Uncoded units**.

Select 2 X's. (Stir Rate and Sugar %).

Click **Contours**.

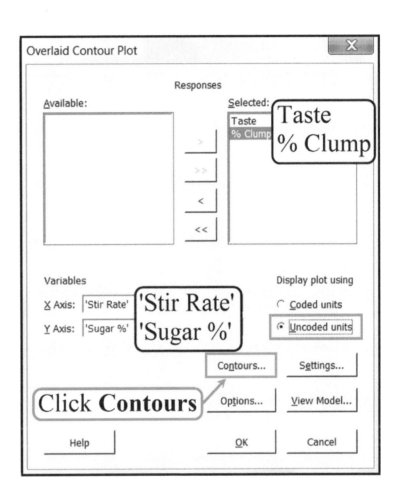

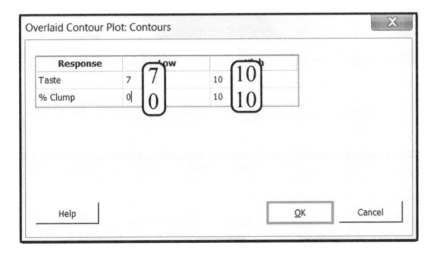

Determine the desired range of values for each Y. In this situation, the graph should show the settings that will produce a % clump less than 10% and a taste value above 7. (The taste scale has a maximum value of 10.)

Click **OK**.

At the Overlaid Contour Plot window, click the **Settings** button.

Multiple overlaid plots are possible, depending upon the settings for those X's not part of the graph.

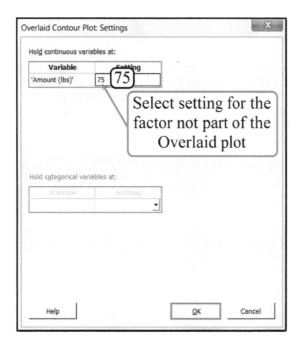

Select the setting condition for those factors not selected as graph variables.

Click **OK** twice.

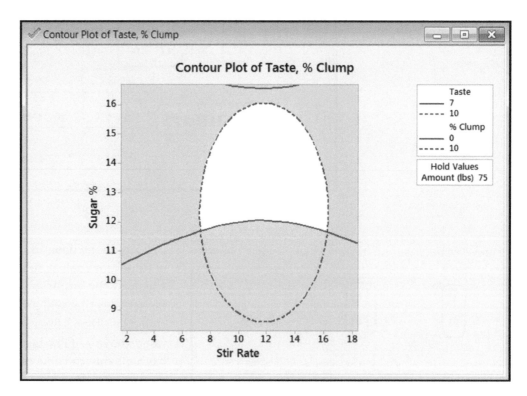

The white area shows the region that satisfies the desired outputs for both Y's.

Use the Cross-Hair option to determine values for Stir Rate and Sugar % as well as for the Y's.

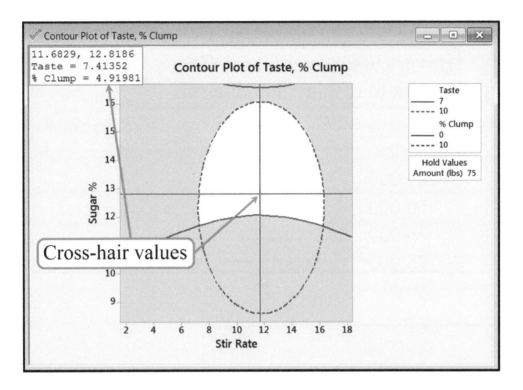

Multiple Response Optimization

Tool Use: Use the Multiple Response Optimization tool in Minitab to obtain an estimate of the inputs that will produce the best value for all outputs. It is especially useful with multiple Y's, when trying to optimize one output may cause another to degrade.

Data Type: Input – Discrete or Continuous; Output - Numeric

Minitab Project: *RSM*

Worksheet: *Candy*

Menu command: *Stat > DOE > Response Surface > Response Optimizer*

It is important to have the last model created for the output to be the desired reduced model. To verify the model currently being used, hover the cursor over the green check mark.

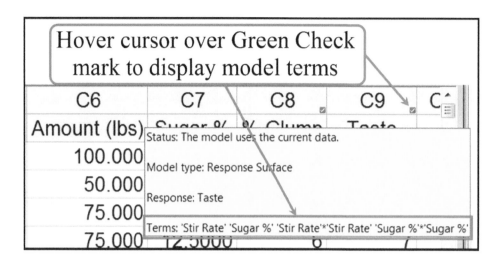

Hover cursor over Green Check mark to display model terms

C6	C7	C8	C9	C
Amount (lbs)				
100.000				
50.000				
75.000				
75.000				

Status: The model uses the current data.

Model type: Response Surface

Response: Taste

Terms: 'Stir Rate' 'Sugar %' 'Stir Rate'*'Stir Rate' 'Sugar %'*'Sugar %'

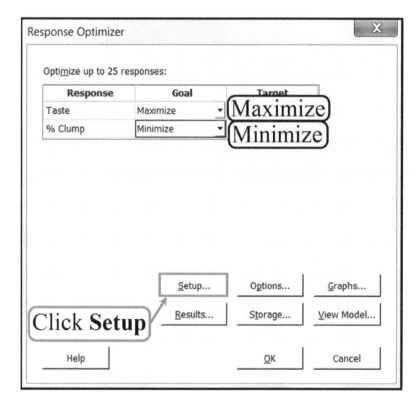

Input the desired Responses (% Clump and Taste).

Select the goal for each output.

Click **Setup**.

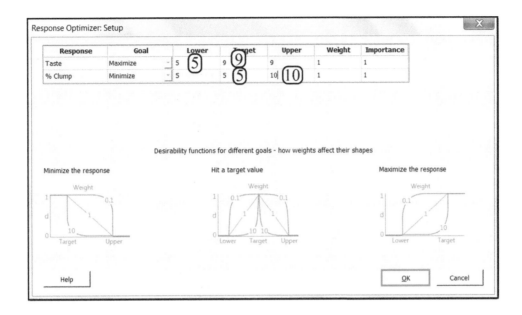

Input the **Limits**, (lower, target and upper as required) **Weights** and **Importance** values for each Response.

Click **OK**.

The goal in this example is to Minimize the '% Clump and to Maximize the Taste. The table below shows which values are required for each goal. The cells containing an 'X' indicate where a value is not required.

Goal	Lower	Target	Upper
Minimize	X	Required	Required
Target	Required	Required	Required
Maximize	Required	Required	X

The optimizer maximizes the desirability (d) value for each Y, and then combines all d values for all Y's to obtain a composite desirability value D. The larger the composite D, the closer the results are to satisfying the Y's goals.

Weight

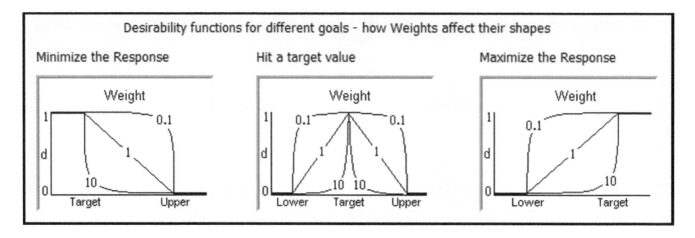

The Weight value tells Minitab how to calculate the individual d value.

- .1 places more emphasis on the lower or upper values. (The d value increases rapidly once the lower or upper limits are crossed.)
- 1 gives equal emphasis to all values. (The d value increase linearly from the upper or lower threshold to the target value.)
- 10 places more emphasis on the target. (The d value remains small until the value approaches the target.)

Importance

The Importance value is a relative number indicating the importance of the multiple outputs to one another. The values range from .1 to 10; Y's with equal values have equal importance. The scale allows one Y to be up to 100 times as important as another. (.1 versus 10).

Minitab calculates the composite D value by using the individual d's and each Y's importance value.

Click **OK** in the Response Optimizer window when complete.

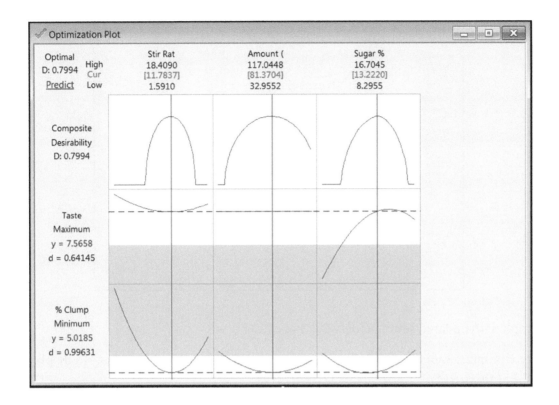

The Optimizer produces a local (but not necessarily global) solution. Inputs can be varied to obtain a more desirable output. One method of doing this is to manually change the values of X's.

Click the red **Cur** value under the factor to change (for **Stir Rat** this is the value 11.7837).

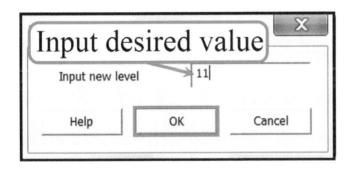

Change to the desired value and click **OK**.

The red line moves to the new value and new outputs are shown.

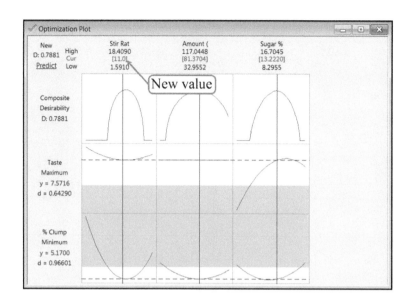

This is the graph with updated settings (new Stir Rat of 11).

The Response Optimizer tool bar allows the user to return to the original settings. To display the toolbar, select ***Tools > Toolbars > Response Optimizer***.

Click the Star icon in the Response Optimizer tool bar to return to the original condition.

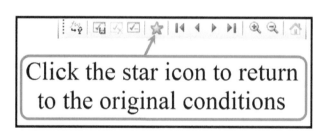

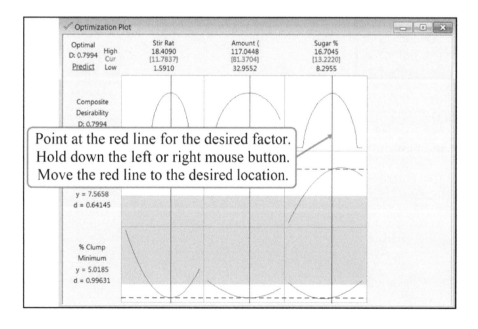

Another method for changing settings is to point at one of the red lines, hold down the left or right mouse button, and move to the new condition. Minitab then updates values based on the final settings of the inputs.

Planning Experiments

The critical step to achieving a successful result is proper planning for a Designed Experiment. Such planning should include discussion of the following:
- Outputs to be measured
- Factors to be investigated
- Design type
- Potential need for blocking
- Potential issues with training
- Potential issues with data collection

All of these issues should be thoroughly discussed and decisions finalized before proceeding to execution of the experiment.

Assuming planning and execution are properly conducted, it is still necessary to confirm results; this involves execution of confirmatory runs at conditions within the design space, but not necessarily at the axial or corner points. If the model does a good job of predicting results, then the model can be used. If it does not, then further experimentation is required.

Modifying Designs

Modify Factors: When using Minitab to create and analyze a designed experiment, it is important to understand the proper procedure for changing existing settings. For instance, if it is necessary to change a factor setting, don't simply change the values on the worksheet; this will create issues with the analysis.

Instead, follow the proper method as described here.

Minitab Project: Changing Designs

Minitab worksheet: *Modify1*

Menu command: *Stat > DOE > Modify Design*

C1	C2	C3	C4	C5	C6	C7	C8	C9-T
StdOrder	RunOrder	CenterPt	Blocks	A	B	C	D	E
11	1	0	1	15	925	10	70	Old
9	2	0	1	15	925	10	70	Old
7	3	1	1	10	1000	15	60	Old
5	4	1	1	10	850	15	80	Old
6	5	1	1	20	850	15	60	New
10	6	0	1	15	925	10	70	New
8	7	1	1	20	1000	15	80	New
12	8	0	1	15	925	10	70	New
1	9	1	1	10	850	5	80	New
2	10	1	1	20	850	5	60	Old
4	11	1	1	20	1000	5	80	Old
3	12	1	1	10	1000	5	60	New

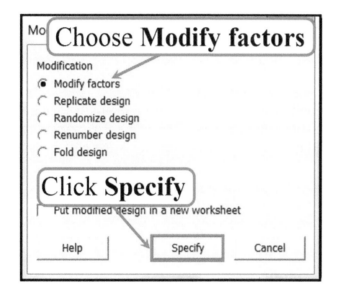

Select **Modify factors**.

Click **Specify**.

Change factor B's low level to 85 and it's high level to 100.

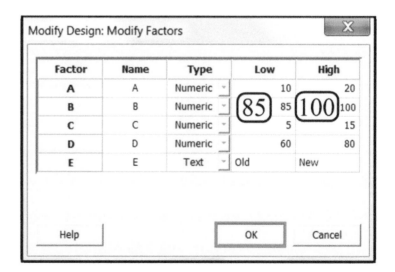

C1	C2	C3	C4	C5	C6	C7	C8	C9-T
StdOrder	RunOrder	CenterPt	Blocks	A	B	C	D	E
11	1	0	1	15	92.5	10	70	Old
9	2	0	1	15	92.5	10	70	Old
7	3	1	1	10	100.0	15	60	Old
5	4	1	1	10	85.0	15	80	Old
6	5	1	1	20	85.0	15	60	New
10	6	0	1	15	92.5	10	70	New
8	7	1	1	20	100.0	15	80	New
12	8	0	1	15	92.5	10	70	New
1	9	1	1	10	85.0	5	80	New
2	10	1	1	20	85.0	5	60	Old
4	11	1	1	20	100.0	5	80	Old
3	12	1	1	10	100.0	5	60	New

Notice that the Center Points automatically change to 92.5.

Minitab allows modification of the **Name, Low,** and **High** settings. The **Type** cannot be modified.

Replicate Design

The Modify Design tool allows for the addition of one or more replicates to the design.

Minitab Project: **Changing Designs**

Minitab worksheet: *Replicate*

C1	C2	C3	C4	C5	C6	C7	C8
StdOrder	RunOrder	CenterPt	Blocks	A	B	C	D
9	1	0	1	15	925	10	137.5
1	2	1	1	10	850	5	125.0
2	3	1	1	20	850	5	150.0
3	4	1	1	10	1000	5	150.0
6	5	1	1	20	850	15	125.0
11	6	0	1	15	925	10	137.5
10	7	0	1	15	925	10	137.5
5	8	1	1	10	850	15	150.0
7	9	1	1	10	1000	15	125.0
8	10	1	1	20	1000	15	150.0
4	11	1	1	20	1000	5	125.0

Menu command: *Stat > DOE > Modify Design*

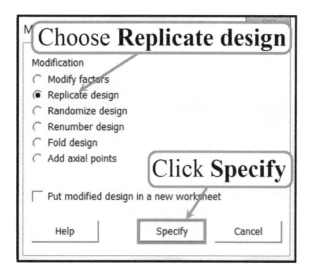

Select **Replicate design**.

Click **Specify**.

Select the number of replicates. For this example select one additional replicate.

Click **OK**.

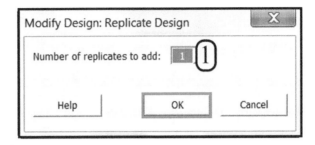

The design is then copied and added below the first replicate, as shown here:

StdOrder	RunOrder	CenterPt	Blocks	A	B	C	D
9	1	0	1	15	925	10	137.5
1	2	1	1	10	850	5	125.0
2	3	1	1	20	850	5	150.0
3	4	1	1	10	1000	5	150.0
6	5	1	1	20	850	15	125.0
11	6	0	1	15	925	10	137.5
10	7	0	1	15	925	10	137.5
5	8	1	1	10	850	15	150.0
7	9	1	1	10	1000	15	125.0
8	10	1	1	20	1000	15	150.0
4	11	1	1	20	1000	5	125.0
20	12	0	2	15	925	10	137.5
12	13	1	2	10	850	5	125.0
13	14	1	2	20	850	5	150.0
14	15	1	2	10	1000	5	150.0
17	16	1	2	20	850	15	125.0
22	17	0	2	15	925	10	137.5
21	18	0	2	15	925	10	137.5
16	19	1	2	10	850	15	150.0
18	20	1	2	10	1000	15	125.0
19	21	1	2	20	1000	15	150.0
15	22	1	2	20	1000	5	125.0

Notice the second replicate is added as a second block.

With multiple replicates, Minitab adds each replicate as a separate block.

Adding Runs to an Existing Design

With some experiments, simply adding additional replicates will not resolve existing issues. For instance, to move from a linear model to a quadratic model, replicates will not provide the required runs. Another situation arises with confounding issues in a Fractional Factorial design.

Foldover

Certain confounding issues can be resolved by performing a foldover of an existing design.

Worksheet: *Foldover*

C1	C2	C3	C4	C5	C6	C7	C8	C9
StdOrder	RunOrder	CenterPt	Blocks	A	B	C	D	E
8	1	1	1	20	1000	15	150	90
7	2	1	1	10	1000	15	125	45
3	3	1	1	10	1000	5	125	90
5	4	1	1	10	850	15	150	45
4	5	1	1	20	1000	5	150	45
2	6	1	1	20	850	5	125	45
1	7	1	1	10	850	5	150	90
6	8	1	1	20	850	15	125	90

This example is a 5 factor 8 run resolution III design. The confounding (alias) pattern is:

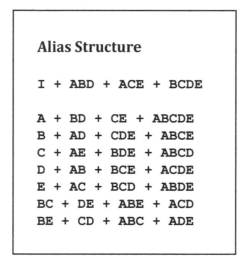

```
Alias Structure

I + ABD + ACE + BCDE

A + BD + CE + ABCDE
B + AD + CDE + ABCE
C + AE + BDE + ABCD
D + AB + BCE + ACDE
E + AC + BCD + ABDE
BC + DE + ABE + ACD
BE + CD + ABC + ADE
```

The Resolution III designs have Main Factors confounded with 2 factor interactions.

To perform the foldover:

Menu command: *Stat > DOE > Modify Design*

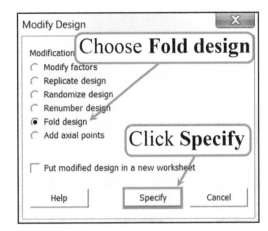

Select **Fold design**.

Click **Specify**.

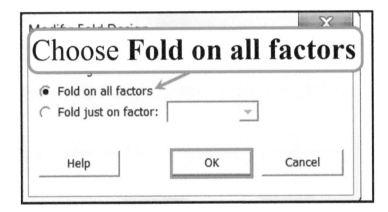

Select **Fold on all factors**.

Click **OK**.

Folding on all factors will change a Resolution III to a Resolution IV; however, it will not change a Resolution IV to a Resolution V design.

Here is the folded worksheet:

C1	C2	C3	C4	C5	C6	C7	C8	C9
StdOrder	RunOrder	CenterPt	Blocks	A	B	C	D	E
8	1	1	1	20	1000	15	150	90
7	2	1	1	10	1000	15	125	45
3	3	1	1	10	1000	5	125	90
5	4	1	1	10	850	15	150	45
4	5	1	1	20	1000	5	150	45
2	6	1	1	20	850	5	125	45
1	7	1	1	10	850	5	150	90
6	8	1	1	20	850	15	125	90
16	9	1	2	10	850	5	125	45
15	10	1	2	20	850	5	150	90
11	11	1	2	20	850	15	150	45
13	12	1	2	20	1000	5	125	90
12	13	1	2	10	850	15	125	90
10	14	1	2	10	1000	15	150	90
9	15	1	2	20	1000	15	125	45
14	16	1	2	10	1000	5	150	45

The new confounding (alias) structure is:

```
Aliases

I + BCDE
Block 1 + ABD + ACE
Block 2 - ABD - ACE
Block 3 - ABD - ACE
A + ABCDE
B + CDE
C + BDE
D + BCE
E + BCD
BC + DE
BE + CD
```

Notice the Main factors are no longer confounded with 2 factor interactions.

Some 2 factor interactions are still confounded with other 2 factor interactions. This is a Resolution IV design.

Folding on just one factor will produce independent estimates for the main factor as well as all of the interactions associated with that factor.

Add Axial Points

The next situation occurs if the Center Points are significant for a factorial design. The significant Center Points indicate curvature, but it does not indicate which factor or factors are causing the curvature. To determine which factor(s) cause the curvature, additional experimental points are required.

Project: **Changing Designs**

Worksheet: *Axial*

C1 StdOrder	C2 RunOrder	C3 CenterPt	C4 Blocks	C5 A	C6 B	C7 C	C8 Results
8	1	1	1	20	1000	15	49
4	2	1	1	20	1000	5	52
1	3	1	1	10	850	5	48
5	4	1	1	10	850	15	45
9	5	0	1	15	925	10	55
2	6	1	1	20	850	5	50
10	7	0	1	15	925	10	56
7	8	1	1	10	1000	15	44
6	9	1	1	20	850	15	48
3	10	1	1	10	1000	5	47
11	11	0	1	15	925	10	58

Analysis shows the Center Point (Ct Pt) is significant.

This indicates curvature exists in the response, but does not indicate which X is causing the curvature.

Additional runs are required to resolve the issue of curvature.

```
Coded Coefficients

Term        Effect     Coef   SE Coef   T-Value   P-Value
Constant             47.875    0.540     88.65     0.000
A            3.750    1.875    0.540      3.47     0.074
B            0.250    0.125    0.540      0.23     0.838
C           -2.750   -1.375    0.540     -2.55     0.126
A*B          1.250    0.625    0.540      1.16     0.367
A*C          0.250    0.125    0.540      0.23     0.838
B*C         -0.250   -0.125    0.540     -0.23     0.838
A*B*C       -0.250   -0.125    0.540     -0.23     0.838
Ct Pt                          8.46      1.03      8.18     0.015
```

The new runs will create a design that contains more than 2 levels for each continuous factor.

Menu command: *Stat > DOE > Modify Design*

Select **Add axial points**.

Click **Specify**.

Select **Default (rotatable if possible)**.

Add 3 center points.

Click **OK**.

The default places the axial points outside the factorial experimental space. Selecting 'Face Centered' places the axial points on the face surfaces of the design cube.

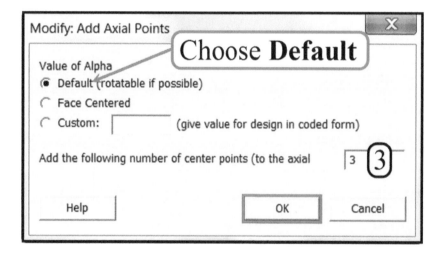

The custom option allows the axial points to be placed either inside or outside the current design space.

Including Center Points is important to assist in calculation of a block effect.

The axial points are run as a second block.

C1	C2	C3	C4	C5	C6	C7	C8
StdOrder	RunOrder	CenterPt	Blocks	A	B	C	Results
8	1	1	1	20.0000	1000.00	15.0000	49
4	2	1	1	20.0000	1000.00	5.0000	52
1	3	1	1	10.0000	850.00	5.0000	48
5	4	1	1	10.0000	850.00	15.0000	45
9	5	0	1	15.0000	925.00	10.0000	55
2	6	1	1	20.0000	850.00	5.0000	50
10	7	0	1	15.0000	925.00	10.0000	56
7	8	1	1	10.0000	1000.00	15.0000	44
6	9	1	1	20.0000	850.00	15.0000	48
3	10	1	1	10.0000	1000.00	5.0000	47
11	11	0	1	15.0000	925.00	10.0000	58
12	12	-1	2	6.5910	925.00	10.0000	
13	13	-1	2	23.4090	925.00	10.0000	
14	14	-1	2	15.0000	798.87	10.0000	
15	15	-1	2	15.0000	1051.13	10.0000	
16	16	-1	2	15.0000	925.00	1.5910	
17	17	-1	2	15.0000	925.00	18.4090	
18	18	0	2	15.0000	925.00	10.0000	
19	19	0	2	15.0000	925.00	10.0000	
20	20	0	2	15.0000	925.00	10.0000	

Next, complete the second block (the axial points and corresponding center points) and redo the analysis using *Stat > DOE > Response Surface > Analyze Response Surface Design*.

Defining Custom Designs

Minitab allows the use of worksheets from other programs. The program will open and analyze them. This is a useful feature because there are situations when it is necessary to analyze a designed experiment that was not created using Minitab. In some situations, however, Minitab cannot analyze the worksheet through the *Stat > DOE* procedure because it does not recognize the worksheet as a designed experiment. This situation can be resolved with the following procedure.

Menu command: (for Response Surface designs)

Stat > DOE > Response Surface > Define Custom Response Surface Design

Menu command: (for Factorial designs).

Stat > DOE > Factorial > Define Custom Factorial Design

The following demonstration uses a factorial design.

Assume a full factorial experiment with 2 blocks 3 factors and 2 replicates; it was created using Excel and an Excel spreadsheet contains both the experimental factor settings and the response.

To analyze this experiment in Minitab, perform the following steps.

Opening an Excel spreadsheet in Minitab

Worksheet: (Excel spreadsheet):   *Custom*

Menu command: *File > Open worksheet*

Under '**Look in:**' Select the directory with the Excel spreadsheet.

For Files of Type select **Excel (*.xls)**.

For File name select **Custom**.

Click the **Options** button.

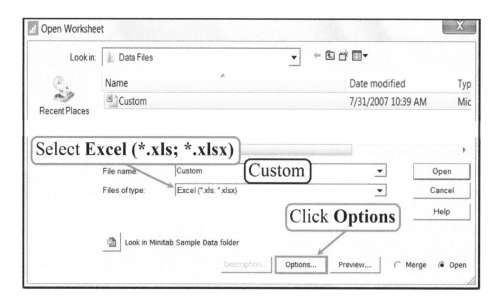

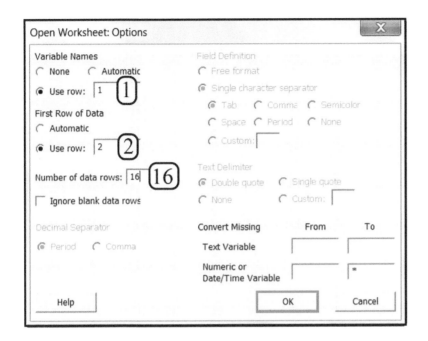

Row 1 of the Excel spreadsheet contains Variable names.

The first row of data in the spreadsheet is row 2 and the spreadsheet contains 16 rows of data.

The **Automatic** option for Variable Names and First Row of Data defaults to the settings shown. The Use Row option is available for those situations where the Variable Names are not in row 1, and/or the First Row of Data is not row 2.

Click OK, then click Preview.

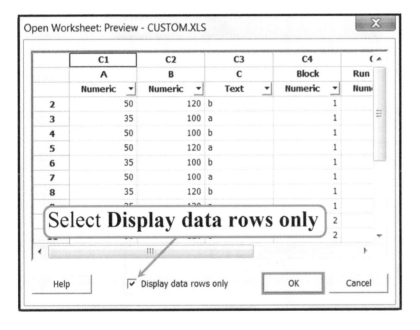

Select the option 'Display data rows only'.

Click **OK**.

In the Open Worksheet window, click the **Open** button.

Below is the Excel spreadsheet opened in Minitab.

C1	C2	C3-T	C4	C5	C6
A	B	C	Block	Run Order	Result
50	120	b	1	1	76
35	100	a	1	2	67
50	100	b	1	3	56
50	120	a	1	4	78
35	100	b	1	5	74
50	100	a	1	6	66
35	120	b	1	7	66
35	120	a	1	8	65
35	100	a	2	9	56
50	120	b	2	10	66
50	120	a	2	11	56
35	100	b	2	12	77
35	120	b	2	13	56
50	100	b	2	14	76
35	120	a	2	15	74
50	100	a	2	16	77

Trying to analyze the worksheet as a factorial design creates the following error:

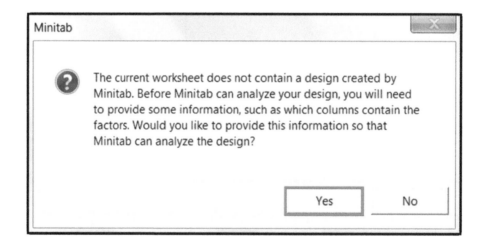

Click **YES**.

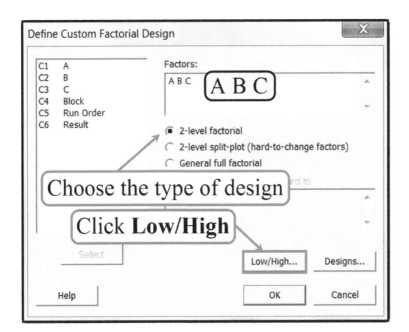

Input the factors (**A B C**).

Select the type of design. This is a 2-level Factorial.

Click **Low/High**.

Input the **Low** and **High** values.

This worksheet is in the uncoded condition, so select the 'Uncoded' radial button.

Click **OK** then click **Designs**.

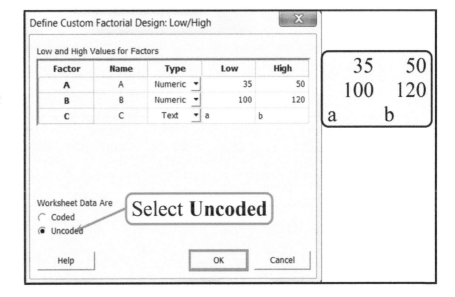

The worksheet does not provide information on the Standard Order, so select 'Order of the data'.

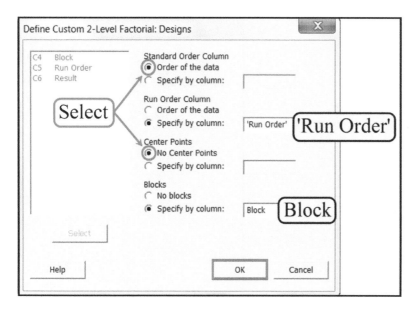

The worksheet contains a column designating the run order, so select 'Specify by Column' and input Run Order.

The worksheet contains no column for Center Points so select 'No Center Points'.

Finally, the worksheet has a column for Blocks; select 'Specify by column' and input **Block**.

Click **OK** (twice).

Analyze the design as previously shown.

Before proceeding to the analysis, check the worksheet to be sure everything is in order.

The final worksheet is shown below:

C1	C2	C3-T	C4	C5	C6	C7	C8
A	B	C	Block	Run Order	Result	StdOrder	CenterPt
50	120	b	1	1	76	1	1
35	100	a	1	2	67	2	1
50	100	b	1	3	56	3	1
50	120	a	1	4	78	4	1
35	100	b	1	5	74	5	1
50	100	a	1	6	66	6	1
35	120	b	1	7	66	7	1
35	120	a	1	8	65	8	1
35	100	a	2	9	56	9	1
50	120	b	2	10	66	10	1
50	120	a	2	11	56	11	1
35	100	b	2	12	77	12	1
35	120	b	2	13	56	13	1
50	100	b	2	14	76	14	1
35	120	a	2	15	74	15	1
50	100	a	2	16	77	16	1

A second method to create a custom design is to define the design before attempting analysis. Start with the original Excel design and open it in a new window.

Menu command:

Stat > DOE > Factorial > Define Custom Factorial Design.

The Define Custom Factorial Designs window opens; proceed in the same manner as previously shown.

Custom Response Surface Designs

The inputs for a Custom Response Surface Design are slightly different than those listed above for Factorial Designs. These differences are shown in the next example.

Worksheet: *Custom Response Surface*

This worksheet contains the necessary runs to be considered a Response Surface Design, but does not have all of the required columns.

C1	C2	C3	C4	C5	C6
RunOrder	Blocks	A	B	C	Results
1	1	45.00	120.00	10.00	128
2	1	58.41	135.00	9.00	126
3	1	50.00	135.00	10.68	128
4	1	55.00	150.00	8.00	124
5	1	41.59	135.00	9.00	127
6	1	55.00	150.00	10.00	132
7	1	55.00	120.00	8.00	132
8	1	50.00	160.23	9.00	126
9	1	50.00	135.00	9.00	131
10	1	50.00	135.00	9.00	121
11	1	45.00	150.00	8.00	163
12	1	45.00	150.00	10.00	134
13	1	50.00	109.77	9.00	130
14	1	50.00	135.00	9.00	131
15	1	50.00	135.00	9.00	133
16	1	50.00	135.00	9.00	114
17	1	45.00	120.00	8.00	111
18	1	50.00	135.00	7.32	121
19	1	55.00	120.00	10.00	126
20	1	50.00	135.00	9.00	139

Menu command:

Stat > DOE > Response Surface > Define Custom Response Surface Design.

Input the factors (**A B C**).

Click the **Low/High** button.

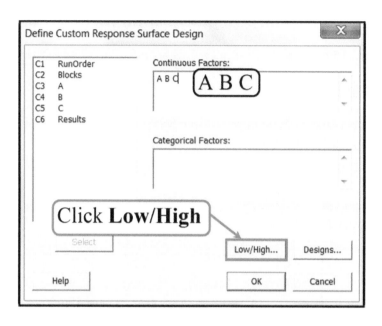

Notice the strange numbers for the high and low; these are the axial points in the design. The correct values should be the cube or factorial high and low values.

The high and low values for the factorial points are:

- A: 45 and 55
- B: 120 and 150
- C: 8 and 10

Obtain this information from the person who created the design.

Input the correct values for the Low and High values.

Updated Low/High screen:

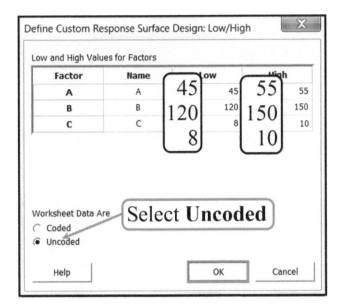

Select the **Uncoded** option for the Worksheet Data.

Click **OK**.

In the Define Custom Response Surface window, click the **Design** button.

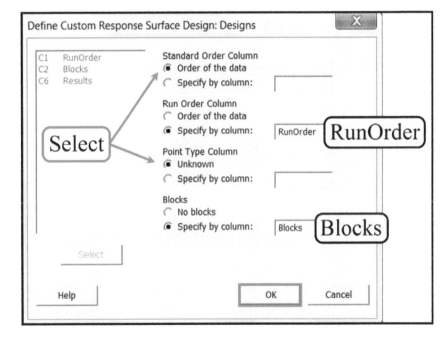

No Standard Order of data exists, so select 'Order of the data'.

A column for Run order does exist, so select '**RunOrder**'.

The Point Type Column is **unknown**

For the column specifying Blocks, select **Blocks**.

Click **OK** (twice).

Here the two requested columns (Standard Order (StdOrder) and Point Type (PtType)) have been added to the worksheet.

C1	C2	C3	C4	C5	C6	C7	C8
RunOrder	Blocks	A	B	C	Results	StdOrder	PtType
1	1	45.00	120.00	10.00	128	1	1
2	1	58.41	135.00	9.00	126	2	1
3	1	50.00	135.00	10.68	128	3	1
4	1	55.00	150.00	8.00	124	4	1
5	1	41.59	135.00	9.00	127	5	1
6	1	55.00	150.00	10.00	132	6	1
7	1	55.00	120.00	8.00	132	7	1
8	1	50.00	160.23	9.00	126	8	1
9	1	50.00	135.00	9.00	131	9	1
10	1	50.00	135.00	9.00	121	10	1
11	1	45.00	150.00	8.00	163	11	1
12	1	45.00	150.00	10.00	134	12	1
13	1	50.00	109.77	9.00	130	13	1
14	1	50.00	135.00	9.00	131	14	1
15	1	50.00	135.00	9.00	133	15	1
16	1	50.00	135.00	9.00	114	16	1
17	1	45.00	120.00	8.00	111	17	1
18	1	50.00	135.00	7.32	121	18	1
19	1	55.00	120.00	10.00	126	19	1
20	1	50.00	135.00	9.00	139	20	1

To refine the worksheet further, the factorial points have a PtType equal to 1, the Center Points have a PtType of 0, and the axial points have a PtType equal to -1.

The PtTypes for each row will be easier to determine if the worksheet is displayed in Coded units. The change to Coded units is accomplished via the Display Design option.

Display Designs

Minitab allows the experimental worksheet to be displayed in either the coded or uncoded view. The uncoded view is simply the actual settings for factors, while the coded view displays the low factorial point as a -1 and the high factorial value as a +1. The other values are scaled appropriately.

To change the view, select:

Menu command: *Stat > DOE > Display Design.*

Select **Coded units** as the Units for factors.

Click **OK**.

The worksheet's values for A, B and C have now changed.

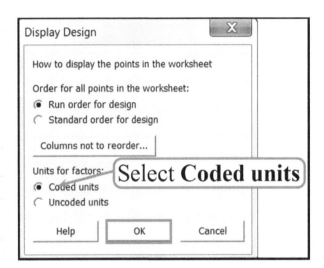

C1	C2	C3	C4	C5	C6	C7	C8
RunOrder	Blocks	A	B	C	Results	StdOrder	PtType
1	1	-1.00	-1.00	1.00	128	1	1
2	1	1.68	0.00	0.00	126	2	1
3	1	0.00	0.00	1.68	128	3	1
4	1	1.00	1.00	-1.00	124	4	1
5	1	-1.68	0.00	0.00	127	5	1
6	1	1.00	1.00	1.00	132	6	1
7	1	1.00	-1.00	-1.00	132	7	1
8	1	0.00	1.68	0.00	126	8	1
9	1	0.00	0.00	0.00	131	9	1
10	1	0.00	0.00	0.00	121	10	1
11	1	-1.00	1.00	-1.00	163	11	1
12	1	-1.00	1.00	1.00	134	12	1
13	1	0.00	-1.68	0.00	130	13	1
14	1	0.00	0.00	0.00	131	14	1
15	1	0.00	0.00	0.00	133	15	1
16	1	0.00	0.00	0.00	114	16	1
17	1	-1.00	-1.00	-1.00	111	17	1
18	1	0.00	0.00	-1.68	121	18	1
19	1	1.00	-1.00	1.00	126	19	1
20	1	0.00	0.00	0.00	139	20	1

The columns with all zeros are the Center Points; change the PtType for these rows to 0.

The rows with all 1's (either +1 or -1) are the factorial points; leave the PtType column at +1.

The rows with 2 zeros and a value larger than either 1 or -1 are the axial points; change the PtType to a -1.

Here is the updated worksheet, noting the new values in the PtType column:

C1	C2	C3	C4	C5	C6	C7	C8
RunOrder	Blocks	A	B	C	Results	StdOrder	PtType
1	1	-1.00	-1.00	1.00	128	1	1
2	1	1.68	0.00	0.00	126	2	-1
3	1	0.00	0.00	1.68	128	3	-1
4	1	1.00	1.00	-1.00	124	4	1
5	1	-1.68	0.00	0.00	127	5	-1
6	1	1.00	1.00	1.00	132	6	1
7	1	1.00	-1.00	-1.00	132	7	1
8	1	0.00	1.68	0.00	126	8	-1
9	1	0.00	0.00	0.00	131	9	0
10	1	0.00	0.00	0.00	121	10	0
11	1	-1.00	1.00	-1.00	163	11	1
12	1	-1.00	1.00	1.00	134	12	1
13	1	0.00	-1.68	0.00	130	13	-1
14	1	0.00	0.00	0.00	131	14	0
15	1	0.00	0.00	0.00	133	15	0
16	1	0.00	0.00	0.00	114	16	0
17	1	-1.00	-1.00	-1.00	111	17	1
18	1	0.00	0.00	-1.68	121	18	-1
19	1	1.00	-1.00	1.00	126	19	1
20	1	0.00	0.00	0.00	139	20	0

To change back to actual factor values, repeat the Display Design menu selections and click the **Uncoded units** option.

Analyze the worksheet as previously shown.

Conclusion

The Improve phase uses both graphical and analytical tools to determine the relationship between critical X's and Y's. This provides the necessary information to shift the team's emphasis from controlling the Y's to controlling the X's.

Control Phase

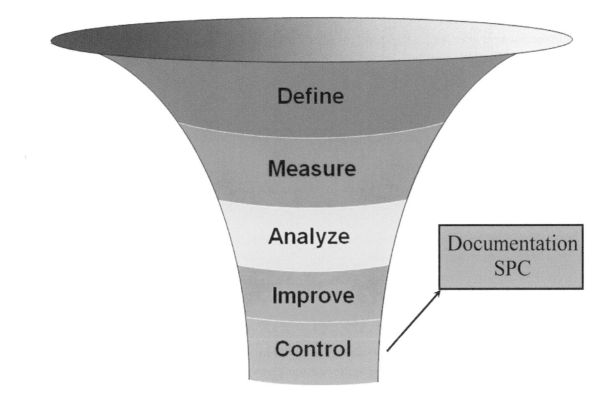

Control Phase

The Control phase of a Six Sigma process is the last step, but is by no means any less important than any of the others. In fact, it is the critical step necessary to ensure improvements achieved throughout the process are maintained over the long-term. Without an effective Control phase, the process will lose any gains made and inevitably slip back to the initial baseline condition.

Tools And Outcomes

During the Control phase teams set up the control charts and tools necessary for proper Statistical Process Control (SPC). A few examples include:

- I-MR Chart
- Xbar R/Xbar S Chart
- P Chart
- NP Chart
- C Chart
- U Chart
- Process Capability – Non Normal Data
- Distribution Curves

All of these tools are designed to set up and/or monitor the processes and procedures necessary to maintain a process in its new and improved condition.

Statistical Process Control (SPC)

Statistical Process Control (SPC) was first introduced in the Measure chapter. At that point in the Six Sigma process, SPC is used as a diagnostic procedure to determine if a process is running in a controlled condition. A controlled condition is defined as having a constant mean and a standard deviation. In the Control phase SPC is used to determine if a process is running in a controlled condition and as a predictive tool.

When setting up control charts, it is important for samples and data to reflect the process in its new, improved condition. Never use data from the old process condition because it will contaminate the control chart findings.

Another common mistake occurs when control charts are constantly recalculated and updated using the most recent data available, rather than the new baseline data collected when the improved process was first stabilized. If the control limits are continually updated using new data, there is a risk of missing key signs of subtle changes in either the mean or the standard deviation.

The best approach is to collect 25 to 30 samples from the process once it is improved and stabilized, and then use that data to calculate control limits. From that point forward, all efforts focus on maintaining the process within those limits. The only time to recalculate control limits is when a change occurs in the process itself.

The examples presented in this chapter all assume the process in question is improved and stable. The overall concepts discussed are applicable to any type of control chart.

Project: **SPC Control**

Worksheet: *Cycle Time*

In an earlier section it was demonstrated how to construct and analyze an SPC chart. In this section, it will be shown how to set the Control Limits while constructing SPC charts.

Menu command: *Stat > Control Charts > Variables Charts for Individuals > I-MR*

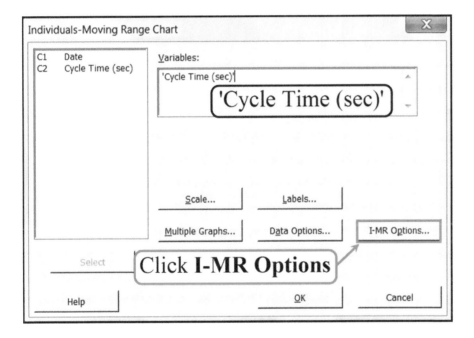

Select **Cycle Time (sec)** as the variable.

Click the **I-MR Options** button.

Click the **Storage** button.

Select both the Mean and Standard Deviation button.

Click **Tests**

Select **Perform all tests for special causes**.

Click **OK**.

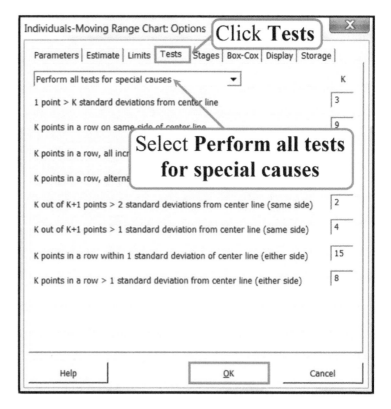

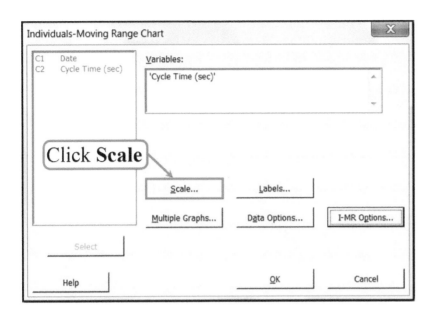

Click the **Scale** button.

Click **Time**.

The stamp column will become
the X-axis tic marks.

Select the **Stamp** button and choose
Date as the Stamp column.

Click **OK** (twice).

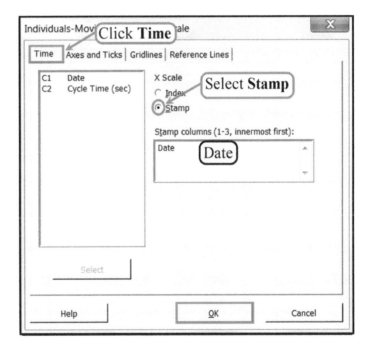

The resulting graph shows a process that is in-control.

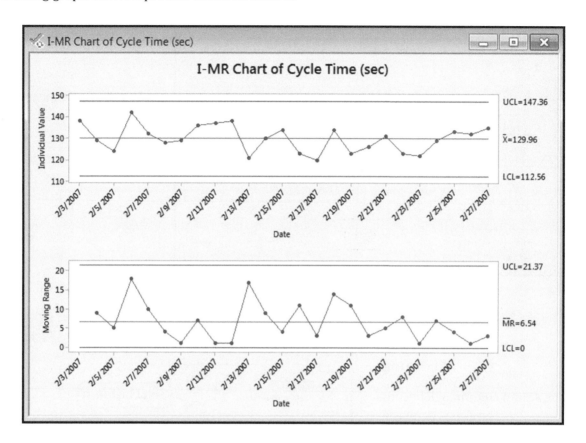

C1-D	C2	C3	C4
Date	Cycle Time (sec)	MEAN1	STDE1
2/3/2007	138	129.96	5.79935
2/4/2007	129		
2/5/2007	124		
2/6/2007	142		
2/7/2007	132		
2/8/2007	128		
2/9/2007	129		

The requested storage of the Mean and Standard Deviation appear in the worksheet. This information will be used to create future control charts.

As the process owner continues to monitor and assess the process, they look for changes in the mean or standard deviation. This is accomplished by comparing future data to the stored Mean and Standard Deviation calculated when the process was determined to be improved and stable.

Worksheet: *Cycle Time 2*

This worksheet contains the initial 25 data points plus 20 additional data points, for a total of 45 points. By simply requesting an I-MR chart, the Mean, UCL (Upper Control Limit) and LCL (Lower Control Limit) will change. Instead, use the stored information to construct the chart.

Menu command:

Stat > Control Charts > Control Charts for Individuals > I MR.

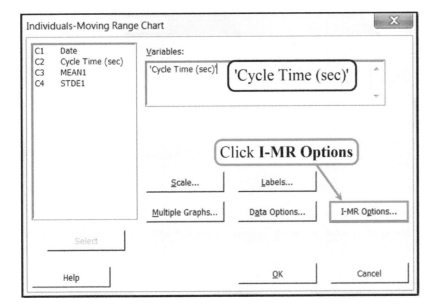

Select **Cycle Time (sec)** as the variable.

Click the **I-MR Options** button.

Select the **Parameters** tab.

Input the Mean and Standard Deviation from the worksheet (Cycle Time).

The values of **130** and **5.8** are rounded from the actual values for convenience.

Click **OK**.

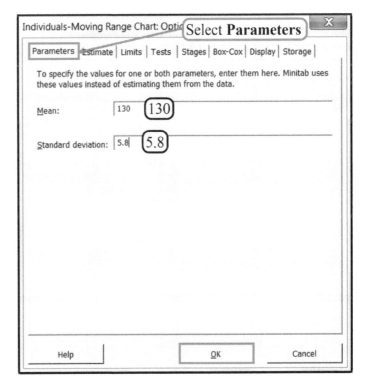

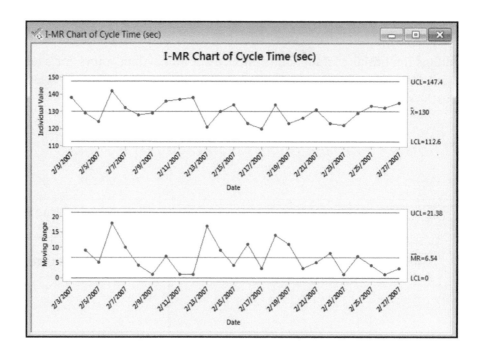

The resulting graph shows the new data with the established Mean and Control Limits.

There is an Out-of-Control condition (9 points in a row above the Center Line) at point 31 (3/5/07). This finding would not be apparent if all the data (new and old) were used to calculate the Mean and Standard Deviation.

X Bar R Chart

If output data is collected as a series of subgroups (more than one item at a time) the appropriate chart to determine stability is the Xbar – R or Xbar – S.

Worksheet: *Xbar - Example*

Menu command:

Stat > Control Charts > Variables Charts for Subgroups >

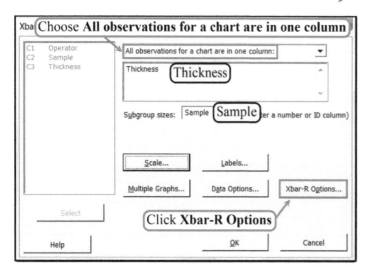

Xbar-R

Choose 'All observations for a chart are in one column.'

Input **Thickness** for the graph variable.

Select **Sample** for the Subgroup sizes.

Click **Xbar-R Options**.

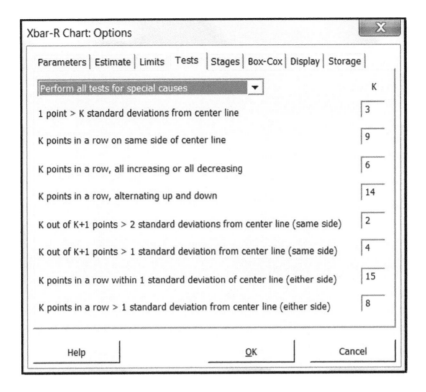

The Test and Estimate tabs will produce the same options as found in the I-MR chart.

Click the **Estimate** tab.

Select the **Rbar** option for the Method for estimating standard deviation.

Click **OK** (twice).

Just as with an I-MR chart, any issues with special causes should be investigated.

In this graph the last 7 points are above the mean.

This does not violate the official rule of 9 or more points on one side of the mean, but it is suspect.

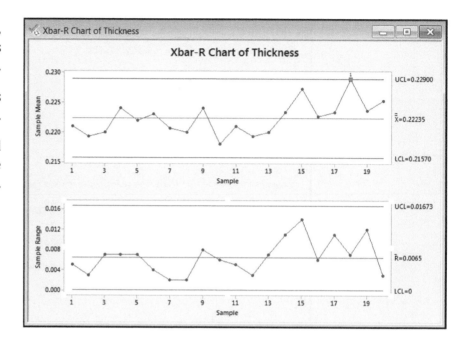

Observing the worksheet, notice that the first ten subgroups were measured by one operator and the next ten were measured by a different operator. It might be interesting to see the differences between the operators. Minitab will create side-by-side graphs displaying information from each operator.

Return to the **Xbar-R Options** screen.

Select the **Stages** tab.

Select **Operator** as the Define stages option.

Click **OK** (twice).

Now each stage is displayed with its associated control limits. This type of graph is useful to answer questions such as, "Are differences seen in the output related to operators?"

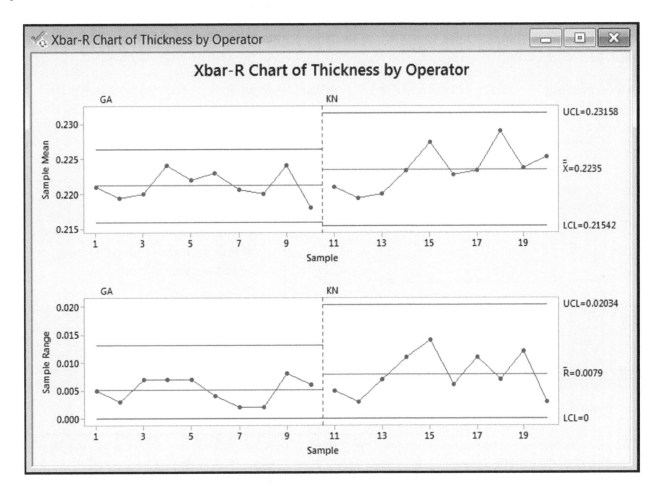

X Bar S Chart

The Xbar S is an alternative to the Xbar – R. In the Xbar S, the standard deviation is estimated using the subgroups average standard deviation. The remaining aspects of the chart remain unchanged.

Menu command: *Stat > Control Charts > Variables Charts for Subgroups >*
Xbar-S

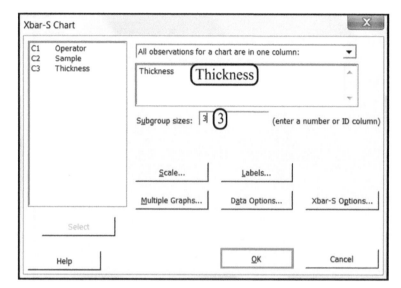

Input **Thickness** as the variable and select **3** as the Subgroup size.

The Subgroup sizes input can be either a number or a column containing the sample size information.

Click **OK**.

The Xbar-S options are the same as the Xbar-R or I-MR options.

The results look the same, only the lower chart is now measuring the standard deviation of the subgroups, not the range.

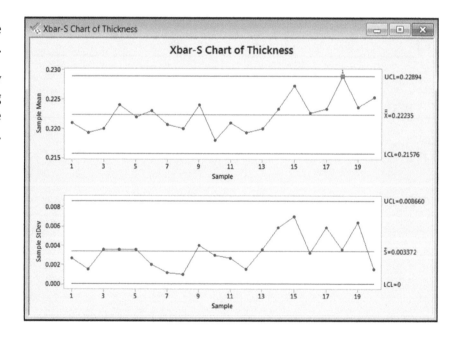

When is it appropriate to use the Xbar – R versus the Xbar – S? It really depends on the specific circumstances. Six Sigma references claim the Range calculation is efficient up to a sample size of 7, and recommend using the Standard Deviation calculation with sample sizes larger than 7.

Control Charts for Attribute Data

Attribute data is generally measured in terms of Defects or Defectives. For Defects, use the C or U chart; for Defectives, use the P or NP chart.

P Chart

This chart plots the samples percent defective, which is used as an estimate of the population's percent defective.

Minitab Project: **SPC BB**

Worksheet: *p Chart*

Menu command: *Stat > Control Charts > Attributes Charts > P*

Input **Number** and **Subgroup.**

Click the **P Chart Options** button.

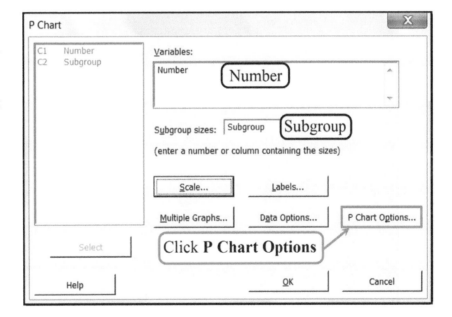

Click the Tests tab.

Select **Perform all tests for special causes**.

Notice there are only 4 tests available for the attribute charts.

The Test criteria can be changed using this screen.

Make the desired changes and click **OK** (twice).

The different control limits are the result of changes in sample sizes.

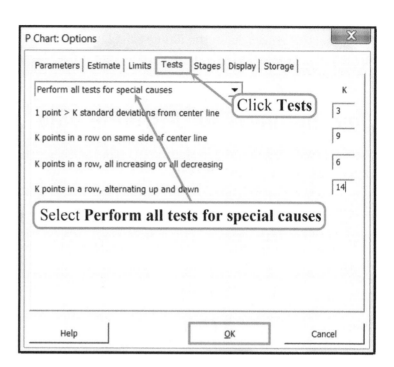

Analyze this chart in the same manner as previous charts.

Check the Out-of-Control points for special causes.

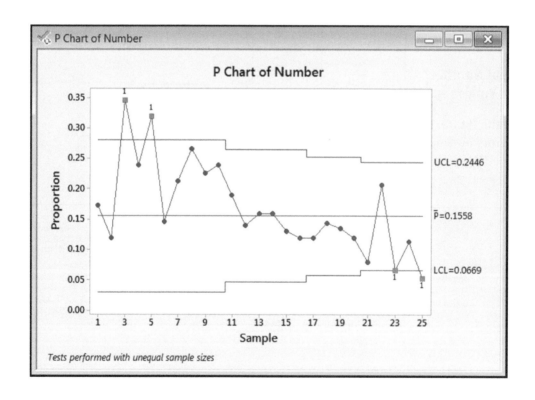

NP Chart

The NP Chart mimics the P Chart; however, with the NP Chart the number of defectives rather than the proportion defective are plotted. Thus, it is simply the P chart multiplied by the sample size N.

Worksheet: *np Chart.*

Menu command:
Stat > Control Charts > Attributes Charts > NP

Input **Errors** as the Variables and **62** for the subgroup sizes. This process looks at 62 items and determines the number of defectives.

The NPChart Options is the same as the p Chart options.

Click **OK**.

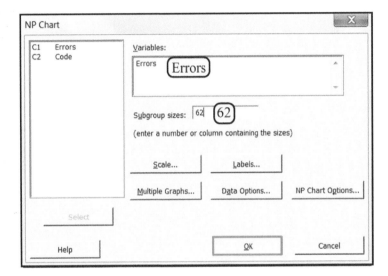

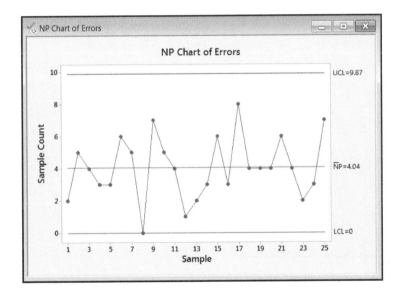

This chart shows the expected number of defectives from a sample of size 62, (4.04).

Anything below 9.87 defectives (upper control limit) can be considered from a stable process with an average number defective items of 4.04.

While Minitab allows the NP chart to be created with varying sample sizes, it is not recommended. Using varying sample sizes results in a chart with varying control limits as well as varying mean values. This makes it difficult to determine the number of defects to expect for a specific sample size.

C Chart

Use the C Chart to monitor the number of defects found in a sample.

Worksheet: *C chart.*

Menu command:
Stat > Control Charts > Attributes Charts > C

Input **Errors** as the variable. The C Chart Options button is similar to the other attribute charts.

Click **OK**.

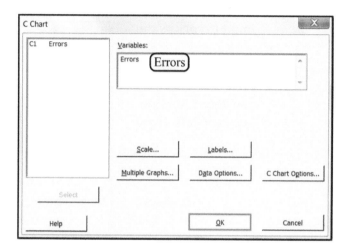

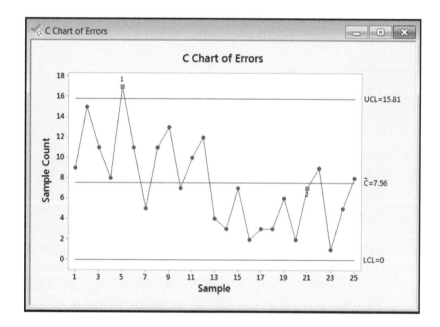

Notice the two out of control conditions at points 5 and 21. These points should be investigated.

U Chart

The U Chart also measures defects, but as defects per unit.

Worksheet: *u Chart.*

Menu command:

Stat > Control Charts > Attributes Charts > U

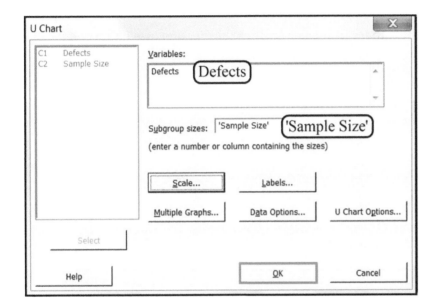

Input **Defects** as the variable.

Select **'Sample Size'** for the Subgroup sizes.

Click **OK.**

Once again, the control limits vary depending upon the sample sizes.

The larger the sample size, the tighter the limits. The 13th record should be investigated for a Special Cause event.

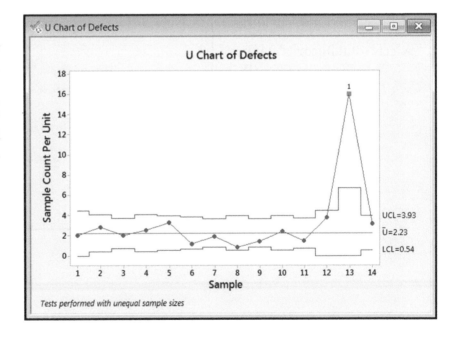

Attribute Control Charts for Special Situations

The traditional P and U charts with large sample sizes will often times experience situations referred to as *Over Dispersion* and *Under Dispersion*.

Over dispersion exists when noise factors cause the process to experiences more variation than is expected based on either the Poisson (for counts), or the Binomial (for proportions) distributions, and under dispersion is the opposite, here there's less variation than expected. In these cases, the regular P and U charts will demonstrate excessive 'Out-of-Control' conditions.

The charts of choice in these situations are the Laney P' and Laney U' charts.

To determine whether the data to be charted suffers from over or under dispersion, use either the P chart or U chart diagnostic option.

In the Minitab project **SPC BB**, select the worksheet *DefectiveRecords.mtw*, (This worksheet comes from the Minitab dataset included with each licensed copy of the software.)

P Chart Diagnosis

Menu Command:

Stat > Control Charts > Attribute Charts > P Chart Diagnosis

Select **Defectives** for the Variables:

Select **'Total Records'** for the Subgroup size. Click **OK**.

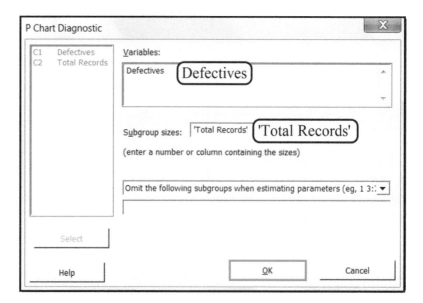

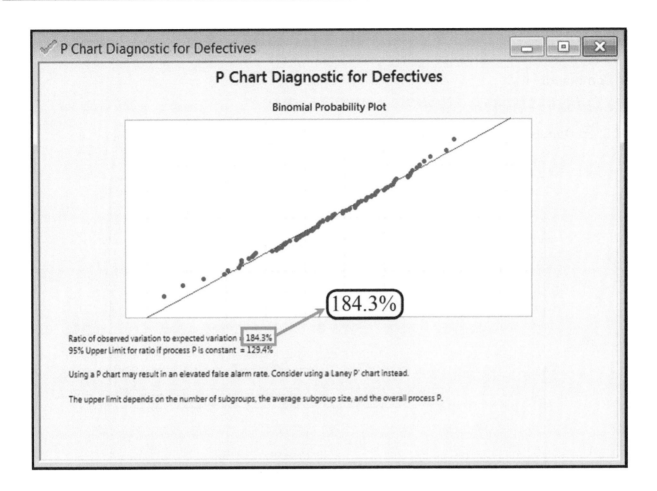

If the 'Ratio of observed variation to expected variation' is greater than 1, (100%), then the Laney P' chart should be used. The results above indicate the value is 184.3%, so the P' chart is the best option.

Laney P' Chart

Menu Command:

Stat > Control Charts > Attribute Charts > Laney P'

The P' Chart Options are the same as shown with the standard P chart.

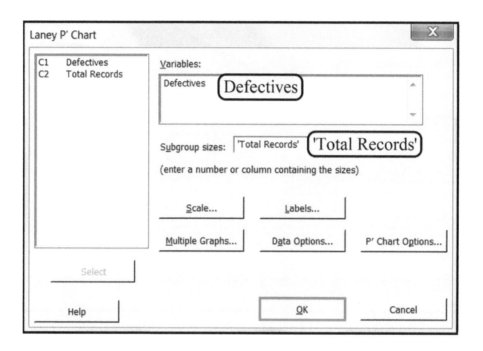

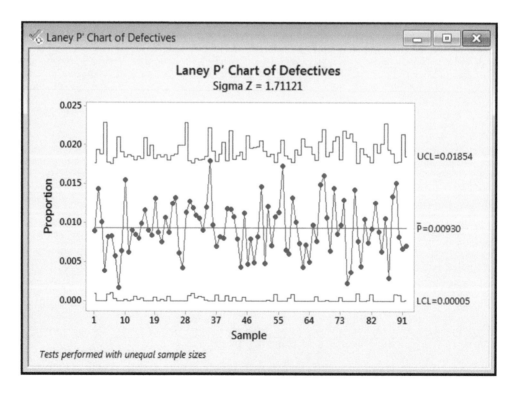

Compare this to a regular P-Chart.

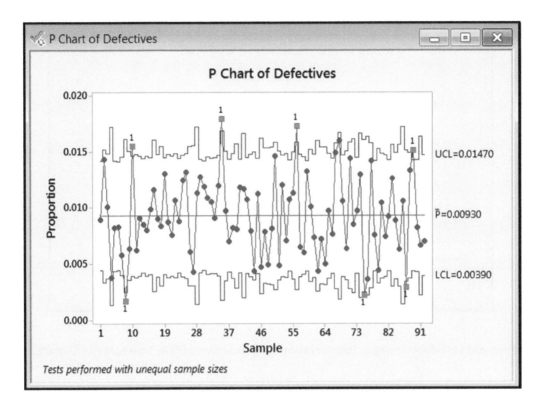

Notice the excessive Out-of-Control points compared to no Out-of-Control points for the P' Chart.

U Chart Diagnosis

The U Chart Diagnosis and the Laney U' Chart work in the same manner. The results of each are shown here.

Open worksheet *MedicationErrors.mtw*

Menu Command:
Stat > Control Charts > Attribute Charts > U Chart Diagnosis

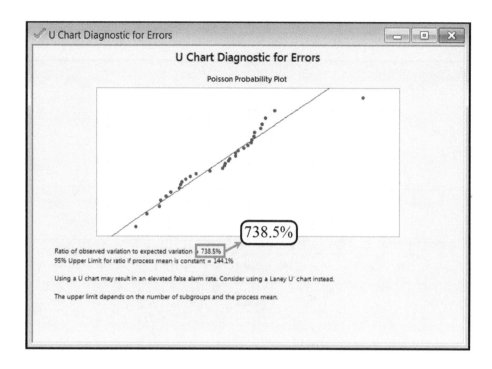

The ratio of observed variation to expected variation is well above 100%, so a Laney U' Chart is appropriate.

Laney U' Chart

Menu Command:

Stat > Control Charts > Attribute Charts > Laney U' Chart

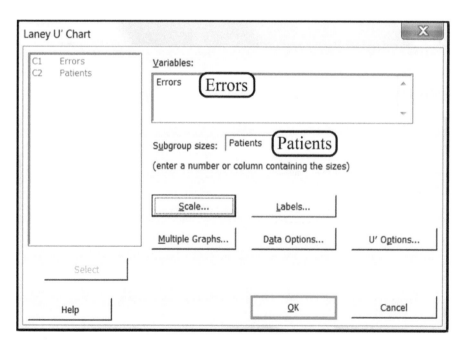

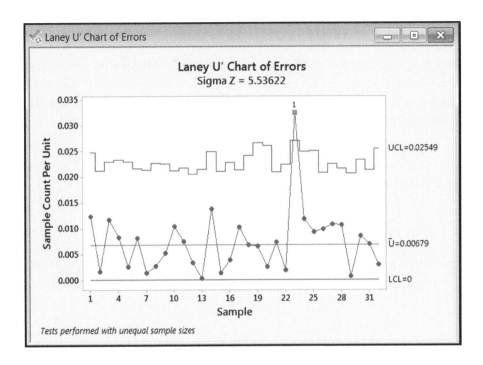

Compare to a standard U Chart.

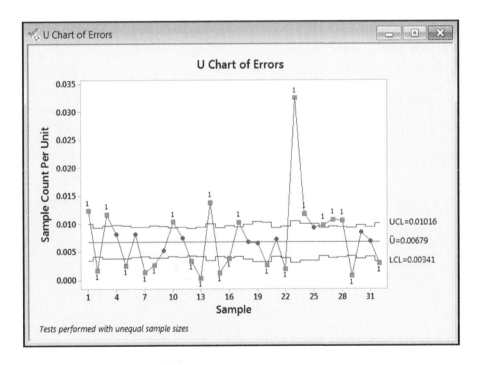

Notice that with the Laney U' chart, there's only one Out-of-Control point verses 22 with the standard U Chart.

To learn more about the Laney P', and U' charts, see Minitab Help.

Process Capability – Non Normal Data

Previous calculations for capability assumed data came from a population with a normal distribution. When this assumption is incorrect, it is important to use procedures to account for the non-normality. Begin with the standard Capability test, demonstrating one of the methods available in Minitab for transforming the data into a normal distribution.

Minitab Project: **Capability**

Worksheet: *nonnormal*

Menu command:
Stat > Quality Tools > Capability Analysis > Normal

This data originated from a process that has a hard limit or boundary at zero. However, the Box-Cox transformation technique requires that all values be greater than zero. Therefore a lower specification cannot be zero.

Select **Skewed** as the Single Column; subgroup size is **1**.

The lower specification for the Box-Cox transformation must be greater than 0, so a small value is used; in this case **.001**.

The upper spec is **30**.

Select **Transform**.

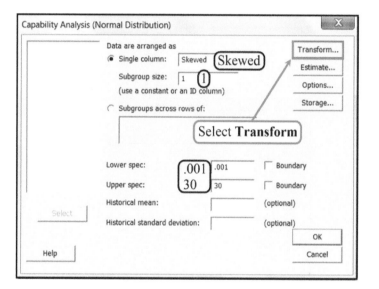

Select **Box-Cox power transformation (W = Y^λ)**

Select **Use optimal lambda.**

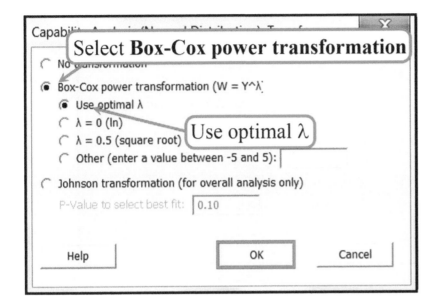

Click **OK** twice.

The results show the transformed data along with the transformed specifications. The original data is displayed in the upper left corner of the window. The capability values associated with the transformed data are more reliable than capability values associated with the non-transformed data.

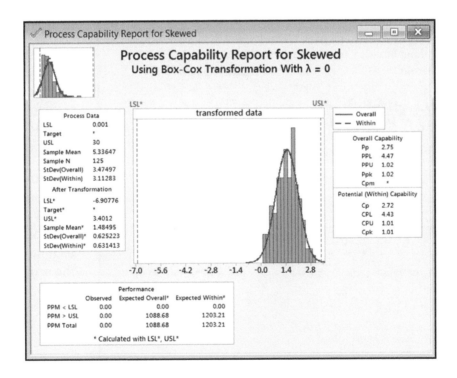

Note: Transformations do not guarantee the resulting distribution will be from a normal population. To make this determination, run a normality test in Minitab. The Capability Sixpack option offers the Anderson-Darling test for normality.

Menu command: *Stat > Quality Tools > Capability Sixpack > Normal*

Inputs for the Sixpack are the same as shown previously.

Select the same Transform options as in the example above, click **OK** (twice).

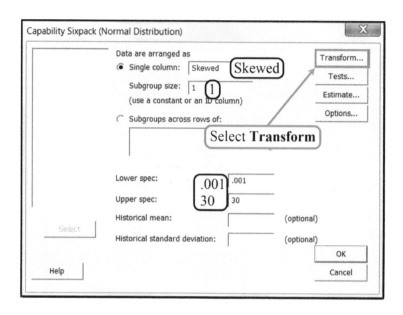

The test for normality found in the Normal Prob Plot indicates whether the transformed data can be assumed to originate from a normal population.

If the transformation does not produce data from a normal distribution, use other techniques to determine the proper capability.

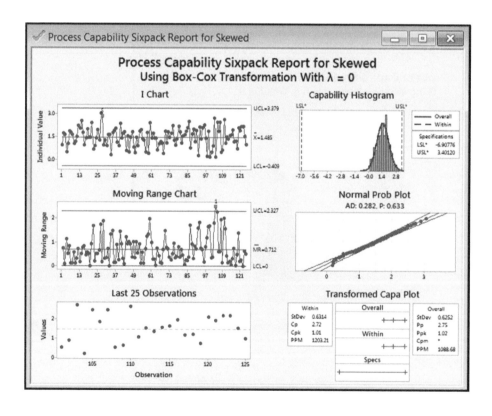

Using Other Distribution Curves

If the Box-Cox transformations are not successful, the next tool to use is Minitab's analysis of non-normal distributions.

Menu command: *Stat > Quality Tools>– Capability Analysis > Nonnormal*

Input **Skewed** as the variable.

Select **Weibull** for the distribution.

Input the Lower spec. as **0** with the Boundary options checked. This lets Minitab know it is not possible to have data below this value, so it will not attempt to determine defects below that point.

The Upper spec. is **30**.

Click **OK**.

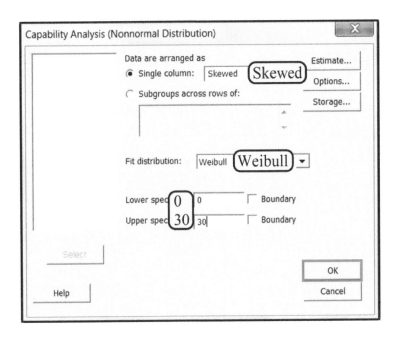

These are the distribution options available in Minitab.

> **Lognormal**
> **3-parameter lognormal**
> **Gamma**
> **3-parameter gamma**
> **Exponential**
> **2-parameter exponential**
> **Smallest extreme value**
> **Weibull**
> **2-parameter Weibull**
> **Largest extreme value**
> **Logistic**
> **Loglogistic**
> **3-parameter loglogistic**

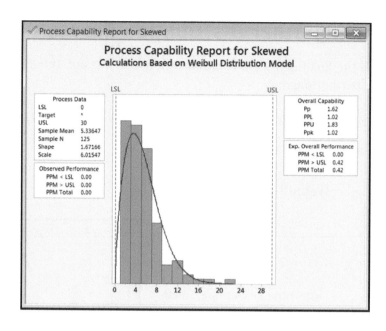

The data remains in its original form, but the capability values are now calculated based on the Weibull distribution.

This same procedure is followed for any of the distributions listed. To determine which distribution is appropriate, use the Minitab option for Individual Distribution Identification.

Menu command:

Stat > Quality Tools > Individual Distribution Identification.

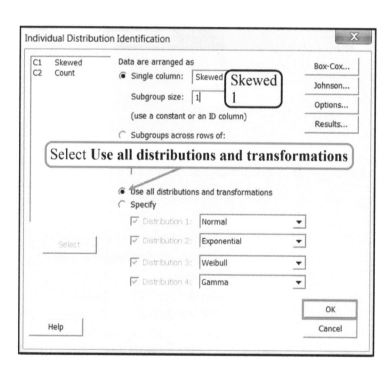

Input **Skewed** as the Single Column.

Use a Subgroup size of **1**.

Choose **Use all distribution and transformations**.

Click **OK**.

The resulting graphs will have p-values for each distribution. Any distribution with a p-value greater than .05 is a possible solution. If the process is known to follow one of the acceptable distributions, use it; otherwise, use the distribution that provides the best fit.

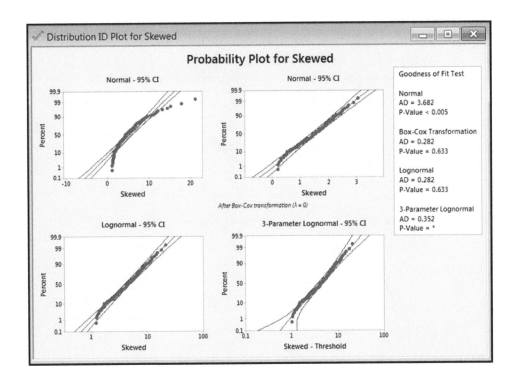

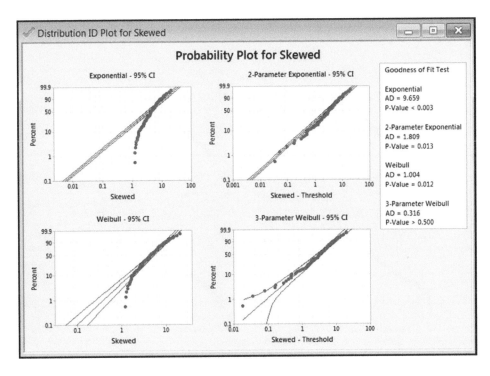

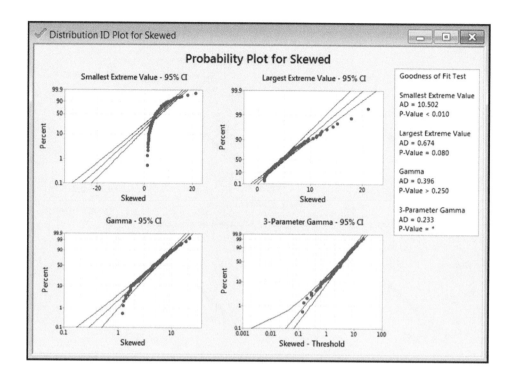

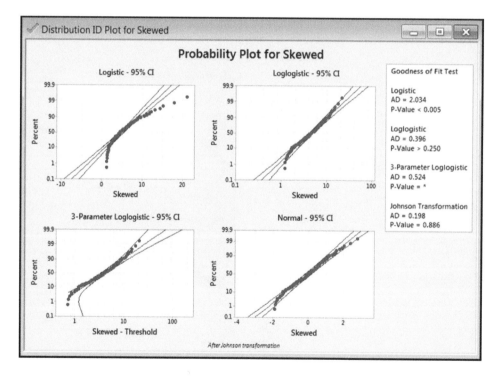

Results indicate the Box-Cox transformation with lambda = 0, the Log Normal, the 3 parameter Weibull, the Loglogistic and the Johnson transform are all possible solutions. Select the desired distribution and run the Capability Nonnormal study as shown before.

Index

Accuracy..80

Accuracy And Precision............................80

Add Axial Points....................................305

Adding Runs...301

Additivity Property...................................81

Alternative Hypothesis.................144-146, 149

Analysis Of The Full
Factorial Experiment..............................240

Analyze Fractional
Factorial Designs.................................270

Analyze Full Factorial With Center
Points And Blocks.................................256

Analyze Phase......................................130

Analyze RSM..281

ANOVA Analysis 162

Assessment...66

Attribute Control Charts
For Special Situations..............................336

Balanced ANOVA....................................222

Bonett's Test 158

Best Subsets Regression 202

Blocks..253-257

Box Plot 46-48

Brush Points 30

C Chart 334

Calculator 29

Center Points..................................253-262

Central Tendency....................................68

Change Data Type....................................24

Checking Process Stability - SPC 74

Chi-Square Analysis 168, 174

Code Data 25

Coefficient of Variation (CV) 69, 71

Columns 3, 13, 14-17

Comparative Studies 150

Comparing Mean and Median 69

Confidence Intervals................................138

Confidence Intervals -
Graphical Display 140

Contour/Surface plots...............................289

Control Charts For Attribute Data 331

Control Phase.......................................320

Copy Columns 16

Correlation 185

Custom Response Surface Designs...............313

Data Manipulation...................................24

Defining Custom Designs 308

Design Of Experiments (DOE) 235, 238

Design Of Experiments (DOE)
With Center Points..................................253

Dialog Boxes 2

Display Designs.....................................317

Display Statistics 72

Dot Plot..40-42

DPMO...120

DPU 120

Equal Variance 158, 162

Errors in Hypothesis Testing............................145

Excel Files 8

Excel Spreadsheet 308

Factorial Experiments............................212, 240

Factorial Plots 260

Factorial Points 237

Foldover...302

Format columns 17

Formulas...18

Four In One Graph 263

Fractional Factorial Designs...................267, 270

Fully Nested ANOVA..............................231

Gage Run Chart 85

Gage Study...88

General Factorial Designs 212

General Full Factorial Design Analysis...........215

GLM..224

Graph Options 30

Graphical Tools....................................40, 130

Graphs of Factors...................................218

Histogram 43, 264

Hypothesis Testing 144, 145

Importance..294

Improve Phase 235

I-MR Chart...................................320-326

Input Data..3

Interactive Nature Of Experiementation 236

Interval Plots With Groups............................143

Jittering..49

Kappa Analysis 103

Kurtosis..71

Laney P' Chart.......................................338

Laney U' Chart.......................................340

Levene Test 158

Mallows Cp 203

Mean (Average)......................................68

Measure Phase.......................................66

Measurement System Analysis (MSA) 77

Median...68

Merge 12

Metrics...36

Minitab Macros 34

Minitab Review 2

Minitab Shortcut Keys...............................33

Minitab's Capability Study 121

Minitab's Chi-Square Analysis 174

Mode..68

Modify Factors.......................................297

Modifying Designs 297

MSA - Audits 110

MSA For Attribute Data............................95

MSA Worksheet 83

Multiple Regression 202

Multiple Response Optimization.....................291

Multi-Vari Graph.....................................233

Multi-Vari Plot 136

NP Chart...333

Null Hypothesis.........................144-146, 149

One Sample t-Test...................................150

Opportunity 120

Other Distribution Curves 345

P Chart 331

P Chart Diagnosis...................................336

Paired t-Test 219

Pareto Chart 59

Patterned Data 20

Percent Defective 120

Planning Experiments.....................................297

Precision...80

Probability Plot.....................................131-135

Process Capability..................................... 118

Process Capability - Non Normal Data............342

Process Capability Six Pack.........................127

Project Charter 37

PtType 280

Random Data 19

Random Samples 110

Randomization...238

Range 69

Rank Data..26

Reduced Model 248

Repeatability..81

Replicate Design 300

Replicates..237

Reproducibility...81

Residual plots 263

Residuals versus Fits 264

Residuals versus Run Order 264

Response Surface Designs....................277, 313

Scatter Plot..57

Shape 71

Simple Linear Regression Analysis 189

Skewness...71

Sort Data...28

Split...10

Spread...69-72

Stacking Columns...14

Standard Deviation.......................................71

Statistical Process Control (SPC)...................320

Statistical Terms 68

Stepwise Function 207, 208

Stratified Samples 112

Subset 11

Summary Statistics.......................................67

Summary Table Options 177

Systematic Samples 115

Text values,....................................22, 213, 252

Tile Graphs 32

Time Series Plot 51

Trimmed Mean 68

Two Level Factorial Designs.........................237

Two Sample t-Test 149, 156

U Chart..335

U Chart Diagnosis 339

Unstack..15

Update Graph Automatically...........................31

Variance...70

VIF (Variance Inflation Factor).......................206

Weibull...45, 345, 346

Weight 294

Worksheets..10

X Bar R Chart 326

X Bar S Chart 330

Z values...120, 122, 123

CPSIA information can be obtained
at www.ICGtesting.com
Printed in the USA
FSOW03n1512161115
13451FS